The Journals of Honoria Lawrence

By John Lawrence

A HISTORY OF RUSSIA
RUSSIANS OBSERVED
THE HARD FACTS OF UNITY
TAKE HOLD OF CHANGE

By Audrey Woodiwiss

COVENT GARDEN THROUGH THE YEARS

The Journals of Honoria Lawrence

India observed 1837–1854

edited by

John Lawrence and Audrey Woodiwiss

HODDER AND STOUGHTON
LONDON SYDNEY AUCKLAND TORONTO

British Library Cataloguing in Publication Data

Lawrence, Honoria
    The journals of Honoria Lawrence.
    1. India – Social life and customs
    I. Lawrence, *Sir* John, *bart, b.1907*
    II. Woodiwiss, Audrey
    954.03'1'0924   DS421

    ISBN 0 340 23919 0

Acknowledgments

This book could not have been produced without the generous help of many people. We are specially indebted to the staff of the India Office Library, and particularly to Dr. Richard Bingle and Mrs. Rosemary Seton, for help that goes far beyond the ordinary line of duty, to Brian Lawrence for the loan of portraits of Honoria Lawrence and permission to reproduce them, to Mr. John B. Denson, H.B.M. Ambassador at Kathmandu, for information about Nepal and to Dr. Percival Spear for advice and encouragement.

Mrs. Venetia Pollock has given most valuable help in the earlier stages of editing and the staff of Hodder and Stoughton in the later stages. Mrs. Hilda Moorhouse has kindly lent us photocopies of some of Honoria's journals and we have found some useful pointers in her historical novel about the Lawrences (*The So Beloved* by "Jane Vansittart", Hodder and Stoughton, 1967).

I have received valuable help with the glossary from the Acting High Commissioner for India, Dr. I. P. Singh, Mr. Francis Sedgwick-Jell and Mr. Abdul Hamid of the Foreign and Commonwealth Office, Professor Sir Ralph Turner, Miss Natasha Lawrence, Dr. Richard Bingle, Col. Henry Lowe, Mr. Theon Wilkinson, Lt.-Col. Keith Robinson and Dr. Percival Spear.

Margaret Dick and Patricia Ward have typed parts of the book with great care and drawn our attention to a number of points of detail.

J.W.L.

Contents

Illustrations

(Between pages 128 and 129)

A miniature of Honoria before her marriage
Henry Lawrence
Henry about 1848
Henry's sister, Letitia
Honoria about 1847
A miniature of their daughter, Honoria
A miniature of their sons, Alick and Harry
A page from Honoria's journal
Silhouettes of Harry, Henry and Honoria
Sketch of Harry in 1849
Sanawar
Henry, by an Indian artist
Honoria on her death bed

Maps

Introduction

Honoria, the wife of Henry Lawrence of Lucknow (1806–57), kept journals throughout her life. These have been used as quarries for quotation over the last hundred years, but none of them have been published before. Intolerant and sometimes prickly, with her "Irish wit" she had a gift for telling phrases. Henry and Honoria Lawrence were greatly admired by their contemporaries and deeply loved by a wide circle of people, both British and Indian. But, since they were careless of dress and other appearances, they raised many smiles.

Honoria Marshall was born on Christmas Day 1808, the twelfth of the fifteen children of the Rev. George Marshall, Rector of Carndonagh, a few miles south of Malin Head, the northernmost point of Ireland. The rectory at "Donagh" was a bleak Quiverful home for the rector's children. From the age of three, however, Honoria was brought up at Fahan, a few miles down Lough Swilly, by her uncle, Admiral Heath. Fahan House is a low house with projecting eaves and a wild garden running down to the lough, which are still preserved almost as they must have been in Admiral Heath's day.

That northern corner of Ireland, where the influence of the Gulf Stream is strong, has a special lush beauty, which remained with Honoria all her days. At first she was homesick for Fahan but in the end "my India" gained her whole heart. She even came to prefer the climate, thinking the hot weather in India less miserable than an English or Irish winter.

Her childhood was happy. She was free to roam and acquired a love of solitude for she did not have other children as constant playmates, although her myriad brothers and sisters were only a few miles away. Instead she grew up surrounded by intelligent grown-up conversation with access to a good country house library. So she acquired literary tastes but of music she knew little and of the visual arts nothing. Small of stature, lithe and active, with fair hair and blue eyes, Honoria was an up and down person whose joys and sorrows, loves and aversions were equally intense.

The Lawrences were cousins from the same corner of Ireland. Henry's father, Lieutenant-Colonel Alexander Lawrence (1763–

1835), was a man of humble origin. He married Catherine Letitia Knox (1774–1846) who belonged to the Irish gentry and they had a family of twelve children, about half of whom were remarkable people. Alexander Lawrence served as an officer in India. He was a very good soldier and a loving father, stern but with "a heart that teemed with affection" (Henry's phrase). Unfortunately he had no talent for either making money or keeping it. So, having a large family, he decided to educate them as economically as possible by sending them to Foyle College, Derry, where their uncle was head-master. They did not come home for the holidays but sometimes visited their cousins, the Youngs of Culdaff near Malin Head, and possibly the Marshalls at Carndonagh and the Heaths at Fahan. But Henry Lawrence and Honoria Marshall did not know each other as children.

Five of the Lawrence boys reached manhood and all of them went to India. Four went into the army and became generals, though most of their work had a civilian character. John, the only civilian by pro-fession, became Governor-General and Viceroy. Henry went to India at sixteen and spent his whole life there, except for two visits home. His life's work as a soldier-statesman and philanthropist in the Punjaub and the North-West Frontier continues to bear fruit after five generations.

Henry had five sisters. His favourite was Letitia, who impressed her contemporaries as fully the equal of her famous brothers, Henry and John. Henry and Honoria regarded her as being, under God, the earthly maker of their married happiness, "my more than sister", "our good angel".

In 1827, Letitia was seriously ill and went to stay at Fahan for a long convalescence. The girl of twenty-five and her cousin of eighteen became lifelong friends. Letitia shared with Honoria her letters from Henry; and her stories about her much loved brother must have kindled a romantic interest, although at the time neither of them knew that Henry was already on his way home from India on sick leave.

As a young lieutenant in the Bengal Artillery, Henry Lawrence fought in the First Burma War. He escaped unwounded but was laid low by the fearful Arakan fever which never left him for the rest of his life. In August 1827 he and Honoria met for the first time, and Henry soon found a reason to return to Ireland and meet his young cousin again. In the spring of 1828, when Honoria was in London staying with her cousin, Josiah Heath, at 24, Bedford Square, Henry also came to London.

Herman Merivale, who knew her at this time wrote: "Well do I remember, after so many years, the impression made on our circle by those fine features and the still more striking figure; the freshness, almost wildness, of that natural grace; the frank, unencumbered demeanour, and the step of an huntress Diana."

During those weeks in London Henry and Honoria met regularly. And nine years later, on her way to India to marry Henry, she copied out all the references to him in the journal-letters she had written to her Aunt Heath in Ireland telling of her doings in London. On April 29th she wrote:

I am tonight absolutely worn out. The weather has suddenly become of a baking heat. At two o'clock Letitia and Henry came from Chelsea, and I was glad to avail myself of Henry's services to escort me to a shoe mart. Having made my purchases in Holborn, I proposed to go a little further to look at Newgate, and when there I recollected that I had never yet seen Father Thames. And as Henry said it was not far, I thought I would go to one of the bridges. I have discovered that in London "not far" implies any space from three yards to three miles, but I did get on, through the very heart of the city which is indeed "the crowd, the home, the shock of men", till we came to St. Paul's and I cannot tell you how disappointed I was in the appearance of it. It is to be sure, wretchedly situated, but it conveys to my mind very little idea of grandeur, and has nothing to my eye to "elevate or surprise". We walked round it and gazed up at it, till we nearly assembled a crowd round us and seeing that it was five o'clock we went briefly on thro' such alleys and lanes and courts, as I can hardly imagine human beings to exist in for an hour, till we got between Waterloo and Southwark bridges. And I have seldom been more delighted, than by the view of the river, its banks and bridges. Henry knows about as much of the geography of London as I do. Namely that the Thames was to our left, Holborn to our right, and Tottenham Court Road before us. So with these indefinite ideas, we made rather a circuitous route, till we came once more to Holborn, where I was so excessively tired, that we got a coach to go home in, having excited no small surprise by our long absence.

By the end of that "memorable walk in the city" they were in love. Yet neither told it to the other. Henry confided in Letitia, but before he could speak of love to Honoria he must have permission, if not from her father, then from someone who could speak for him. Angel Heath, the daughter of Admiral Heath of Fahan, was sixteen years older than Honoria and was like an older sister to her. She was staying with her brother Josiah at 24, Bedford Square and it was to her that Henry spoke. Looking back after nearly ten years Honoria recognised that her cousin Angel was "a pearl of price", but thought her "peculiarly unfitted to sympathise with her own sex". With the best intentions Angel told Henry that as he had no money, no prospects and poor health, he must not think of marriage.

Henry felt bound by this ruling. Later meetings confirmed their love but nothing was said by either of them. Honoria went back to Ireland and Henry to India with his health more or less restored and accompanied by his younger brother, John, the future Viceroy. He did not write to Honoria, but he did not forget her.

Back at Fahan, Honoria tried without success to forget him. Her long solitary ramblings had given her a love and knowledge of nature and she now also threw herself into the study of books. Living in a remote country house in Ireland, she somehow learnt French and Italian, read the New Testament in Greek and learnt enough science to follow with interest the proceedings of the British Association for the Advancement of Science.

At that time the destiny of all young ladies was marriage. Failing that, they became unoccupied spinsters. But the only man that Honoria wanted to marry was on the other side of the world and she was unwilling to sit idly at home. Therefore, to the annoyance of her family, she prepared to be a governess.

On the death of Mrs. Heath in 1831 Honoria left Fahan but it is not known where she lived for the next few years. In 1831, however, she fell ill, and this illness reduced her almost to despair. Little is known of it except that it was long, severe and depressing. It seems that she had injured her spine during one of her rambles, and for the rest of her life she had much pain. She afterwards attributed her illness to her own neglect of "the rules of health", and later she was haunted by the fear of madness.

In 1833, when she recovered, a clergyman by the name of Briggs proposed marriage. She accepted him but could not go through with it and looked back on the incident with repulsion. Meanwhile, returning to India, Henry, with the help of his brothers organised a fund for the support of his mother in her old age. By 1833 that was completed and he was seconded from the army to a congenial civilian job as a revenue officer. At last he could think of marriage.

All this time Letitia considered herself honour bound not to tell Honoria of Henry's love for her but in writing to her she had been careful to keep her tactfully posted with Henry's news, thus preparing the way for a change of fortune without giving the secret away. At last in July 1833 Henry wrote to Letitia: "Really I think I shall be mad enough to tell her my story; try to make her believe that I have loved her for five years and said nothing of my love. The thing seems incredible, but it is true." Letters took four months or more between England and India. Thus Henry's letter crossed Letitia's telling him that their father was dying and that Honoria was engaged to Mr. Briggs. It was only to Letitia that he could then write: "Had I but tried, as one in his senses would have done, to gain her heart, matters might have been managed. If anyone is to blame, I am the culprit, as I am the sufferer. The chances are now very many against my ever being married. This I say, not as a boy of seventeen, but as one – though unattractive in himself – not easily captivated. Tell me always where and how she is. Keep up your correspondence with her." So Henry turned to his work with a fury, measuring more fields and riding more miles in the Indian sun than anyone else, listening to everyone, reconciling village quarrels and imposing a light and equitable tax on every cultivator in his area.

Having broken off her engagement, Honoria revolted against the useless life that lay before her. "The unemployed energies, the unsatisfied desire for usefulness would eat me up." So she became a teacher at Prior Park School, Ashby-de-la-Zouche. "People thought," she wrote afterwards, "that I was disgracing myself and them by trying to be useful and independent, instead of occupying the pleasant post of living among my friends. And at the time I was rather touchy on the point."

Letitia, moved by Henry's last letters, and knowing that Honoria was no longer engaged, told her of Henry's love for her. So in March, 1836, Honoria wrote to Henry saying that she would marry him. He received the letter in June but his joyful answer did not arrive until the autumn. It was then decided that Honoria would go out to India on the first boat on which she could get a passage after February 1837, and that she would meet him in Madras or Calcutta. But she had to leave England before she knew whether Henry had got her letter telling him when to expect his bride. Her journal describes the heart-rending delays before they met, but these were more than made up for by sixteen years of happiness. Henry and Honoria Lawrence were singularly well suited to each other, and James Abbott describes her in an eastern expression as "the female power" of her husband.

The story of the British Raj is little known nowadays, except to those who remember it, but it is time now to reassess its achievements and failures. This is Honoria Lawrence's book, and in it she says little of public events, but the background of the later chapters is the remarkable influence that the Lawrence brothers exercised throughout India and also in Britain.

Henry and Honoria Lawrence both gave their lives to India. And her journals and letters show their fascination for its variety, their enthusiasm for its people and their love and interest in all around them. But they were also Protestant Northern Irish Victorians and these journals show Honoria grappling honestly with a tension between what she believed and felt and what she saw. Gradually her comments on Indians and their customs became more sympathetic, until in the end she was more at home in India than in Britain. Educated but unsophisticated, she had never been to a theatre before she went to India. Unconventional and careless of appearances, she was deeply rooted in traditional values. Her journals give an early Victorian picture of early Victorian India. Much has changed since then but very much remains as it always was. On recent visits to Nepal and Rajputana about half of what I saw would have been utterly strange to Honoria but the rest remained exactly as she describes it.

In editing Honoria Lawrence's Journals for publication we have had to omit much more than we have included. In particular, being religious and thoughtful about her faith, Honoria was always considering the ways of Providence. So she theologises and moralises at length. We have omitted most of this but have tried to keep enough to show the character of her belief. An ever present sense of Providence is a *leitmotiv* of these journals.

As one might expect, she wrote much about her children but we have only included a little of this. Her sometimes excessive solicitude for their moral growth ought not to obscure her continual pleasure in their company.

For Honoria Lawrence there was little difference between a letter and a journal. All her journals were addressed to someone, to Aunt Heath, when she was young, to Henry or some friend after her engagement and marriage, and latterly to her children in England. And her letters were journals. In 1840 she wrote to her sister-in-law, Letitia: "I find myself continually journalizing, when I want really to tell you about ourselves. And I believe it is the best way. It is horrid to hear only in a general way of those we love. And a picture of the day on which one happens to be writing is generally the best *vignette* to illustrate a letter." Sometimes she wrote two journals of the same period. There would be a journal addressed to Henry which "relates to our own immediate feelings", and a "public journal" in which "external objects are noted". These latter took the form of letters to an unidentified friend and were evidently intended to be read by other members of their circle. Later she wrote journals for her children, and then forgot what she was doing and started addressing Henry or her friends.

This was typical. Both she and Henry were wildly unmethodical. They saw that this was a fault and Honoria tried to cure it by laying down detailed plans for the use of their time. When they failed to follow one plan, she made another; but that was not followed either.

The Lawrence papers, which I inherited on the death of my father, who was the grandson of Henry and Honoria Lawrence, amounted to over a hundred bundles of manuscript, most of them exceedingly interesting. For the last thirty years they have been on permanent deposit at the India Office Library, where they have been well cared for and are being steadily bound into volumes, a delicate and most laborious task. These papers were originally collected by Sir Herbert Edwardes in order to write the biography of Henry Lawrence, but he died before he was able to complete the task. His widow thought that the effort had accelerated his death, and it must be acknowledged that these papers are not easy to handle. Scholars have worked on parts of them but they have not been systematically used as a whole, in spite of the devoted labours of J. L. Morison, Maud Diver and others.

There are gaps in the record, for some of the Lawrence papers were lost during the lifetime of Henry and Honoria, and others were destroyed in a fire at the end of the nineteenth century. Some were mislaid, some are very hard to decipher, some are disintegrating and others are bewilderingly out of order. Yet what remains gives a vivid picture of every stage of Honoria's married life. We cannot hope to have made no mistakes but we have done our best to establish the correct text. We have corrected obvious slips but we have not tried to improve the original. Added words are in square brackets. We have sometimes had to bring together sentences and phrases that are not consecutive but we have not altered the order of words. We have allowed ourselves a free hand in punctuation, and have corrected some eccentricities of spelling; but others we have left.

In Honoria's time there was no generally accepted system for the transliteration of Indian words. So competing versions of the same word were current and Honoria was not consistent in her choice. Neither have we aimed at consistency. Indian languages have a short vowel which is halfway between the English a in bat and u in but. Hence Kurrachee for Karachi, and with equal reason. Ranjit Singh is now the accepted form, but our ancestors generally wrote Runjeet. And the long a has at certain times and in some places been pronounced like aw in awful, while at other times and places it is pronounced ah. Hence forms such as Affghaunistaun which we have not adopted. We have however kept Punjaub for Punjab or Panjab. In general we have tried to modernise enough to make the text easy to read without destroying the atmosphere of the original.

The immense burden of deciphering and transcribing has fallen on Audrey Woodiwiss. The final choice of material to be included is our joint responsibility. The introduction, notes and connecting material are by me.

The present book has been in gestation for four years and during the next two or three years I hope to complete a life of Henry Lawrence, with the aid of a grant from the British Academy and continuing help from Audrey Woodiwiss. After that I propose to edit a selection of the Lawrence manuscripts now at the India Office Library. This programme would not have been possible without the selfless and sustained help given by Mrs. Cecily Holland and Miss Mildred Gibbs. Mrs. Holland was a missionary of the Church Missionary Society who, after her retirement from India, spent a day a week for some years working without any remuneration on the Lawrence papers at the India Office Library. When she died her work was taken up by another C.M.S. missionary, Miss Mildred Gibbs, who taught history for many years at St. John's College, Agra. Alas! Miss Gibbs died while this book was with the printer. She and Mrs. Holland went through many of the files and volumes most relevant to the biography of Henry Lawrence summarising, quoting the most important passages verbatim and occasionally adding their own shrewd comments. Their combined notes come to about 750,000 words. I take this occasion to express my warmest gratitude to them in public. May they rest in peace.

John Lawrence

ONE

Passage to India

Honoria had not seen Henry for nine years. Their friend James Abbot, whom she describes in Chapter Thirteen of this book, describes her on her arrival in India. "She was not beautiful in the ordinary sense of the term; but harmony, fervour and intelligence breathed in her expression."

Having embarked on board the *Reliance* she began the first of her journals addressed to her future husband. After landing in India she stayed with Major and Mrs. Hutchinson in Cossipore near Calcutta. While waiting for Henry to meet her there, she resumed her journal.

On board the *Reliance*, Northfleet, Monday April 3rd, 1837
In this first moment of finding myself alone in my cabin – in this hour when I have broken the tie of all early associations and, trusting implicitly to you, have embarked for a foreign land, how should I occupy myself but in pouring out my heart, first to God that he may direct and bless us, and then to your beloved self, for whom I cheerfully encounter these trials.

Miss Mackey* is not yet arrived, nor is the cabin yet put to right, but while my efficient servant, Phebe Saunders, is arranging my things, I seat myself on a box and take out this book which I got on purpose to hold the journal I mean to keep for you. It will be my chief delight while put up here. And now do you ask what I feel? Why, chiefly thankful delight that I am actually on my way to you, and strong hope for the future.

Tuesday April 4th
Dearest Harry, I keep before my mind your advice about shipboard life, and I think I shall be able to subdue my naturally open demeanour

---

*With whom she shared her cabin.

and be staid and reserved. When I think that in this little cabin we shall meet, that here we shall see each other, and be overpaid for all the cares and troubles of the last nine years, my spirit rises in elasticity and I fear nothing.

I rose at seven this morning after a not very pleasant night, dressed and then read the Bible with Miss Mackey. She seems a pleasing unaffected girl, and being the only candidate for matrimony, except Miss Stewart, among seven or eight and twenty men, most of them single, she will probably have her share of admirers. She and her party went out to breakfast, and long may they do so, for then I have the cabin all to myself. I occupied myself in reading, working, arranging, etc. till four when we dined. I found my location on the Captain's right, three from him, between Mr. Wynyard and Mr. Plowden. The dinner was to me most disagreeable. The very circumstances of sitting down so large a party, with the consequent strife of tongues and clatter of knives, is quite bewildering to my head. Besides the conversation of the gentlemen to my right and before me, was not suited to my taste, even as a listener. I accordingly looked, I fancy, as black as thunder and gave monosyllable answers to those who spoke to me, returning to my cabin as soon as the cloth was removed.

Before long I had a message from Mrs. Stewart, asking to see me. She is first cousin to Mrs. John Stokes, and I had been specially commended to her. I think that in her I shall just find the matronly friend you would wish me to have. I went to tea in the cuddy, and afterwards had a visit from Captain Warner who was polite "*all'ultimo signo*", offering to walk with me, and perform all other knightly service. I did not ask him to sit down, for I don't want visitors. So he soon made his bow.

Oh! that I could send a carrier pigeon to tell you that I actually am on my way, for there are you my darling, sickening in deferred hope. However, you are surely getting my letters and learning from these how gladly I forsake all others to cleave only unto you. There is but one cloud in my prospect, at present no bigger than a man's hand, but which I dread overspreading our sky. I mean separation. For among all the Indian couples I know I scarcely perceive any who have not been parted for a long term of years.

Wednesday April 5th

Another day over, and not a very pleasant one, for we have had a contrary wind and have lain, or rather pitched at anchor all day, and most of the party have been very sick.

My bed was made just in time, for I began to feel very queer. However, by lying down I escaped any violent sickness, and I have been stretched flat till a few minutes ago, when perceiving the ship more steady, I got up to undress, and now before I put out my candles, I hold my nightly chat with you.

Thursday April 6th

Captain Warner came a little before noon to ask me to walk, so I went out for half an hour and found myself much the better for the exercise. I was determined to tell him how I am situated, for as Annette sagely remarked to me, "His being the Captain gives him no dispensation against falling in love." So I took my opportunity when he told me he has a brother in the Bengal Artillery. I quietly replied "Very likely I may see him for I am going out engaged to marry a gentleman in that service." My voice was quiet enough I fancy, and the crimson I felt mounting to my temples was concealed by my bonnet and veil. Having made known my engagement also to Mrs. Stewart and Miss Mackey, I suppose it will be no secret to anyone on board, and it is my desire to be looked on as a married woman. This saves all troubles.

Captain Warner is decidedly a gentlemanly man, with tact and good taste. Captain and Mrs. Davenir amuse me much. He is a Mulatto, a very nigger in his aspect. She with a broad unmeaning fair face, and little stiff curls like a doll's over her head. These little people do so ogle one another, and appear so happy in their connubial state that it does one good to look at them. Miss Mackey is a lady-like, simple, in-experienced, well disposed girl. Her brother ought to be pleasing, he has the qualifications for being so. Yet he delights not me. He seems too much of an animal, and he always smells of tobacco. Dearest Harry, surely you do not smoke? I abhor every form of tobacco, from pig-tail to cigar, from Lundy Foote to Prince's Mixture, from a *hookah* to a curley pipe. Mrs. Stewart is the big blue-bottle fly among the ladies; she is evidently conscious of her station, but is neither over-bearing nor condescending, a clever kind-hearted woman of the world, I take it. Miss Stewart [is], to my taste, very pretty and engaging. The only people I envy are those ladies who have their lords and masters with them, not that I am in danger of coveting my neighbour's husband, but I feel miserably half-ish. Well darling, there is a good time coming.

Friday April 7th

Writing to you is almost the only enjoyment in which I can yet take an interest here. You have often in your letters referred to your desire of engaging in the political department, and thankful am I your ambition takes a civil, not a military, turn. With the latter I could have no sympathy. An army appears to me of no value except as it tends to the preservation of peace and life. I am persuaded that this is the result of well trained troops. My soul loathes aggression and conquest. But the ambition to hold an influential station where a man can repress wrong and encourage right, is just what I can enter into with all my heart, though the jealousies, rivalships and disappointments which beset this path are no trifling evils. Perhaps you may smile at this grave statement from a woman, yet, no – you will not.

We do and must influence the character of men, and therefore we ought deliberately and conscientiously to form our opinions, that our weight may be thrown into the right scale. I will tell you what I believe to be one of the strongest feelings in me: desire after influence. Not the love of sway, or carrying my point, which I see in many; but the power of influencing minds. This feeling is one reason why teaching is a positive pleasure to me. I know few pleasures to compare with seeing a human mind take its moulding from my hands, and this has been my passion from childhood. My earliest [ambitions?] were of writing a book which would make other people think just as I did.

Saturday April 8th

I have been looking at your picture and reading your letters, dearest, till I can almost fancy I see and hear you. The worst part of the voyage is that so long a time must pass without tidings of you. You can understand what I feel, by your own suspense till you had replies to your letters of June. Tho' even then you heard of me. Sometimes I am rather ashamed at the contents of my letters, for they would better beseem a girl in her teens, than one of my sober age. But it seems as if the last nine years were wiped away, and my heart as fresh and young as when we parted. Take the consequence then, for much of what I am, you have made me.

Sunday April 9th

We are in the Bay of Biscay, as my tempestuous writing may indicate, but I get on famously. This is the first Sabbath at sea, and I cannot express my delight that one week is over, that I am some one hundred miles nearer you than I was on Monday last.

I take up my pen, in defiance of the floor being half perpendicular. I have no uncomfortable feeling except that my head is rather giddy. My situation at dinner has generally been more to my mind, near Captain Warner and Captain Cobb and Colonel Wilson. These generally ask me to take wine. Two or three of the young men who I suppose knew no better have otherwise asked me and I have gone through the form, but not recognised them on deck, so that now they let me alone.

Tuesday April 11th

Yesterday evening I began a work I had reserved for the sea, in reading and tearing up heaps of old manuscripts. As I looked over these records of past thoughts and feelings, there was a strange mixture of pleasure and pain. They seemed to me belonging more to some other person than to myself, and gave me the impression of a young, ardent, misdirected mind, striving after something better than it had attained, yet without stability of purpose, taking its colour from surrounding objects, yet adding a line of its own. The papers worked over consisted of fragments of tales, odd verses and couplets, sketches of sermons, chronological tables, abstracts of mythology, grammar etc., lists of derivations and definitions. Collections of scripture reference, opinions of books read. All, all begun, but scarcely anything ended. It reminded me of the feelings with which I have walked on the seashore and looked at the broken shells, all of which wanted value from being imperfect.

Saturday April 15th

Yesterday after dinner I went out on deck with Mrs. Stewart. We walked with Captain Warner and then sat down. The stately vessel with all her sails spread "walking the waters like a thing of life". The moonlight on the snowy canvas, the figures of the men as they moved about the rigging, now in shadow, now in light, the picturesque effect of the light at the binnacle, shining on the rough countenance of the steersman, the murmur of the little waves, the shouts of laughter now and then from the groups of young men on the other side of the deck, who were playing at leap frog and such like games. All was so new to me, so magic in its effect on me, that I sat like one entranced. And think you, love, I forgot a sentence in one of your letters, where you say that you never look on the stars without thinking of me? No, indeed, and your presence was so strongly with me that I could have spoken to you.

Today passes much as yesterday, and now I think I have got into a settled plan, which is this. I rise at seven and have a little quiet time for thought before eight thirty, when Phebe brings me my breakfast. Then she settles the cabin and takes her own breakfast. About ten o'clock Miss Mackey, myself and our servants, sit down, read a part of the New Testament, and have prayers. Then I set myself to be busy at reading and writing till twelve when we have lunch. After that I take half an hour's constitutional on deck, come back and occupy myself again till three thirty, when we dine. After dinner I lie down for half an hour and then go on deck, where I remain till eight. Then we have an hour's light reading or chat. At nine we read some of the Old Testament, have prayers and are in bed at ten. I shall not long like nine hours abed, but I was worn out with want of rest the five months before embarking.

I have got Mill's British India to read.* My books besides are: Scott and Henry on the New Testament, Thornton on the Old. For lighter reading I have got *Kenilworth*.

Sunday April 16th

I have often asked myself what I expect in married life. Perhaps it is hardly wise to anticipate the details of an untried condition nor, unless I deceive myself, will these very materially affect my happiness. I think I have great power of adaptation, and can reconcile myself to outward circumstances, if but all be right within. What I look to is merging my own being into that of another, having no separate interest, joy, responsibility – that last word must be taken in a restricted sense. This is what my heart has yearned after, what I had deceived myself by thinking I had found, but which I now do verily believe to be in store for me, if our merciful Father permits our union. I could not have believed any man could so enter into a woman's feelings as you do, for it seemed to me that the difference of apprehension which mental and physical constitution created was the great bar to happiness in married life. And having come to this conclusion, I had made up my mind that if I ever married I must be satisfied without this sympathy, or look for it only from female friends. But your letters convince me that you are strung so that the chords of your mind will respond to that which wakens mine. Surely there will not be less of this when we are face to face, than there was while sea and land divided us.

I can hardly guess how I shall be affected when we meet, but I fear I shall be paralysed, and that you will not know what to make of me, for intense feeling generally deprives me of the power of expression. A sort of shyness comes over me, I think what a great baby I am, and in short feel very like a fool.

Thursday April 20th

I accomplished at dinner a manoeuvre that delighted me, namely getting away from Major Beatson's neighbourhood. There was a leg of the table very much in my way, so I asked Mr. Wynyard to change places with me and then got between him and little Johnnie Stewart.

Friday April 21st

Latitude 18° 47″. In reading the account of the Hindoo Code today, I

---

* *The History of British India* by James Mill, the father of John Stuart Mill. James Mill, Jeremy Bentham's "warmest disciple", never visited India but wrote in several volumes what became a standard history. "His powerful though rigid intellect was applied to the support and extension of the positions he shared with Bentham." *D.N.B.*

was much interested in trying to note the points wherein the system must be improved by the survey. The evils must have been great indeed in levying the land tax under the old regime. Dearest, how I love to think of you as the useful and honourable instrument of good.

I hope you are an admirer of Wordsworth.★ He is my companion at breakfast, and I feel better always after reading him, but I want someone to share the pleasure.

Saturday April 22nd

Sometimes I fidget myself by thinking you will not get my letters saying in what ship I come in time enough to meet me, and that I have clean forgotten the name of the people I am to be with. Or I fancy, should you be ill and John come to meet me, I should not like to give him by mistake the reception due to you.

Sunday April 23rd

Latitude. 11° 0′. We passed the sun today at 12°. How delightfully we are getting on. My love, what hourly dangers surround us! Just as I finished the above line, I saw a blaze on the side of Miss Mackey's couch. Her swing lamp hangs just above, and the socket not having been properly screwed in, it fell out with the candle. There was no one but myself in the cabin, but most providentially I saw the accident at once and had the presence of mind to snatch up the candle and put my hand on the place where it had fallen.

We changed climate with a rapidity which is very trying. This day fortnight the thermometer was at 42°. Today, it is 81°.

Tuesday April 25th

In the morning there was a perfect calm, the appearance of all struck me much, the look like moulten silver of the sea, blending with the white haze of the sky. Some of the gents went out in a boat, and brought back as spoil some Portuguese Men of War and Mother Carey's Chickens. I have got one of each, the latter Mr. Warner promised to have stuffed for me. I wish I could preserve the former, which delights me by its delicate transparency, its brilliant colours and beautiful form.

Wednesday April 26th

The day has been sultry, but I do not find any inconvenience from the heat while I sit in my cabin *déshabillée*, that is to say no clothing save a chemise, dressing gown, and a pair of slippers. How I am ever to go clothed like a civilised being in India is more than I can divine.

★He was.

In reading Mill I am surprised to find how he depreciates the testimony of Sir William Jones in all Oriental matters. I am divided between my desire that you should not find me ignorant altogether, and that you should be my sole teacher.

I am persecuted by finding likenesses between the people at table and the dishes on it. Captain Cobb is the image of a shoulder of mutton. Captain Davis is like a dried reindeer's tongue and Mr. B., who sits near me, is exactly like a piece of crispy, brown roast pork. These odd notions dance before my eyes very often, and I find myself sometimes on the verge of laughing aloud at my own whimsies.

Thursday April 27th

"The Captain's compliments and there is a homeward bound ship in sight," were the first words I heard this morning. Up I jumped and finished my eleven letters.

Monday May 1st

There was a shoal of porpoises and dolphins gambolling about. I love to look at these creatures which seem made merely "to take their pastime in the deep" and to be created for the purpose of enjoyment.

Wednesday May 3rd

Another day nearly a "*dies non*" for I have been really ill. Towards 7 p.m. the rain ceased and I crept out like a bird of darkness, and in my Indian-rubber shoes, defied the wet decks and got a walk which has done me a power of good.

Sunday May 7th

Latitude 6° 26″. Last night before I had been half an hour in bed, I was roused by Miss Mackey being in violent hysteria. For two and a half hours she continued in fearful paroxysms. We had Mrs. and Mr. Mackey and the doctor. Four of us could not hold her. When I looked at her and thought how liable I had once been to similar attacks, I was much moved. It was a great mercy that I was well enough to be up and of use to the poor sufferer. She got two hundred drops laudanum but did not sleep till towards noon today. Now (at 3 p.m.) she is in a tranquil slumber. A visit from the doctor has closed our adventure. I asked the little man about my bathing to which he objected. And then, when I said I did not like to give up the comfort, he said "I'm quite aware how pleasant it is, and I wish I could partake of it myself." Thinks I myself, a droll notion! Partake my bath!

Thursday May 11th

A fair wind carrying us seven to eight knots. A ship in sight. What news does she contain for me? We spoke the ship who proved to be a Frenchman from Rio, I was amused at the politeness of the Captain who in reply to our "*D'où venez-vous?*" said: "*Et d'où venez-vous, s'il vous plaît?*"

Friday May 12th

I go on with my pleasant task of copying your leters. You say you "have nothing to offer me but unbounded love". And what more, dearest, can mortal give to mortal? Yes, or rather what more can the undying spirit give to its kindred immortal? We each of us tried to be sufficient to ourselves, and to find in intellectual pursuits and in friendship, a substitute for one object, and we have both learned the fallacy of such attempts, that we were formed, as Coleridge says "to find in another being the complement of our own".

Wednesday May 17th

My calculations about your proceeding is, that you will take advantage of the rains to come down the Ganges, and be at Calcutta in June, as I promised to sail as soon after February as I could. It is a very great blessing to me that I do not habitually fear, though my heart sinks when I reflect that my latest news of you was in January.

They are getting up a play on board. One of the servants who knew nothing of it was down on the lower deck, and met Mr. Maitland, a great hulking man, walking with a drawn sword, and exclaiming "give me some green spot where I may lay me down and die". The poor woman ran off in a great fright to tell her mistress that the third officer had lost his senses.

Wednesday May 24th

There is a man who sits just outside my port to cool the wine and I sometimes talk to him. Yesterday I asked him about a strange sail he had seen, "Is the ship in sight, Jimmie?" "No, Ma'am, she's nearly discernible out of sight, she ain't no bigger than a duck now."

Friday May 26th

We are in a gale. The sea is a glorious sight rising in mountains, the waves crested with white, and showers of spray ascending and descending. But I have not seen much, for we have had the dead lights on except for a few hours. I am neither sick nor frightened, but I feel excited by the elemental air.

Saturday June 3rd

Another wearisome day is over. The gale has freshened and we are bumping about in great style. For a few moments today I believe we

27

were in danger. Owing to some mistake at the wheel we were taken aback, and the ship turned completely round. I had got up before breakfast, being weary of lying late in the morning and at ten I was lying on the couch with my eyes shut, and very sick, when I heard a crash. I ran to the port and seeing some men on the chains letting down ropes, it struck me there was a man overboard, and in the horror of the thought I lost every feeling of illness. All day I continued to stitch away vigorously, being unable for anything else.

Sunday June 25th

Are we within two days of Madras? May you this moment be more tranquil than I am!

Monday June 26th

My best beloved, here we are off Ceylon but too much in the clouds to see it.

Tuesday June 27th

We have since been running eleven knots and expect Madras to-morrow. Shall I hear from you at Madras?

Thursday June 29th

5.30 a.m. Who shall describe the feelings with which I have just looked at the land?

Friday June 30th

At 9 a.m. we dropped anchor, having made the passage in eighty-one days eight hours, the shortest ever known. Captain Warner went ashore immediately and I begged him to call at the post. At two Captain Warner returned. No letter for me. Then my heart did fail me.

After a short visit on shore, which is described in the next chapter, Honoria returned to the *Reliance*, to continue her journey to Calcutta.

Sunday July 2nd

I lay down last night hoping that this morning would find us a good many miles nearer to Calcutta. In this hope I fell asleep and slept soundly too, very glad to be in a swing cot instead of on a couch. Before sunrise I was up, and on looking out, lo, the Custom House stared me in the face, and I found we had not been able to get up our anchor. I was greatly vexed but comforted myself by thinking that these things happen not by chance, and every day we are delayed gives more time for you to meet me at Calcutta.

Thursday July 6th

We are now in Diamond Harbour. I spied a boat putting off from the shore and by the glass I saw P.O. on the flag. A letter boy was sent on board by her. No letters for this ship. Oh Harry, we shall be up tonight. Mr. Maxwell said so at dinner. Will you be on board, dearest, this very night? You must have heard by this time of our arrival. Every brig, barge, dinghy, that comes in sight, I set the glass to, for I think you may be on board.

Saturday July 8th

Mr. Mackey has had a letter from shore. Oh Harry, when shall I?

Cossipore, Sunday July 9th

It seems a century since I last opened this. Such a variety of feeling has passed through my mind. I continued at every moment to expect you as we went up the river. I paced about my cabin like one demented. Captain Cobb came in to see me, and afterwards Captain Warner. To each I gave the same reply: that you or someone by you deputed would come for me and I would remain on board till then. At one we dropped anchor at Coolie Bazaar. Every moment I then expected you. Captain Cobb was going ashore and I begged him to call at Watson's. I saw boat after boat put off and I was left the only one on board except Mrs. Cobb who awaited her husband's return; back he came, told me he had seen Dick,* and thankfulness to hear of you helped me to bear what was certainly a grievous disappointment. I determined then to go ashore with the Cobbs to the hotel.

And then when I got into a room alone I did give way to the poignant disappointment. After a good hearty fit of crying I washed my face, and returned with a composed mien. Presently Dick came, rather a broken reed in an emergency, and in a very short time Major Hutchinson made his appearance. Then I was quite relieved, but as Mrs. Hutchinson had not arrived I could not accompany him back, so I slept at the hotel, and at seven today Dick came for me and brought me hither. I am delighted with the Hutchinsons. And now that I have collected my thoughts, I am really at rest in my mind. I wrote you three letters today, and I repeat what I have there said, that I am perfectly satisfied at your not being here, feeling as I do that we each did our best to arrange what seemed to us most desirable and that a higher hand has over-ruled our steps for some wise end. Let us not lose our privilege as Christians of feeling a Father's hand in every event.

*Dick was the youngest of the Lawrence brothers. Known in the family as "Dick, the star that would not shine" he was born in 1817 and died in 1896 as a Lieutenant-General.

Cossipore, August 13th, 1837

Your letters, my own dearest Harry, are always delightful, but some-how those I got last night were peculiarly so. Every word even the simplest expression, filled me with delight, and gave me a thrill of happiness that is almost too much. You may say you fear I think you long in coming. Would you have it otherwise? Perhaps dearest, you too much pride yourself on keeping your word, and it has been good for you thus to have been led by circumstances to an involuntary departure from it. I should indeed be wholly undeserving of your love, if anything could lead me to doubt it after all you have done and suffered for me.

You tell me that "pet expressions and endearments are not at all in your way". I have seen how flimsy a texture mere billing and cooing is, in the daily wear and tear of married life and, as to any demon-strations of affection in the presence of others, I think it perfectly intolerable and indelicate. So I think we are agreed on that point, as on the other you allude to on dress.

When I was getting my outfit, I used to bother Letitia to know what was your taste and, everything I looked at, I used to say – "Would Harry like that?" She used to say "Never mind he'll like anything you wear. He used to admire that hideous red gown you were wearing in London." As to ornaments, I meant exactly what I said when I once wrote requesting you not to buy any for me. The few trinkets that I have, lie month after month unworn, and if you were to cover me with jewels they would have no value to me, except as your gift. And for the barbarous things called ear-rings, when I was six years old my ears were pierced. Before I was twice that age, I took the rings out and have always said that nothing should induce me to wear ear-rings, unless I were married and my husband insisted on it. Now as you are not disposed to make this a test of my obedience, you see such trinkets would be of no use.

I will tell you one thing in which my notions have altered; I used to think and say that if married, I should like my husband to give me an allowance for my own expenses, and I used to fancy it would be very disagreeable to ask for money if I wanted it. But now I think so differently that it would make me uncomfortable to have any portion called my own, for I find that we are so completely one that there is no room for such an arrangement.

It is now after breakfast, and I have just got your dear letter of the 5th. Surely you will be here today. When I read what you say about change of quarters my first feeling was disappointment. Must we then give up the camp life, and be all the year round on our good behavior? My heart does bound to think that your labours are appreciated, and your merit known. Besides I want to go over with you the very ground that you have trod alone, to see the spot where you first wrote to me. I love you more and more for thinking of others as well as ourselves in the proposed change of place.

I have just been called away to give the *dobie* a rowing about tearing my clothes. There is nothing, except the mosquitoes, so disagreeable to me here as having a man to wash for me, but I suppose I shall get used to it. Truly dearest my eyes fail with looking out for you. I feel very much inclined to cry, but the days when tears were a relief are over, and to shed them makes me now so really ill that I try to repress them. Nor are you, my beloved, on a bed of roses, though your anxieties are mitigated by the very circumstances of moving.

August 15th, 11 a.m.

Hope is certainly a very persevering lady, beginning as she does every morning to build up the castle which had been thrown down the night before. At seven thirty Miss Mackey and her brother came to see me. I have asked her to be my bridesmaid. I hope you will approve?

9 p.m. Today was trying. First of all the hourly expectation. Then the Mackeys spending the day, and really it is no lounge to be agreeable to people for twelve hours on a stretch. When they were gone a drive was proposed. I thought, shall I go? And I would have rather stayed but then I thought it would do me good so I said to Mrs. Hutchinson "It's too late for the steamer tonight, so I'll go." We went a little way and as we came back in the dusk, Mrs. Hutchinson exclaimed "There's Mr. Richard Lawrence." I looked and sure enough there was a man in a military frock, and a buggy standing near. I felt certain you and Dick had somehow come together, and that you were upstairs. All my blood seemed turned to lead, and I could not speak or stir. We drove by the stranger. Mrs. Hutchinson bid me get out of the carriage. By a great effort I did so and thought I should have dropped to the ground. The Hutchinsons thought just as I did and would not come up. I got upstairs, paused, heard no sound, stopped in the lobby, looked into the drawing room. The lamps were not lighted, and there was still no sound. I entered the room, ran to the verandah, and seeing no one concluded there was something amiss, and Dick was afraid to come and tell me. With this idea I was running down again when I heard a strange voice and ran back. Mrs. Hutchinson followed me to the verandah, and told me it was some Mr. Lamb who was come to drink tea here. And then I could refrain no longer, but shed the tears that had long been ready to burst.

We are now on the eve of a solemn engagement – of the greatest change, except death, that can befall mortals. And as you say, ours is a peculiar union. But its very peculiarity gives it value in my eyes. The more we are to one another, the greater our happiness. One cause why

31

so many fail of domestic happiness is, in my opinion, their not sufficiently relinquishing all previous connections so far as they interfere with the claim of husband and wife. I am prepared for our both feeling rather foolish at first. I am, no more than you, given to express strong emotion by word of mouth, but we shall soon understand one another, my beloved. I believe that I am often, though unintentionally, brusque, and Letitia used to talk of my "knock me down manner". But, for people who are to be happy together, the great point is not so much being free from all peculiarities of manner, as a perfect understanding of one another.

August 16th

I have begun with a new stock of patience.

Do you know, my Henry, that the thought of death is most intimately associated in my mind with marriage. Is not our very vow, "till death us do part", and "so long as ye both shall live"? And, but for a hope full of immortality, how could we endure the thought?

August 17th

My hand shakes so much I can hardly write. About noon a *chuprassee* came and told Major Hutchinson there was a Sahib below who wanted him. My heart beat. Mrs. Hutchinson in a few moments sent to know who it was, and the man said "Lawrence Sahib". Before I had time to know exactly how I felt, Major Hutchinson came back to say it was Dick, who, seeing the steamer last evening thought you had been in it, and expected to meet you here. Poor Dick was a sad put off. I cannot help expecting you every moment. I do not think I can stand six more weeks of the state I have been in, since this day six weeks ago we reached the Sand Heads.

Later that day Henry arrived. See p. 48.

Two

First Impressions

Honoria gives her first impressions of India while still on board the *Reliance* and continues them in a letter to an unidentified friend.

MADRAS

At 9 a.m. on June 29th, 1837 I was still on board the *Reliance* when I came in sight of Madras. Long before it was possible to see, I had my head out of the port as far as possible to see if the land was in view.

The day was bright and clear, and very hot. Behind us lay the wide waste of waters we had traced. Before us was the land which we most of us contemplated for the first time and looked at as our place of sojourn for many a long year. The sea was perfectly smooth except near the beach, where the long unbroken line of surf dashed against the shore. We were just opposite the Custom House, and several other buildings which stand close to the water. From the ship, these looked very well, the pillars and porticoes giving a general showy appearance. The novelty of all the scene, and the sight of land at all, made me interested in what I saw, but in itself the view would soon be wearisome. All was glaring and flat except a very faint outline of distant hills behind the town. No vegetation relieved the eye, there was nothing to give the idea of "A home in which the heart could live".

The water was perfectly speckled with boats of which catamarans chiefly attracted my attention as being most novel. Three logs of wood are lashed together, the middle one is rather longer than the other two, and a little turned up at one end. A raft is thus formed, which barely floats, so that at a little distance it is not visible above the surface, and the men appear sitting on the water. Some catamarans had only one rower, but most had two. These men were very dark, nearly naked and most repulsive looking. Among them all I did not observe one countenance that had a decidedly human expression, all looked like mere animals, they were mostly bareheaded, and had the head shaven, except one long thick lock at the crown. Some of them wore silver rings on their toes, their limbs were slight and pliant, and, as well as their bodies, generally covered with thin black woolly hair.

The catamaran is moved by a long broad thin paddle, rounded at each end, and held by the middle; the rowers sit face to face, in a kneeling position resting on their heels, so as to show the soles of the feet, which, as well as the palms of the hands, are white. Sometimes when the raft itself was not seen, it was amusing to observe the men, apparently squatting on the water, and brandishing the paddles at one another. They row by sticking rapidly first at one side, then at the other. These men bought fruit for sale in large flat baskets, made of bark. How these are kept dry is more than I know, for when I was afterwards going through the surf, I saw men and cargoes and all, washed clean off. But such a trifle seemed to cause these amphibious beings no manner of inconvenience. Their hands soon reappeared above the surf, they swam about, regained the catamaran, and plied their paddle as if nothing had happened. I am told that sharks are rarely found within the line of surf; were it otherwise the poor boat men would have little chance of their lives.

The *masoolla* boats are almost equally curious, they are shaped much like half the rind of a melon, only more concave and the end more pointed upwards. They are formed of planks sewn together with cord made of coco-nut bark, and are caulked with the same, without any metal being used in the construction. There are bars or rather branches of trees, laid across the top, the men sit on one and rest their feet on the next. The oars are merely long pliant boughs, with a broad piece of wood tied to one and all together looking like ill proportioned malt shovels. These play in ropes, by which they are tied to the gunwale. The accommodation boats, intended for passengers, have one end planked, cushioned seats and an awning over head. At the stern a man stands, steering by means of a long oar, likewise tied to its place. Thus the whole make is of the rudest kind, and appeared particularly uncouth after the neat shape and high finish of an English vessel, but the wood and fastenings of the *masoolla* boats are all so pliant and elastic that it yields to the wave and lives, where a boat of ours would founder.

Our ship was soon besieged with boats and swarming with natives, some bringing fruit and vegetables for sale. Others were *dobashes*, or servants, come to engage themselves to the European. These latter wore white robes, and had altogether a better air and countenance than the boatmen. There was one group of our party that I pitied very much, they were cadets for Calcutta, who were alive to go ashore and spend two or three days at Madras. All were ready each with his carpet bag, containing no doubt the brilliant scarlet jacket that so many were burning to exhibit. Their plans were arranged and they stood on deck talking together, and watching a nice looking boat that approached, and which they intended should take them ashore. And so it did, but not as they anticipated. Out of it stepped an official, presenting a printed paper as his credential and telling them that they must accompany him, for, it seemed, a new order had been issued by which no cadets for any Presidency were to go at large on shore in India till they had reported themselves and been reported upon. The poor youths were thus condemned to pass in the barracks two out of the three days they were on land.

Next morning at seven o'clock I went ashore; the passage through the surf was much less formidable than I expected. After riding over two or three high waves, the boat was thrown high and dry on the beach, two men were ready with an armchair set on poles, in which they carried me out of reach of the tide.

Before I had been five minutes on shore I had proof of the native indifference to truth. I was stooping to pick up some shells when a Hindoo custom house officer came to examine my trunks and, excusing himself for interrupting me, said, "I will bring you plenty shells tomorrow." He then opened my trunks, went through the form of lifting up one or two parcels, and shut up all. Mr. Cotterill's conveyance was waiting for me. It was a palanquin carriage, shaped like an oblong box with a well below for the feet, holding four people and Venetianed all round. The driver was a native in European dress, than which nothing can look worse. Alongside of each horse ran a man with a *chowree*, which is a long tuft of grass, hair or feathers fastened on a stick, and used for whisking away flies. These men wore a sort of short petticoat and vest of striped blue cotton cloth, and on their heads a wide flat cap of the same.

The buildings on the beach appeared on a close view, very shabby. They were much weather stained, and the want of glass windows gave them a ruinous aspect. As we drove along a road raised like a causeway on the beach, the surf dashing ceaselessly on the left, and to the right a long line of European buildings, every object amused and interested me. Sometimes we met a Moslem wearing loose white trousers, and yellow slippers with turned up toes. Sometimes a woman carrying her infant astride on her right hip, her right hand supporting the child who sometimes takes its nourishment there, while with the other hand she supports a burden on her head. We met a young English officer cantering along, or an older one carried in a palanquin. We also saw numbers of *hackerries* or bullock carts. These cattle are generally of a dingy white, with long upright horns, and miserably meagre. They have large humps on their necks, the cart is made with a long pole, at the end of which is a transverse bar that is laid across the bullocks' neck, so as to rest just between the hump and head. This looks very painful, and many of the poor creatures were sadly galled.

Turning from the seaside, we came to a large piece of bare ground, very arid and dreary looking. It was fenced round by small coarse pillars of brickwork, with a rough railing between them. Narrow foot paths intersected it, looking even more white and dusty than the surrounding ground. Carrion birds hovered over it. This is where the natives burn their dead, and Mrs. Cotterill told me it was a shocking place to walk through, on account of the mutilated, half consumed remains left there.

Though we had left the beach and its buildings fairly behind us, there was still little verdure. There were indeed along the road many tulip trees, but they had suffered so much in a late storm that they looked stunted and miserable. Only here and there a large bell-shaped blossom peeped out.

One of the first things that strikes a stranger in India is the inefficient way in which the natives labour, the "much ado about nothing", the "great cry and little wool". Very unlike the workmanlike business at home. Here were men at work to repair a wall that had been damaged in the gale. They crouched on the ground and used a small trowel, in which they lifted up, each time, a little bit of mortar that they dabbed against the wall a great many times. I felt inclined to run up and take a trowel in my own hand to show them how it ought to be used.

At nine o'clock I reached Mr. Cotterill's house which stands near the Scotch Kirk. A large building with a high spire, but having the same tawdry half ruinous look, which struck me in all the public buildings at Madras. It is odd enough that both there and at Calcutta, the Scotch church should have a spire out-topping all others. I believe they were so made out of contradiction to Bishop Middleton, who forbade their having any spire at all. Very much akin to Christianity, certainly, the conduct of both parties! Or, as Von Rausner says, "What sort of a Christian Lion must the Brahmin have inferred from such a paw?"

On entering the house, my first feeling was strange familiarity, surprise at finding how true had been my previous notions of Indian arrangements. The lofty and shady rooms, and the perfect tranquillity was a delightful contrast to the confinement, glare, noise and motion of the ship. The house was nearly square, having in front of the lower storey an open portico, with a verandah over it, into which the upper rooms opened. The walls were covered with white *chunam* or plaster, and the floors matted. Every room had fixed in the walls several branches, with sockets for lamps, and glass bell shades round them.

Each room had also many lofty folding doors, and windows made like such, which open from one room to another and upon the verandahs. The windows have on the outside Venetians, and inside, glass doors, which are closed during the day to keep out the hot air. To exclude the insects and glare there are likewise cheeks or screens made of very small slips of bamboo, placed horizontally, and woven with thread. They are painted green, and have often thin muslin covering the middle part; they easily roll up, and are let down by being untied. The doors from one room to another are likewise Venetianed, and when locked back show other doors of fluted silk, like a chiffonière, which do not fill up the whole space, but leave two or three feet open above and below, to admit the air. On the windward side are hung mats, called *tatties*, made of the fragrant kuss-kuss grass. They are constantly kept wet. The air that passes through them is delightfully cool. But the most important article of furniture in an Indian house is the *punkah*, an oblong frame of light wood covered with canvas and painted white. It is hung edgewise from the ceiling so low as just to clear people's heads, and at the lower edge it has a fringe or frill, being otherwise ornamented according to taste. If the room is large it has several *punkahs*. They are moved by a long string from the middle, which is constantly pulled. The current of air thus produced is very agreeable, indeed almost indispensable to Europeans during the hot weather.

Another point striking to a stranger here is the multitude of servants, and I don't think I shall ever get over the dislike I have to seeing them lie, stand and sit about the doors or even in the room, for in some houses the *punkah* is pulled by a man inside. And where there are children, they are always carried or followed about by servants. The natives do not, certainly in general, understand our language, and old residents seem to think no more of their presence than of so many tables or chairs, but to me the restraint is very irksome.

Indian houses are built universally, as far as I have seen, on the plan of having the rooms open from one another, without intervening passages or lobbies. This too adds to the publicity of our life here. All the houses I have seen in this country have the rafters bare, only painted. This is, I believe, lest the white ants commit their ravages undetected, but it has an unfinished comfortless appearance, and it is strange to look up from damask couches and rosewood tables to a ceiling with naked beams.

In this climate people always live on the defensive. Every thing is liable to spoil, the ants attack every species of wood and paper. The beds are surrounded by a gauze cage to exclude the mosquitoes. During the rains every sort of coloured clothes are liable to become spotted and discoloured, and half of a lady's time is employed in taking out the contents of her trunks and exposing them to the sun, which in time fades them. Insects get into the binding of books, and every thing on the breakfast table must be covered to keep out the flies. But these evils are felt as such only at first. Nor are they, to me, so disagreeable as the cold at home. But I am confounding present thought with first impressions, and must return to Madras. While I was there, the weather was very warm, the thermometer 90° in the house.

We went out to dine towards St. Thomas's Mount [in] Chindera-pettah, a part of the station entirely native, I could only take in a general impression of dark figures sitting on their heels, or lying down under open sheds where their goods were disposed on the ground for sale. Children up to seven and eight years old, running about quite naked, their heads shaven, except the tuft on the crown. Getting clear of Chinderapettah, I was struck by the languid, listless, parboiled effect of the ladies who reclined in the open carriages, and especially of the children, who poor little dears, looked truly like hot house plants. Among the gentlemen on the road, there were more who seemed beer drinkers than bilious subjects.

Dr. L.'s was the first house I had seen at night in the country, and I was struck then as I have been since at the darkness of the rooms by day, and their lightness by night. While the sun is up the Venetians are kept closed, and the shade is such that I found it difficult to read, but in the evening everything is opened to admit the air. Each room has from eight to twelve or more pairs of sockets fixed in branches to the white wall and all looks brilliant and cheerful. The candles and lamps on the table must have glass shades and wire tops to screen them from the perpetual breeze of the *punkah*. When you seal a letter you must go into the corner to be out of the way of the *punkah*. If you shake pepper on your plate at dinner, you must hold up your hand to prevent the *punkah* from blowing it all into your face. When you are writing, if you do not lay a weight on the corner of the paper, the *punkah* whisks it up against the pen.

In India the houses have no bells, the servants being always within call. In Madras the call is "Boy", a corruption, I believe, of *Bahee*, or brother. In Bengal it is "*Qui Hie*", "Who is there?", from whence the English in this Presidency are commonly termed *Qui hies*. The Madras people are called Mulls and those of Bombay Ducks. But my learning does not extend to giving you any etymology for these terms. People in the upper provinces are Mofussilites, *Mofussil* meaning any place beyond the station. And the up country folks in turn call those of Calcutta, "Mahratta Ditchers".

To return to my brief sojourn at Madras. We left Dr. L.'s house early, by eleven o'clock. I had dismissed the *ayah*, who made her *salam* wishing me "plenty good night". But I was too much excited, too hot, and too restless to have a good night. I sat up writing till my eyes ached, and then lay down, but not being able to sleep I escaped from my green gauze cage and wandered about the adjoining rooms, quite unconscious of the misery I was preparing for myself. Alas! I did not then know the treachery as well as venom of the mosquitoes. The little wretches bite so gently that one hardly is aware of their presence, except from their buzzing, but this I heeded not, nor was it till twenty-four hours afterwards that I found my feet, arms, neck, all covered with white lumps accompanied with intolerable irritation.

In the afternoon I was obliged to go on board, for the ship was to be off early next morning. Mr. Cotterill accompanied me, and as we had an hour to spare, I took the opportunity to look at the Custom House, and the motley groups assembled in its portico. Here were troops of fishermen, sitting and lying on the ground, boat-men crowding up for custom, talking very fast and very loud, and all at the same time. They seem to have the facility of articulating without shutting their mouths, for while they chattered, there seemed no closing of that awful chasm, a ring of black lips, outside a rim of white teeth, and within this setting a tongue and throat dyed red by the stuff the natives constantly chew called *pan*, a mixture of which the chief ingredients are *betel*-nut, cardamoms, *chuna* and occasionally opium, with some crimson dye.

Then came beggars whining in just the same tones as our own street mendicants, salaming by putting both hands to the face, and bowing the head. One woman went on doing this, and then touching her stomach to show she was hungry. She looked as if she was, and I pitied her but could not help laughing at her child, a little fat, merry thing of five or six years old, who imitated all its mother's tones and gestures, looking up in my face, and then patting its stomach which looked already fuller than it could hold.

Here too were Armenians, fairer than the Hindoos, and better dressed, wearing long muslin robes, and tall peaked caps. There were Chinese, looking as if they had walked off a teacup, their dull yellow skin, flat features and long narrow black eyes, being a great contrast to the Hindoo countenance. They wore trousers, a loose upper dress, like a long skirt, and a broad brimmed conical straw hat. And seated on the ground, men who seemed to be keeping accounts, writing with a sharp stylo on long slips of palm leaf.

By this time the surf was rising rapidly, and as I could not get an accommodation boat, I took the first that offered, where I sat, un-comfortably enough, on one of the bars laid across the gunwale, with my feet on another, keeping fast hold lest I should be upset or washed off. The surf is much more formidable when facing than when coming ashore with it. Every surge that came hissing and foaming towards the little boat, rising like a mountain, and crested with white foam, seemed as if it must overwhelm us. But accidents rarely occur. The boat rides over the wave, and I escaped with only a sprinkling of spray. When we had got into smooth water the head boatman came up, salaming, to ask for some additional pay for having brought me so well through. In general the demand is made beforehand and, if refused, the passenger gets a good ducking.

We were soon alongside the ship, and till I then saw her I had no idea of her enormous size. The chair, made like a small barrel with one side cut away, was lowered. I got in, was wrapped up in a flag, the boatswain gave a whistle, the chair was hoisted up, and once more I was in my floating prison. There was some delay in our weighing anchor, and it was tantalizing to be in sight of land for twenty-four hours more, but in the afternoon of July 2nd we got off.

CALCUTTA

Cossipore, August 1837

Owing to our singularly rapid passage I had outstripped the letters which announced my coming. And the arrangements for my landing were not, therefore, just as they were intended to be. At 3 p.m. I went ashore in a *bholia*, a long narrow boat pointed at each end, the after part covered in so as to form a little cabin, Venetianed and cushioned round.

Hotels are but of recent establishment in Calcutta, hospitality in India, as in other half-civilised countries, being a matter of necessity. But as the influx of strangers increased, the inhabitants must have felt their entertainment rather a tax, and public accommodations have sprung up. The best hotel is Spencer's, to which I went, and which is really a noble one. The sets of rooms so well arranged that parties do not interfere with one another, and the attendance is excellent.

I landed with a lady and gentleman who had been fellow passengers and we got very nice apartments, a sitting room, with two bedrooms and dressing rooms opening off it. But four pairs of lofty doors threw the whole pretty nearly into one. Stranger still was it to see men act as chambermaids, making beds, arranging the dressing tables etc. Certainly the difference in colour and costume makes a wonderful difference in our notions. A black form does not give the idea of indelicacy and exposure, though nearly naked, and the white robed bearers going into a bedroom do not give the least of the feeling it would do to see footmen there.

The following day I came here, and have been for the last three weeks with very kind friends, Major and Mrs. Hutchinson. There is in this house a dear little girl of four years old, and it is very curious and pretty to hear her speak two languages with accuracy. English she knows from her parents, and she chatters Hindustani with the servants. She is often my interpreter and translates as quickly as I can speak. Her two elder sisters are at home, and this is the sad part of Indian life.

Do you remember our reading the Memoir of Thomason?* I now see the truth of what he says respecting the disruption of domestic comfort in this country. As far as children are concerned, this is dreadful, just as their minds expand, and they require and begin to appreciate parental care, they must be sent among strangers and grow up ignorant of their parents. Or else the wife must leave her husband to be with her children.

I daily see the benefit of not having quitted home so young as most ladies who come to India do. Leaving England before they have had much experience of life there, they persuade themselves that the annoyances, which arise from the fact of ourselves and those around us being only human beings, are exclusively Indian.

During my short residence in this country, I have been struck with the depth of colouring with which the scenes of existence are here painted. Life is so uncertain, disease so rapid, there are such lengthened separations, and so many uncertainties in the conveyance of intelligence, that I feel quite bewildered at the startling occurrences I hear of.

When Mrs. Hutchinson came out, she had as fellow passenger Mrs. F., a lady who had gone home for her health; her husband had come to Calcutta to meet her. He immediately got into a little boat, intending to await her arrival at a certain point. A breeze sprung up, which was against the boat and upset it. Mr. F. was never seen again.

A friend of Major Hutchinson's had gone home and there met a lady to whom he became attached, but not deeming it then pertinent to marry, he returned to India, and afterwards wrote asking the lady to come to him. She did so, but by a train of circumstances somewhat resembling my own, the gentleman was up the country at the time of her arrival. She came immediately to Cossipore, and he set out to join her as soon as he heard she was come. Some weeks elapsed before he could reach her, and I can well understand her anxious and impatient feelings. He was daily expected, when she was taken ill of cholera, and in two days died. The frightful rapidity of death and all belonging to it in this climate obliged immediate interment. She died in the morning and was to be buried in the afternoon. Just as the funeral was about to start, a boat stopped at the steps leading to this house, the gentleman stepped out, and was barely in time to see her remains and follow them to the grave.

*Thomason was a famous chaplain of the East India Company, the father of Mrs. Hutchinson and of Henry Lawrence's friend James Thomason, afterwards Governor of the N.W. Provinces.

I have spoken of servants in this country, and I have further to say that I think the system respecting them, exceedingly hurtful to one's mind. You hire your servant at so much a month, they do your work, and you have no further concern with them. If they do not please you, you dismiss them, they make their salam, and next day you are surrounded by new faces. At home every conscientious person feels responsible to a certain degree for the moral conduct and religious instruction of his domestics as well as the duty of consulting their comfort. Here the difference of religion does away with the first, and the habits of life in a great measure obviate the second, and it is difficult for the master and mistress to recollect that their servants are responsible immortal beings.

I was surprised to find among Europeans the prejudice of caste and that many of them object to a low caste native simply on that ground, as much as a Hindoo would. The obsequious manner of the servants annoys me greatly. I do not mean they ought not to be respectful, but a man's standing with folded hands waiting for his master's orders seems to me more like devotion than service. The train of domestics in an Indian establishment is entailed by the impossibility of getting one to do anything he does not consider his work. Your bearers will not take a teacup off the tea table. Nor would the *khitmutgar* pull the *punkah*. I asked Mrs. Hutchinson yesterday how many servants they had, she replied "I am not sure, but we are very moderate people, I can soon reckon." The number amounted to nearly thirty. An *ayah* (waiting maid) and underwoman, a sweeper, the sirdar (head) bearer, mate-bearer, and six under-bearers. A *khannsamah*, or house steward, three *khitmutgars* or attendants, and a *bawarchee*, or cook, the *malee*, or gardener, *bheestie* (water carrier), *dobee* (washerman), *durzee* (tailor), a coachman, two *saeeses* (grooms), two grass cutters, and a man to tend the goats, two *chaprassees* (men to go messages) and a woman to keep off the bodies which float down the stream by the house. All these servants will only wait on their own employers. Everyone going visiting takes his own. A lady who came here for a week lately, brought two women, two *Khitmutgars*, two bearers and a *durzee*. I have still my *balatee ayah*, or English maid, whom I brought out. Valuable as she is I shall not be sorry to part with her, for it is difficult in this country to have a European servant without making a companion of her. She sits all day in my dressing room and, when I go in and see her there so uncompanioned, I cannot but speak to her with a sort of familiarity I would not use had she society of her own rank.

While on the subject of servants, I may add a few words about their costume. The *khitmutgars* are Mussulmanns. No Hindoo of any good caste would touch our food. In Calcutta the Mhugs or Burmese act as cooks to the Europeans. And among the Hindoos themselves, the poorer Brahmins earn their livelihood as cooks. Their caste being the highest, no one is contaminated by eating what they have touched. The term *khitmutgar* literally means servant, but is applied only to table attendants. They wear white trousers of white muslin, a long upper vest, somewhat like a dressing gown, of the same and a belt or sash generally of white, edged with some bright colour. On their heads turbans of white muslin, with a wide brim made of *shola* (a light wood like elder) and covered with very minute folds of muslin. In many establishments they have a livery denoted by a colour folded in with the sash and turban. The bearers or *kahars* (who hold somewhat the place of footmen) are Hindoos. Their turbans generally consist of one piece of cloth, folded round and round the head, and often have I admired the graceful waves in which they lie. The bearers wear a short tightly fitting vest which closes at the right side, to distinguish them from the Mussulmann's who fasten theirs at the left. Instead of trousers the bearer has a long piece of cotton cloth, folded round the hips and tucked in at the waist. The women wear a wide petticoat of white or coloured chintz, a tight jacket with short sleeves, and a long piece of muslin, a *chuddar*, which is thrown over the left shoulder, one end hanging down as a mantilla, the other folding round the head as a hood. All when out of doors wear shoes, generally of yellow or scarlet leather, with turned up toes, but they never come into the house with them on. Indeed a man could not show more disrespect than by coming into your presence with covered feet and bare head – such are the different notions of politeness. By an odd burlesque very high titles are given to persons whose occupations are least esteemed. The man of lowest caste, who sweeps the ground and would eat after a Christian, is called *Mehtur*, (*Maître*) or Prince, and a taylor, who is not much more in esteem here than his brethren of the thimble are in Europe, is called *Kalifa*, or King.

Going in from Cossipore to Calcutta we passed through the Bang-bazaar, a very long range of the native town, sufficiently disagreeable in itself, but to a stranger very amusing. The streets were always crowded with bullock carts, coolies carrying loads on their heads, banghy-bearers, carrying their burthens suspended from each end of a long elastic piece of bamboo, laid across one shoulder. Buggies, (gigs or cabriolets), with the hood put up to exclude the sun, perhaps a fakir shouting out for charity, and exhibiting an arm which for years he has held in an erect position, till the flesh has wasted away, and the nails are like birds' claws. Africans, Chinese and Armenians each with their distinctive characteristics of feature and dress. A *ruttle* or idol car on high wheels with a raised platform on which are frightful images. And, never to be forgotten, the *cranchee*, a four wheeled carriage which looks like a ghost of a deceased Hackney coach. It is drawn by two *tattoos* or small shaggy native horses. The harness is of rope and as in the *hackerries*, there is a pole with a transverse bar resting on the horses necks. On a low seat behind the steeds sits the driver, generally a dirty, wild looking man, with a quantity of matted hair and wielding a whip long enough for a four in hand. This conveyance is used as you may suppose, only by natives, and within it may be seen perhaps six fat men, covered only round the loins, so that as they squat in the *cranchee* they seem quite naked, their skin shining with oil, and of a peculiarly disagreeable yellow hue, which the natives acquire as they grow fat. The carriage thus filled, looks like a nest of lizards. And away it flies, over rough and smooth.

All these glowing under an Indian sky, and rattling, creaking, shouting, pushing, grunting along make such a confusion as to me was more bewildering than the crossing from the Mansion House to the Bank. The buildings on each side were quite in character with the scenes in the streets. Being chiefly shops, open in front, raised a few steps, the wares spread on the ground, and the owners squatting and lounging beside them. Among the goods were cotton clothes of all descriptions, brass and earthen pots, shoes and caps, sweetmeats and grain. All sorts of inferior European hardwear goods. Chinese toys and pictures, fans of every kind, women's ornaments of glass and tinsel, wreaths of flowers for the temples, *hookahs* of all kinds, and of course house furniture.

Of a Sunday, after having the shade, coolness, and quiet of church it was quite stunning to come out to such a scene. On this road we passed two temples, which stood in the street as houses, but the wide doors were always open. When lighted up at night I could see within a frightful many armed figure, before which stood a priest with a hand *punkah*, fanning the idol. The sight of these horrors, gives great force to the scriptural appeals and remonstrances on the absurdity as well as crime of idolatry. At night the shops looked very pretty, being lighted up with many little lamps, and the people within kindling their wood fires to cook their food or prepare *metahee* (sweetmeats). Or perhaps the merchant seated cross legged on the ground, with an open book spread on his knee, summing up his day's accounts, or a more literary character in the same posture, following his studies or reading aloud in a chanting tone, and keeping time with his body which he swayed back and forwards.

Some huts in the suburbs were formed wholly of matting, and so open that when the light was burning we could see in. One in particular I used to admire; it was a forge, and the whole building was of semi-transparent matting. We used to pass it in the dark when returning from our evening drive. And very picturesque was the half-veiled view of the interior. The bright flame rising and sinking and the swarthy workmen leaning over the blaze.

Among the sights in and about Calcutta, I used to be amused at seeing a native young gentleman or two in an English buggy. Their white robes and soft limbs look so unfit for even the exertion of driving and the appearance of all is such an odd mixture of Europe and Asia, that few objects attracted my attention more.

In the crowded streets of Calcutta one is struck with seeing so few women. Only the lowest description, the oldest and the ugliest are seen abroad. The younger are generally pretty, but age very early, and before thirty look very old. The *pan* they chew discolours the teeth. Their skin wrinkles, their eyes become bloodshot and their flesh flaccid. They then are very hideous, and the more so from the ornaments with which they load their persons. The women marry very young, my *ayah* has with her her daughter, a widow aged thirteen. Elephantiasis is a very common complaint among the females, affecting one leg with frightful swellings but not affecting the general health.

Most of the upper class of Europeans in the Presidency have houses out of town, especially about Chowringhee, a part bordering on the river and very pretty; each house is detached and surrounded by a compound, or enclosure laid out in garden and shrubberies. The houses are upper roomed and have generally flat roofs surrounded by a balustrade and open porticos in front. I saw but little of English society in Calcutta, but some points struck me as characteristic. One was that the conversation continually turned on home. "When do you go home?" "We hope to go home in two years." "He's going home next cold weather." "They are going to send their children home next season." "I took my furlough and went home five years ago." And when the papers come in of a morning the first questions are "Any news from England?" "How long were the last steam letters coming from England?" "When does the next ship sail for England?"

One piece of luxury at the Presidency astonished me. It was American ice. It is packed surrounded with jam in the ship's hold and arrives with wonderfully little loss. A lump of it put into a glass of wine is as great a luxury as can be tasted in this climate. Indian etiquette is in some respects different to English. "May I take a glass of wine with you?" "Thank you, I'll take beer," sounds at first very odd. Moreover, here the signal for the ladies rising from the table is given by the principal lady guest, not by the mistress of the house.

The richer natives in Calcutta are imitating European manners, equipages, and buildings. Near Cossipore is a house with large grounds belonging to a Hindoo. We went into the grounds one evening to look at his pet rhinoceros. There were four or five of these curious creatures, walking about tame and grazing or rather grubbing in the earth for roots. Their keepers sat by, but their office was only to watch that their charge did not wander away. The animals were perfectly tame and allowed us to pat them, they followed their keepers and are quite harmless.

It is the univeral feeling that in Calcutta, where the wealthier natives mix a good deal with Europeans, their Hindoo prejudices are fast giving way, not I fear to the Gospel but to English science and literature. Good however must be done by the extension of knowledge, and by a breach being made in the seven fold shield of *dustoor* (custom) which has so long defied improvement.

We were struck when reading the observations in *Saturday Evening* on the Grecianising Jews how much they applied to the Anglicised Hindoos of Calcutta. European female teachers are employed as day governesses of some rich natives and I heard a very intelligent Englishman, who had been long in the country, notice the great change when respectable native ladies were seen taking a drive in an open carriage. Some Hindoo gentlemen even eat with Europeans, and at the Hindu College the youths are instructed in the English language and literature. Though they nominally continue Hindoos, they are in fact Deists. Government seminaries for the diffusion of education without any direct attempt at proselytising are established in all large stations. One lad who had been brought up at the college used frequently to come to Major Hutchinson. He was a fine, intelligent looking fellow, who seemed thirsty after information. He had a pretty correct idea of the outline of Christianity and spoke of the absurdities of Hindooism but seemed untouched at heart by either "the sinfulness of sin", or the beauty of holiness. This lad spoke English very well, and one day brought us a composition of his own in that language, a rambling essay on the advantages of science.

In the Indian papers and journals there are frequent contributions from the students, generally correct as to grammar, and shewing a considerable knowledge of our standard authors, but the questions are elaborately brought in and the style is universally bad, inflated, full of false metaphor and frequently a mere caricature of Gibbon's inversions and circumlocutions.

The sensuality of Hindoo faith and practice is so gross that to them the self denying doctrines of Christianity must be peculiarly distasteful, and the daily habits of falsehood and licentiousness must almost incapacitate their minds from comprehending the Christian standard of morals.

I went to see the Orphan Refuge of Mrs. Wilson and was much delighted with her and her labours. She is a widow and has an asylum for female orphans about eight miles above Calcutta on the Hoogly. The building is large and commodious, standing within an enclosure which opens by a *ghat*, flight of steps, on the river. We entered and, walking across the courtyard, we found ourselves at the door of a room which is a chapel. Here on the matted floor were seated a hundred girls, their ages varying from three to twelve years arranged in rows of twenty-five each, the little ones in front, the older behind. All were dressed exactly alike and exquisitely clean and, not being disfigured with ear-rings and nose-rings, they looked simple and child-like. The dress consisted of one large piece of white muslin bordered with crimson, and each girl's name worked on it. This is called a *saree*. The girls all looked healthy and happy and either there was, or I fancied, much more intellectual expression in the countenances of the elder ones than I had seen in any other female. When we entered they were singing the evening hymn in Bengalee, and it was very sweet to hear a hundred young voices join in its simple music, especially when one thought from what they had been rescued.

Mrs. Wilson is an elderly woman, of lady-like, quiet, firm demeanour, with an intelligent, benevolent countenance. Nothing in her manner enthusiastic, but like one who had counted her cost, and given herself heart and soul to the work she had chosen. She prayed in Hindustanee, and afterwards, as we were there, in English. She wished us to question the children and we asked them of some of the leading facts and doctrines of the Gospel, Mrs. Wilson acting as interpreter. The children answered readily and intelligently. We then went into the school room which is large, clean and airy, the Venetians light green, the walls white, the floors matted. Off it opened the sleeping rooms, one a large dormitory, where the girls spread their mats and blankets, the other and smaller room had *charpaees* or bedsteads, and was the hospital. Going out of this building, and crossing a parade court, we entered a long room where the children eat. Down the middle was a channel for water and on each side sat the girls, each pair provided with a brass plate of rice, with a seasoning of fish, or *dal*. At the top of the room were Mrs. Wilson's two assistants, who were I fancy country born, i.e. half caste young women. They superintended the distribution of the food. All the domestic habits of the girls brought up here are native, and while their minds are educated they are not unfitted for simple life. As they grow up they are married with native Christians, and some of the very young ones we saw were betrothed. They do needlework beautifully, and it is sold for the benefit of the institution. The upper part of the house is appropriated to Mrs. Wilson and her assistants, all seemed clean, orderly and cheerful, and I never looked with more respect on any being than I did on Mrs. Wilson.*

*The Lawrences became her lifelong supporters.

THREE

Marriage and Honeymoon

Henry and Honoria Lawrence were married very quietly on August 21st, 1837. Two weeks later they embarked on a pinnace that conveyed them up the Ganges to Revelganj, whence they went by land to Gorakhpur. This chapter consists of extracts from her journal to Henry and a letter to a friend.

Journal to Henry

Thursday August 17th, 1837
9 p.m. You arrived my Henry. I need not say more to make us both recollect that hour. We parted at eleven that night. August 18th I joined you on the verandah at six. We were happy, yet not wholly so. At heart I had a constrained feeling as we talked. After breakfast you and Richard went to Calcutta. I went to my room and lay down. You returned about 5.30 p.m. That night I sat with you. At 1 a.m. you went to Barrackpore.

Saturday August 19th
You returned after breakfast. You went to see the foundry. In the evening we sat by the river and talked.

Sunday August 20th
Not a very comfortable morning. We scarcely saw one another till after church, and then only in the presence of a third person. In the evening we sat in the verandah. We read together. About eleven that night I left you, feeling it was our last good night.

Monday August 21st
[Their wedding day] I was astir before six. At eight you came to me. We went down to breakfast. At nine thirty we left this house. And

48

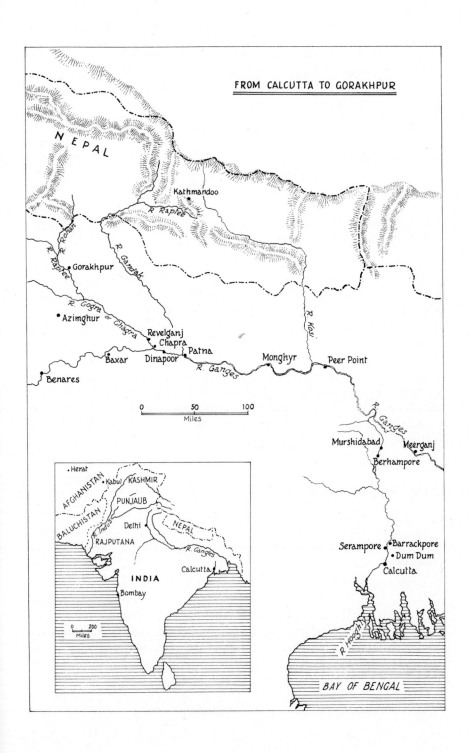

FROM CALCUTTA TO GORAKHPUR

NEPAL

Kathmandoo

R. Raptee

R. Rohan

R. Raptee

R. Gandak

Gorakhpur

R. Kosi

R. Gogra or Chagra

Azimghur

Revelganj
Chapra
Patna

Baxar
Dinapoor

Monghyr

Peer Point

R. Ganges

Benares

0   50   100
Miles

R. Ganges

Murshidabad

Meerganj

Berhampore

Serampore

Barrackpore

Dum Dum

Calcutta

R. Hoogly

BAY OF BENGAL

Herat

AFGHANISTAN

Kabul   KASHMIR

PUNJAUB

BALUCHISTAN

R. Indus

Delhi

NEPAL

RAJPUTANA

R. Ganges

INDIA

Calcutta

Bombay

0   200
Miles

then Harry! – We came home, and thank God, our first hour of our union was given to Him. We remained in the drawing room till eleven that night.

Saturday you and Dick went to Calcutta. I rummaged your papers, looked over your clothes, and enjoyed my new privilege so to do very much.

August 23rd

We rather made fools of ourselves. We rose early and went out boating. And in the evening went out again.

Tuesday August 29th

We went to Dum Dum. Came back very tired, found the Hutchinsons returned. Began to be on our good behaviour.

Wednesday August 30th

We were working at the Theodolite, very hot. You went to Calcutta. On your return you found me in bed and ill with fever. Of Thursday I remember little.

Tuesday September 5th

We embarked on the pinnace, and then, dearest we fairly felt that we were afloat together, that we had each other and no one else to look to for comfort. We shall neither of us forget how we sat that evening and looked at the banks of the river, talking of the past, the present, and the future.

Tuesday September 12th

Wrote a tragedy this morning.

September 22nd

Time passes, I know not how. "One long sunshine holiday" of happiness.

September 30th

Arrived at Seeta Khoond. Several small tanks walled in. One is filled by a hot spring of very clear pure water. On our way home climbed a rocky eminence. Came back to the pinnace, heartily glad to be in our own place again.

Henry inserts a description of this tiring day and ends:

Mrs. Lawrence is requested in future not to be so frisky and to take all opportunities, when fatigue is before her, to spare herself by lying down when she can, shutting her eyes and opening her stays. There are a hundred ways of making the best of a bad bargain and she's the cleverest cook who makes the best broth out of the fewest materials.

October 7th

I shall not without pain leave our little ship where we have passed so many hours. We are entering afresh the cares and duties of an active life; you to resume old habits, only modified by the addition of a wife; I to try my steps in a new path under your guidance. We have here learned that we can be all in all to one another, but have recognised the Giver of our precious gifts.

Letter to a friend

We are in a pinnace. It is fifty-five feet long but not drawing above two feet of water, with two masts, and rigging somewhat like a yacht, but ruder. It has sixteen oars, but we proceed chiefly by sailing and tacking. The pinnace has a poop, covering about two-thirds of its length, and forming the cabins. One fifteen feet square; the other fifteen by twenty feet and about seven feet high. These two rooms venetianed all round, having a *purdah* or curtain let down from the outside during the heat of the day. The heat has been oppressive, the thermometer being 90° and 92°. We have had one rather severe squall, but I have not yet seen anything like the violence of the elements that I expected in this climate. Indeed I think our western ideas of the horrors of India are vastly exaggerated. I have not yet seen a snake, except one in the water, though I am not yet reconciled to the great cockroaches which creep out from the crevices of an evening. Nor was I much pleased to see a scorpion walk deliberately across the floor a few days ago, nor to find a centipede making a bed of the slipper I was about to put on. One of my greatest annoyances is the prickly heat, which is a red rash breaking out over the body with an infinity of little watery specks excessively irritating.

We are, on board, about forty souls, ourselves, our servants, the *manjee* (commander) and crew. The boatmen are called *dandees*, from *dand*, an oar, and the profession is followed by both Hindus and Mussulmanns. Our men are dark, spare and active, most of them young, for their work does not favour long life. They wear mainly a waist-cloth and small skull cap of white or coloured cotton. The *manjee* is in no way distinguished from those under him, except that instead of pulling the ropes, he steers and gives orders, which he delivers in a sort of loud, prolonged chant audible at a good distance.

There is no part of the costume where the natives shew such variety of taste as in the arranging of the hair. And this does not as far as I can see depend on religious distinction. Some cover the head with a load of folded cloth, others wear no covering on it, and have the hair cropped close. Some wear little caps and the hair reaching down to the shoulders, where it is cut square across. Others have a broad line shaven from the forehead to the nape of the neck, and others cut off the hair above the forehead from ear to ear. And it is not uncommon to see the whole head shaven except one long tuft on the crown. The Mussulmanns have generally fine beards. But the Hindoos almost always shave theirs.

You would be astonished what absolute rags are the sails of country boats, and still more so that these tatters do carry along the vessel. Except in boats that are partly of European build, the bamboo is one of the chief materials, forming masts, helms, oars, spars, anchors. If there be no wind, we track by a rope fastened to the mast and pulled by a set of the *dandees*, who walk on the bank. Sometimes they are obliged to go through the water, and even to swim a considerable distance. They seem to feel neither heat nor moisture and they roll about in the river, their grinning black faces appearing above the water.

Often have I seen a man wash in the stream the piece of cloth that forms his dress, wring it out and then wrap it round his body, while the *manjee* shouts to them calling them his "*babas*", or children.

They are all a most loquacious race, and their chief pleasure seems to be smoking a "*hubble-bubble*" or pipe, a cocoa–nut shell or small hollow globe of wood which has a long tube inserted at the upper part, with a little earthen saucer on the top, where the lighted tobacco is placed. The globe is filled with water and from one side of it projects another tube, to which the mouth is applied and thus the smoke is inhaled through the water. The *hubble-bubble* is the chief refreshment of all the hard working classes, as the *hookah* is the grand recreation of the idle. We sail or track along until sunset, when we lie to, close to shore, and anchor, or rather *lagao*. That is: several ropes are put out from the boat, each having at the end a strong bamboo stake which is driven into the ground, and so we are secured for the night.

As soon as we are fairly *lagaoed* all hands are at work; some chopping firewood, intent on improving their supper; some going into the water carrying a net stretched between two bamboos shaped like the letter Y, and on his head a light basket into which he puts the little fishes as he catches them; others who are further advanced, lying down after supper to rest. The strong red glare of the fire, falling on their bronzed figures, and lighting up their bright, black faces looking very picturesque. Of a moonlight night they sometimes sit up very late, talking and laughing; the wit among them telling stories, or the whole group discussing the price of grain.

We get up about daylight and after a cup of coffee go on deck, where we sit till the sun drives us in. We then dress and are ready for breakfast at nine o'clock. During the day we read, write and otherwise occupy ourselves till towards five o'clock, when we dine, and afterwards go on deck. When the pinnace comes to, we land and ramble or sit on the shore till eight o'clock. Then we have tea, and busy ourselves till ten o'clock. I should like our voyage to last for months, it is so free from care, so unshackled, so independent of any enjoyment beyond what we have in each other's society, intellectual pursuits and the fair face of Nature.

We have sometimes met a *budgerow*, and seeing a white face has caused us all sorts of speculations. A *budgerow* is smaller generally than a pinnace, and more foreign in its aspect. It is a light and speedy vessel, but it does not admit of cooking on board. And where there is a separate cook boat, people have often the pleasure of seeing it wind-locked all day on one side of the river, while they are detained on the other.

We have seldom seen the Ganges at its full breadth because of the many islands which divide it into channels, sometimes not more than half a mile wide. Besides, it winds so much as to look more like a succession of lakes, than a continuous stream. The banks have been a good deal varied but their present clothing is *moonge* or *jeplassee*, a tall coarse grass ten or twelve feet high with a feathery head of white downy seed, presenting in places a surface so unbroken, so unspotted as to look like a heavy fall of snow. Balsam, purple, white, red and variegated abound in the hedges, and are planted round temples and tombs. The blossoms are laid as offerings on the shrines, and are afterwards thrown into the river, which I have seen quite enamelled with them.

What would you say to see the boatmen who pull us along by a rope push their way through a whole wilderness of *dhatura*, which also hangs its beautiful bells in every hedge and nook? Some of its blossoms are tinted round the edge with a reddish purple. Every variety of cactus and aloe is used for fences, and when well planted they are quite impenetrable. There are beautiful creepers festooning from tree to tree, or matting over the ground, some of the convolvulus family, others with a small bright blue blossom of the *digitalis* species. We see multitudes of two or three varieties of the palm, which have the characteristics of smooth, slender stem, and round head of drooping leaves, but lack the graceful feathery leaves and curved outlines of the coco. All trees of this sort shoot from the earth, as if they had attained their full growth under-ground, the completely formed head rising from the ground like the crown of a pine and the stem gradually lengthening. The peculiar mode of growth of these plants, reminds me of Milton's idea of the fully formed animals rising out of the earth, at their creation.

Barrackpore is on the right bank of the river, on the opposite side stands Serampore, a Danish Settlement. We did not land there but it looked a clean compact town, the buildings chiefly white and the whole having a more European air than anything else I have seen in Asia. Here is the celebrated Baptist Mission which in the work of translation and every other effectively useful measure leaves far behind every other mission in India. When Doctor Marshman came out to this country, our government refused him any countenance or even toleration. He therefore put himself under the Danish protection, and for years he has been a burning and shining light in the land. His son is following in his steps, and the printing-press at Serampore is constantly sending forth useful publications and reprints. It issues a weekly paper called *The Friend of India*, exceedingly well conducted, a decidedly religious paper, but temperate and liberal, and edited with such good sense and sound judgement that it is always quoted with respect by the other periodicals, which manifest a very different spirit.

The Indian Press was relieved from censorship only three years ago by Sir Charles Metcalfe who was temporary Governor-General then. The newspapers in this Presidency at least are universally of what is termed liberal politics, that is, opposed to the Tory party at home and generally advocating an enlarged policy towards the natives. But except *The Friend of India* they are generally of a very low stamp, full of gross personalities and miserable attempts at wit.

People generally leave home so young that their political predilections have not taken a very strong bias, or they have been here so long that the actors they remember have passed away, and the newcomers excite but a vague feeling of interest. The terms, that "Scoundrel O'Connel", "that noble Duke of Wellington", "the enlightened policy of Lord Mulgrave towards Ireland", "the faction that would overthrow the Church and the Throne" though used here, do not at all convey the pungency of party spirit that they indicate with us.

In the morning Henry took me to see the park and parade ground [of Barrackpore]. The newest objects to me were the Sepoys going through their military exercises, and a stud of elephants. The native troops wear a uniform like the English and very ugly it looks on them.* To my civil eye they seem to perform their exercises with

---

*When Henry Lawrence formed the Corps of Guides he clothed them in khaki and gave them comfortable native dress. They were the first troops in the world to wear khaki.

great precision. Their lines appeared to abound with holy men, whose residence is always indicated by a little red triangular flag placed on a tall slender bamboo. As to the elephants, I was quite astonished to see about twenty, young and old, some standing in stalls under covered sheds, some taking their food and cropping great branches of trees much as we eat water cress.

We continued our course up the river without adventure till September 12th, when we reached Berhampore. Here there is a great manufactory of silk, chiefly of a light and thin, but very strong description. Before we had been an hour lagaoed, we were visited by the *copra-wallahs*, cloth merchants bringing silks for sale. Each opened his bundle praising his own goods and disparaging his neighbours, thrusting a piece of silk towards us, and recommending it "*Scatch plat*" (Scotch Plaid) or "*Bailatee*" (English) or whatever he thought would be most acceptable. One day at Cossipore a *boccas-wallah* (box man, pedlar) was displaying his goods. Mrs. Hutchinson took up some stockings, saying to him in a tone which I suppose he thought disparaging, "These are English?" The man spoke a little of our tongue, and immediately said "It's, Mem Sahib, not Anglees. Liverpool, Mem Sahib, Liverpool". I hate buying from the natives, they always ask twice or three times as much as the thing is worth, or as they mean to take, and then when they are offered less they hold up their clasped hands saying "*Hum gurreeb admee*," "I'm a poor man," looking all the while as sly as possible, and as if they enjoyed having taken in the "*Feringhees*" (Christians, a corruption, I fancy, of Franks).

September 16th

We entered the Great Ganges and our *manjee* came to ask a *bugis*, or present, for *Gunga-gee*, (Mr. Ganges).

During this week we had some glorious sunsets, sometimes the sun rushed down like a red-hot ball through the clear blue sky till it dipped behind the hills, rapidly sinking till but a golden speck remained and then disappearing, to be succeeded by a rose coloured tint, bathing the whole western sky through which the evening star shone like a lamp. Other evenings the sky was heaped up with masses of purple clouds, the silvery sun lighting up their edges. This is constantly succeeded by lightning, indeed I do not recollect one evening since I came to the country without vivid flashes, generally to the westward. We are in the land for enjoying all skiey influences. And we have no barring and bolting out of these beauties but can at any hour go to the verandah, or the tent door to look out. One feature however, I miss, the dark masses of cloud which at home we so often see at night, sailing across a clear sky. Nor do we here see "a sable cloud turn forth her silver lining on the night". As far as I have seen in this climate, the nocturnal heavens are either perfectly transparent or covered with a mist more or less dense.

As we advance up the river, the number of boats increases. Sometimes when we go on deck of a morning there are fifty or sixty sail in sight. Relieved against the red eastern sky, they remind me of the spectre ship seen by the "Ancient Mariner".

September 20th

I was amused at seeing a herd of buffaloes swim across. They resemble large coarse dark grey cows excepting in the setting on of the head, which in a buffalo is very peculiar. The forehead is nearly on a level with the back, so that the long curved horn lies almost on the shoulders, and the chin is poked straight out. The creature has always the look of staring at you with a vacant enquiring countenance. And there is something very ludicrous in its air. They swim well, the heads alone appearing above water, and the driver holding by the tail of the hindermost.

September 21st

Off Peer Point. Peer means a holy man, and Peer Point is the residence of one. *Fakeers* or religious mendicants belong to both Mussalmanns and Hindus, whose faith is in many things blended, though there must always be a grand distinction between the eaters and the worshippers of the cow. On the summit of one rock overhanging the stream, was the *fakeer*'s hut, and a little to the left, up the hill, one Hindu temple and the ruins of another, quite overgrown by a *peepul* tree, a kind of aspen, which strikes its roots into every crack and fissure of a building, and soon loosens the stones. The seeds are carried by birds, and are often deposited on the bark of another tree, where they take root, and completely smother their abode. There is among the natives a superstition that if a man who has planted a tree, dies in debt, the creditor comes in the form of a *peepul*, roots itself in the tree and destroys it.

September 29th

Reached Monghyr a city once famous in Oriental story, and fortified strongly after the native fashion, with a fort having thick mud walls, faced with brick and a deep wide ditch. The brick facings are fast going to decay, and the *peepul* is rooting itself in the turrets.

There are several *ghats*. *Ghat* means a passage, but is particularly applied to the passages leading down to a river; these are sometimes merely rude steps cut in the clay, but the better sort consist of a regular flight of stone and brick steps, with a gateway at the top. One of these at Monghyr attracted my attention. The steps were at the early hour we saw them crowded with people. Strings of women to draw water, clothed in their graceful flowing attire, their wrists and ankles decorated with ornaments, which though generally mere baubles, are not the less picturesque. Each balanced on her head a *ghurrah*, the red earthen vessel in which they draw water, and which seems formed to be inconvenient, being shaped like an orange with a wide circular [rim?]: it rolls about at a touch. However it is the only water pitcher used, so I suppose it has its advantages. Down [the women] were filing. Some were stooping to fill their vessels, others were placing on their heads those already full.

In the shallow water were troops of bathers, men, women and children, all paddling and swimming about, like so many frogs; some who had emerged from the bathe were drying and twisting up their long hair. Others were washing their *cummerbunds* (waistclothes) by beating them against a stone and others, who had finished this operation, were girding on their still wet clothes.

September 24th

The Hindu and the Mussulman religions read us a lesson as to public acts of charity, and were the Christian name to be swept from India tomorrow, it would leave few memorials in the shape of works for the good of the natives, such as the digging of tanks, sinking of wells and planting of topes.

Within a few days there were two deaths among our crew: one poor old creature had looked dying from the time we set out. Poor old man! He had no relatives on board, and the other *dandees* would hardly give him water to drink, and only interfered to prevent his taking nourishment from us "because he was a Hindu". It was pitiable to see the withered shrunken form lying on the deck, hardly covered by a dirty blanket, and most painful to feel that we could do nothing for him. I was quite relieved when he died, and his remains were thrown overboard. And was there an immortal spirit sojourning in that form? In the perplexity that will arise from such a sight, there is but one resting place for the mind, "Shall not the judge of all the earth do right?".

The other death was of a young man, son to one of the *dandees*. He lay for several days nearly insensible. His father's grief was very affecting. The old man used to sit on deck hour after hour supporting his Baba's head, appealing to him in the most wailing tones, and weeping bitterly. His comrades too in this case shewed feeling; one after another would come and sit by him, but the patient could not be roused from his lethargy. He had high fever on him, a lightening pulse, hot skin, and swollen throat, but because he was insensible to what went on, and did not speak, they all declared it was not fever but that a spirit had got into him, and they would not allow him to take medicine from us. Night after night, when we lay to, "Wise men" were brought from the shore to exorcise the spirit, but as you may suppose the poor sufferer died under such treatment. Him they buried, and when all was over, the bereaved old parent used of an evening to sit apart on deck, not caring to prepare his food, but "put his face between his knees" and looked indeed as if his "occupation was gone".

October 5th

At Dinapoor we went on board in the evening in the midst of wind and rain, and all night the gale continued increasing. We were most uncomfortable for the two following days. The pinnace pitched to and fro on her moorings and our goods tumbled about the cabin. Having no glass windows we were obliged to keep the Venetians closed to exclude the rain. The air felt like a wet blanket, and the clothes we put on of a morning seemed as if they had been soaked in spray. I felt as if I had been dipped in a honey pot.

At Revelganj we left the pinnace. Set off at three p.m. in palinquins. The night was beautiful but the roads were all but impassable. The storm last week laid the country under water. The man who had posted our bearers reckoned the stages differently from those who carried us, and in the middle of the night we were set down, the men refusing to take us any further; after some difficulty, they did carry us to the next stage. We reckoned on reaching our halting place by eight in the morning. At nine, however, we were still short of it, and as the sun was not very hot, we stopped in a grove of bamboos. Among the beauties of the vegetable world, this is conspicuous, from one root or bunch of roots, scores and hundreds of stems arise to the height of sixty or eighty feet, each perfectly straight tapering to the top, feathered with bunches of long narrow leaves and leaning from the centre outwards, so that the clump has the shape of a hearse-plume. But in the aspect of the bamboo, there is nothing funereal. It is a bright green, its stems covered with a thin verdant bark, beneath which is the beautiful natural yellow varnish of the cane. This tree is the resort of fireflies. At night they seem like drops of light shaken from the branches.

Journal to Henry continued:

October 10th

10.30 a.m. In a *palkee* contrived from my sea cot in a most Robinson Crusoe like fashion. We left the pinnace and continued *daking* till 8.30 a.m. this morning, having missed our bearers, left behind our *petarrahs*, forgotten to put tea in the *palkee* and divers other moving accidents. But, darling, why should these things ruffle us? These are our appointed trials sent to teach us forebearance and self-government. Excuse the lecture, my own Harry. Roads in places very bad, sometimes over morasses and *jheels*, sometimes merely a path through a field.

Burra Ganj, October 11th

Alas darling, too soon does the teacher require to be taught. Before many hours I was peevish and irritable, and that to your dear self. We started at 3 p.m. and at four got to the house of a charitable indigo planter, who gave us a cup of tea. Reached Meerganj at six, got into a buggy and had a delightful drive by moonlight to the bungalow which we are now in. The furniture consists of a table, a cot, and two chairs, but there is a good roof to keep out the sun. We have *khana*, *panee*, soap and water, clean clothes, books and writing materials. Above all we have each other.

Henry replied:

Our dawn trip was a most disastrous one, the bearers at no stage of the tour being ready, and then being vile jawing fellows. I feel that I was more like a maniac than aught else for twenty-four hours. But instead of peevishness I saw nothing but the utmost sweetness and gentleness in you, my darling.

Hatimpore, October 13th

Reached the Jurie where we were ferried over in a most primitive manner. Two boats, each hollowed from a single trunk were lashed together, and on this the buggy was placed. We afterwards crossed in the same way. The bend of the stream looked like a lake with steep banks overgrown with jungle. On the banks were some travellers seemingly waiting to be ferried over. As we came in sight, the boat pushed off from the opposite side, the men standing up in it and shoving it along by tall bamboo poles. The water like a mirror reflecting the whole, beautiful butterflies and birds flying about and the wood-pigeons cooing from the surrounding thickets. The jungle consisted chiefly of Mimosa, three species. Long running creepers festooned many of the bushes, and the ground was enamelled with wild flowers. There we were, darling, the only two Europeans, and all the world to each other.

As the sun went down the moon shone out and we had a lovely drive in the clear night, passing through patches of wood and lanes bordered with bamboos all sparkling with fireflies. The native villages among the trees very picturesque. Their low thatched roofs overgrown with gourd-like creepers. The inhabitants standing and sitting in groups outside in the moonlight. Here and there a large single tree, under which lay a herd of cattle, seeming to enjoy the cool evening as much as we did. We reckoned on finding a tent, and at 8 p.m. we saw among the trees at sunset our servants seated and fires lighted. All this was very pretty but we were somewhat aghast to find no tent and a *charpoy* spread under the canopy of heaven. However, you found in the *tope* a matted shed where our bed was placed. We got a fine plump *moorghie*, and we have been very comfortable but for the swarms of insects, which even the mosquito curtains did not exclude and which bite me unmercifully.

Yesterday the 12th we were up before sunrise, and after perfunctory ablutions and summary toilette, performed after most rural fashion under a tree, we got into the buggy and went over such a road "if road it might be called, which road was none". Joke the first was your getting out and carrying me over some *jheels*, and afterwards walking through such places that your clothes were all wet except your *banian*. When we came halfway, you took off your own clothing, girded the *Pushmina* round your loins and put on my cloak to the great astonishment apparently of the niggers, who stared at seeing a sahib so attired.

Here we got letters and papers. Before nine we crossed the Ghagra, and after half an hour's driving reached the tent at Kussur Thana. Here we were made amends for all our troubles, finding all comfortable; and after breakfast and bath we were very snug.

Henry interposes:

At 11.00 p.m. while you are snoring like a young rhinoceros, I again take up the book to testify how good a traveller you are, how courageous by land and water, and how gentle and forbearing to your cross husband.

Puttrah, October 15th
Yesterday read, wrote, and at 4.30 p.m. set out for Pycowly. The road a wheel track through fields or no track at all through swamps and *nullahs*. "Crackskull Common and Featherbed Lane" were nothing to it, but we got safely to our tent, which was cheerful and where all was bright and right.

Started this morning at five thirty. After we had gone a little way I was astonished at the politeness of the natives, who showed us the way, smoothed the road and shoved on the buggy. I soon learned this was not all disinterested benevolence.* As we came near the village

*They had reached the district in which Henry had authority.

you pointed out the old *Fakir*'s abode. When we got to our own tent, the traps were not there. And funny enough, we were immediately greeted by an envoy of his holiness, asking permission to send a breakfast. We pushed on however, to Reade's camp,★ quite a Canvas City, which we reached about nine, and here we are, at home and busy. I do not recollect ever feeling better than for the last few days.

★E. A. Reade, the Collector of Gorakhpur, was a lifelong friend.

FOUR

At Gorakhpur and In Camp

The honeymoon was over, Henry Lawrence went back to work. He remained very much a professional artillery officer all his life and served in several campaigns, but his great life's work was in civilian administration. At this stage of his career he had been seconded to the Revenue Survey and it was in this work that he acquired his deep knowledge of Indian village people and their problems. This – together with the villagers' knowledge that he loved them – gave him an extraordinary influence over them. He had a hot temper, and Indians resent the loss of temper more than Europeans do, but they forgave him.

Honoria explains later in this chapter what the Revenue Survey did. But why was it important? Immediately before the British conquest India had fallen into an unparalleled state of anarchy upon the break up of the Moghul Empire. In particular the relatively fair and efficient system of taxation established by Akbar in the sixteenth century had collapsed. Tax gatherers and marauding armies took what they could get, often leaving the peasants to starve. Records had been destroyed, populations had shifted and it was no light matter to discover who a given field belonged to, who was liable for the tax on it, and to assess a fair tax. If the assessment was too high, the cultivator went bankrupt. If the assessments were consistently too low, the state itself would be bankrupt, for the land tax was the chief source of revenue.

It was not easy for a foreign power to grasp a system of land holding and taxation that was entirely strange to them. Systems of land tenure differ as much in India as they do in Europe but in general a right to cultivate certain land and a right to collect the tax on it are recognised, rather than property in land, as understood in Europe. Serious mistakes were made, sometimes by giving rights of ownership which native custom did not recognise, sometimes by fixing the tax too high and sometimes by leaving it fixed at the same level for ever. Yet the Revenue Survey removed many great injustices and in the end imposed an equitable and fairly administered taxation such as India had never known. The Lawrence brothers were consistently in favour of light assessments and the consequent extension of cultivation. There was no shortage of land in India till towards the end of the nineteenth century. So the extension of cultivation became easy, as soon as it became known that a man would always be able to reap what he had sown.

In 1838 the British had already been for a generation the "Paramount Power" in India, from Cape Comorin in the South to the Himalayas in the North and the River Sutlej in the West. The Honorable the East India Company, John Company for short, or the Company Bahadur, as the Indians called it, had long been under Parliamentary control and its commercial functions had ceased to be important. Its hitherto invincible army consisted of some European regiments and more numerous native regiments under British officers. To the end of the Raj about a third of the total area of India consisted of Native States under their own Rajahs. These conducted their internal affairs in their own way, subject to the informal but strong influence of a British Resident or Agent.

The Company ruled its own dominions through a small Civil Service recruited by personal nomination of the Company's Directors. The pay was good but the task was strenuous and the climate hard. So weaklings did not seek entry into the Indian Civil Service. Its ranks were supplemented for various purposes by secondment from the Company's army. The ablest officers tended to gravitate to the Political Service, which is how Henry, George, and Richard Lawrence came to do civilian work. John was the only one of the Lawrence brothers who entered the Civil Service at the beginning of his career.

Journal to a friend

1837

Gorakhpur is a large military station and has several civilian residents. So there is what is called "a good deal of society". In this country the étiquette is for the newcomers to call on those whom they wish to know. At least this is the rule for bachelors. A married man does the same but his wife waits to be visited by the ladies.

Nothing can be duller than the society of a small station in India. It is worse than a country town at home, for here the climate produces languor and there are few topics of public interest. English politics excite comparatively moderate feeling and the local events are seldom very wonderful. The station when we were there contained only two single ladies who were talked of as "the big spin" and "the little spin" (spinster). When I heard their merits discussed, I rejoiced at not having entered the place as a spinster. But when I saw what life in the cantonment was, I especially rejoiced that I was not to be pinned down to one spot and live such a life as ladies there. They may rise early but, I fancy, do not generally. Breakfast about ten, and soon after visitors begin, chiefly gentlemen, and long indeed are their visitations. Any man who has nothing else to do comes and "bestows his tediousness" on the ladies, who rarely go out during the day. So the morning passes, till two or three o'clock, when tiffin is announced, which is generally like a regular dinner and to which visitors often remain. After this, the ladies retire to their rooms, and I suppose to take a sleep till about sunset, when they go out for the evening drive on the same dirty road where they have driven a thousand times before, meeting the same faces they have met a hundred times. Coming in from the drive there is dinner, then coffee, then bed, for in this country people retire very early. And so passes day after day, till the corps or the civilian is removed and then they settle down in some other place to plod on the same round.

The dinner table in this country strikes a newcomer. The company look English enough, except for the sallow complexions. The gentlemen's dress, which is entirely white, pleases my eye greatly. The linen jacket looks so cool and clean I wonder it is not adopted in summer at home. The arrangements of the table, too, are much like what we are used to, but on looking up from the circle of guests, one is immediately struck by the complete belt of black faces and white muslin dresses that surrounds it. Every person brings one or two servants, who stand behind their master's chairs, and give the party its Indian look.

The cook-house is always apart from the dwelling. And the distance which the dishes are carried, as well as the swinging of the *punkah* over them, makes the food generally cold, despite the hot water plates. The cooking differs little from our own, except in the regular curries and mulligatanees. Mutton and fowl when boiled are encased in a covering of thick paste, made of coarse flour and water. This is taken off when the dish is brought to table. The meat is much more juicy and tender than when boiled without a covering. I was surprised to find so many English articles of food in India. All kinds of preserves, jams and dried fruits. Sauces, potted meat, and fish, cheese, and biscuits are to be seen in every house. Soda water, which in this climate is largely used, is called by the natives *Balâtee pânee*: English water. The vegetables, pease [sic], asparagus, turnips etc. are all tasteless. And I was astonished to find the fruit so insipid. Pines [sic] are stringy and coarse, oranges tough and dry. Mangoes are occasionally good, but for the greater number taste of turpentine. The plantain is like a mealy pear. Guavas, some people like very much, but their peculiar flavour is to me disagreeable. There are pears that are very good for preserves, but not fit to eat raw. The custard-apple is full of black seeds surrounded by a pulp something like custard. But I have tasted nothing so good as a melon, a pear or a strawberry since I left home. At Calcutta I saw a very nice fruit called the Alligator pear. The fleshy part is eaten with salt and pepper, and tastes like the best cream-cheese.

Of all practices in Indian society I detest the *hookah*. And it is utterly barbarous to see it brought in before the ladies retire. There is a stand somewhat like a large candlestick, on the top of which is a silver receptacle for the charcoal balls and perfumed tobacco. The lower part of the stand is filled with water and into one side is introduced the long snake-like tube, with its gay mouthpiece. All the finery and perfumery do not take off the disgustingness of the practice, and of its expectatory accompaniment. It is strange to see a gentleman sitting after dinner with the snake taken lovingly under his arm, the mouthpiece held gently between his lips, whence it is occasionally withdrawn that he may address the lady next to him, to whom he breathes forth alternate smoke and compliments. Cigars are bad enough, but they are not taken in company. It is only their determined smokers who are afterwards redolent of them. But the *hookah* is a nuisance not to be borne, and I wish every lady in the country would express the same opinion.

In this *zillah* the mango *topes* are among its principal beauties, as well as advantages. To plant a *tope* is amongst the natives an act of religion and certainly one of benevolence. So much are these trees esteemed that a Hindoo will not cut down even one that is decayed, and I never observed one that appeared wantonly injured. The shade of the mango is so dense that it defies the sun, and does not favour the growth of weeds or jungle. It is in leaf all the year round, changing its foliage in March, but never becoming bare. The mango grows to a great size, especially in this district, where it rises to eighty or a hundred feet. A few feet above the root the trunk generally parts into two or three diversions, which sub-divide into large branches, running upwards very much as a pear tree grows. But when a tree stands detached, it throws out its arms on every side, and looks not unlike a fine oak. After passing through jungle or even over fields when the sun has set, there is a dry warm feeling immediately on entering the tope. The trees are regularly planted in rows, so that standing in the midst, there is in every direction a lofty green vista, forming a noble avenue up to the camp.

In this district the villages are generally very picturesque. The houses are low with drooping eaves, generally mantled over with *kuddoo*. In damp soils both walls and roof are frequently made of matting. Almost every village has its tope, its clump of bamboos, its detached *tar* trees and its tank with a white temple beside it. The ground clear of forest is generally well cultivated. As there is seldom any division between the fields except a slight ridge of earth thrown up, the country looks like one gigantic park varied by masses of planting, and occasional clumps of shrubs and detached trees.

Near Gorakhpur there is a road, lately cut through the forest and which was laid out by Henry. This road extends in a straight line for miles. Its long vista of road level cut through the thick trees is very pretty. There is no human habitation in sight, and we did not meet a single traveller. In one part we saw numerous prints of wild elephants' feet. They abound in the forest, but are not dangerous unless a single one is met. We were mounted on a tame one.

About a mile from the station there is a holy place called Gorucknaught. A succession of mango *topes* gives two or three miles of shade, and in the heart of this there are many tanks and temples. They are square, white buildings, with dome shaped roofs, and arched entrances; the ground about them is kept exceedingly neat and clean and contains some splendid single trees with seats built round them. There are also pretty gardens, with balsams, jasmines, tuberoses and other flowers for the worshippers to make garlands of.

Near the temple is a burying ground, for, though burning is the usual mode of disposing of a body among the Hindoos, yet some of the more sacred dead are buried. There were tombs of mason work raised over the *mohants* or priests and the same on a smaller scale over the *cheelahs*, or novices. The place swarms with *fakirs*, a most disgusting race, generally stout able-bodied men, daubed with ashes and filth, and more nearly naked than even the other Hindoos. They are impudent to the greatest degree, and with all their dirt and nudity, have a pampered appearance. Nothing human can be more horrible than they look. And we know that they practise every abomination.

One morning before sunrise we were driving through Gorucknaught, and hearing a great noise of drums, bells and horns we turned up to one cluster of temples. The largest temple was lighted within, and showed a shrine upon which I did not observe any figure, but heaps of flowers, feathers, scarlet cloth, tinsel, shells and all sorts of trumpery. Outside a troop of *fakirs* blew horns, beat drums and struck upon large bells that hung in the verandah. The worship, as far as we saw, was this: a priest with his face all muffled up except the eyes, stood before the shrine holding an earthen lamp, or rather cup of oil with many lighted wicks round its edge. This he waved slowly round his head, then turned to the right, then to the left, and bowed to the shrine. We turned away sick at heart. Oh when will the "saving health be known among all nations"?

Gorakhpur is a missionary station, and has a very pretty church and parsonage house, with a missionary school for boys and one for girls. A few miles off there is a farm belonging to the missionary society, and likely to be very productive, being chiefly newly reclaimed forest-land. Here Mr. Wilkinson has built a church and a bungalow, both very pretty objects. They stand on one side of a large tank, just opposite to a Mussulmann place of worship. It is to be hoped that the decay of the latter and rise of the former indicate the conditions of the two faiths. This farm, from its sequestered position, is particularly useful, as giving a place for locating the converts and keeping them apart from the heathen.

There is a race course a mile round, and the horses are ridden, some by their masters, some by jockeys. A Hindu jockey is a droll object. Nothing can be more unbecoming to natives than our costume. The riding cap above the dark face, and the slender limbs clothed in hotter inexpressibles and gaiters give the idea of a dressed-up monkey. These, and the European spectators on horse-back or in carriages, all attended by their *syces*, and the natives in their white robes and gay turbans, had a very picturesque effect. Quite unlike any of our home ideas. Nor must I forget the old red-faced colonel mounted on an elephant whose scarlet trappings shone in the evening sun, the field officer sitting just behind the *mohout*, and a pale skinny subaltern occupying the less dignified post in his rear.

Journal to Henry

Sunday October 22nd

We had some discussion last night on the observance of this day, and I told you, dearest, the truth, that our Sundays had been my least happy hours since our marriage. It is our indispensable duty to make up our minds as to how the Christian Sabbath is to be observed. My beloved, seek God's teaching on the subject, follow it simply, and then we shall pursue our occupations with a cheerful quiet spirit. My own view is that our rule ought to be the entire suspension of worldly business. The exceptions must be determined by circumstances. My love, I do not like to seem as if I were your teacher, but circumstances have led me to the consideration of subjects which your attention has not thus been directed to, and I now implore you to consider the matter. I should like to take some one book of Scripture for Sunday and pursue it regularly on that day, for a longer time than we give to reading in the week. Studying the New Testament in the original, reading such works as Milton, writing on matters connected with religion, all these would vary the day's occupations, and make "the Sabbath a delight"

October 24th

Dined at Mr. L.'s. Conversation chiefly about horses and Mr. Treaves "a most gentlemanly man, whom you could not help liking". A civilian who had gone home, kept horses at Newmarket, became intimate with the Prince Regent, got letters from him to Lord Hastings, been placed in a responsible and lucrative trust in Calcutta, been suspended only because he neglected his business, and left everything to his *baboo*, so that the very *chuprassees'* places were sold. Applied to be reinstated, directors refused, Marquis of Hastings gave him a letter to the Rajah of Oude, desiring him to provide for Mr. Treaves. And "a capital berth he must have had of it", for he died in two and a half years "worth four *lakhs* rupees". The story attracted my attention as Mr. Thomson⋆ told it with all the naiveté of a worldly man, who lays open his notions without an idea that he is showing his own want of principle, or lack of moral vision to distinguish between right and wrong. The whole tale was told as if its hero had been one of the most fortunate and enviable of men. How will such stand at the last day?

Counia, November 1st

Yesterday at 4.30 p.m. we left Gorakhpur. Every mile we advanced in the jungle I felt my spirits rise. All our annoyances seemed left behind, and my mind regained that tranquil elasticity "which in the crowd and bustle of resort" is much impaired. We left the buggy at a piece of water which the people called a lake, but which looked more like a river. We crossed in a canoe. On the other side was our elephant. I could hardly believe that I was myself, bestriding the *hattee*'s neck with my feet on the *mohout*'s hinder parts. We dismounted to cross the Rohan, which is so deep that the elephant swam across it. A man last night told us it would take a week to go by river from here to Gorakhpur.

November 3rd

This has been a quiet pleasant day. You went out early and then there was the delight of expecting you and welcoming you home. All the morning you were busy and I enjoyed the tranquil pleasure of sitting quietly by. "The English enjoyment" as Rousseau called it "of sitting silent in the same room". In the afternoon a delightful ride on the elephant through the jungle, with very large trees, many beautiful creepers and shrubs.

Camp Goolurya-Serai, November 4th

We were astir early and off by six. Set out on a *hattee*, crossed the Rohan, mounted our *tats*, rode to the Chilwa, crossed it, got on another elephant, rode through the forest. On the plain got into the buggy and reached camp a little past nine. I cannot express the pleasure I find in the successive lovely days, "cloudless clime and starry skies". There is a creeper abundant here, it has a slender stalk thickly clothed with leaves of a delicate pale green. Each leaf looks like two leaves joined

⋆G. P. Thomson was an Additional Judge at Gorakhpur.

near the stem, folded so that it looks like a butterfly, with its wings half-closed. The leaves are from two to four inches across, and some of the young ones that are tinged with red and have tendrils near them, look wonderfully like the insect. We have seen no game but two or three peacocks, and the wood-pigeon cooes incessantly. Some bird which I have not yet seen, has a shrill cry in the morning like Puck-er-oh, Puck-er-oh. Flashes of green parrots, a few herons.

Gorakhpur, November 5th

We came in here yesterday evening and had some very happy hours of conversation, in which we talked over what might be our future way of spending our time.

Dhuria bazaar, November 8th

We had a quiet and pleasant Sabbath. Received the Sacrament, not I hope and believe as a mere form. Monday we paid visits, and did botheration of settling, and at 4 p.m. "away to the woods away".

November 11th

My beloved, I have been trying to look into myself and find out what is wrong, when I recollect what my intentions and expectations were, and find how far my doings fall short of these.

November 12th

My chief deficiency is, I think, in making the most of circumstances. When I am settled down in a routine I can adhere to it steadily, and fill up every hour, but if I get off my track I am all adrift, my time slips by and I am altogether unhinged. This is a disposition peculiarly unfitted to the life I now lead. Let it then be my endeavour to be always prepared with some occupation, and to be satisfied with the employment that is most convenient, without considering whether it be the one I at the moment might fancy. Since our marriage I discover in myself an impatience and irritability which I did not formerly give way to.

Tuesday November 14th

Sunday we had more bustle than usual, but some pleasant hours together. Yesterday you went out surveying early and did not return until eleven. In the evening we drove out. Noticed a beautiful grass of which they make fences here abouts. It grows twelve or fourteen feet high, has a slender stem and a fine feathery head of silky blossom, the leaves are rough and coarse and are used for chopping [i.e. thatch]: they are called *serput*, and the plant *serraria*.

On Sunday evening we rode to the Raptee, embarked in L.'s boat.

Noticed square mounds of earth at every twenty or thirty yards. They were about eight feet square and four or five feet high, and the Brahmin's brothers who were with us said they were as a defence against the wild elephants. This seemed very absurd, and I mentioned it to G. but he said it was quite true, that a very small drain or mound will stop an elephant, as it is afraid of a trap. When a drove are making an inroad, if one of the young ones should fall down, the whole flock stops till it rises.

Saturday November 25th

Yesterday evening darling you shewed me how to plot, and today I did two villages. How pleasant was it even to fancy I was helping you.

Mhoodkowly, December 8th

Came here to Rind's camp yesterday evening, Rind's tents and appointments very neat, but oh, such talk! I should die of it, or go mad. An incessant stream of self conceit and scandal, and eating and drinking interlarded with profane expressions. The whole perfumed with the *hookah*, which at this moment makes my head split, and my hand shake.

I should like that our tent had more of the method and neatness of this, for I think both time and temper would be saved thereby. But were this one of Tippoo's shawl tents, I would not take it, and the etceteras, in exchange for our little single pole.

Secundra, December 10th

At our old quarters. Dearest, why do we not oftener speak of the home to which we look forward? Sometimes, when I consider my own happiness the next thought is, how soon it must be over! But, I say to myself we shall never be parted. There may be a separation by death, for a time one of us may have to finish life's journey alone, but as compared to what follows, this is but like an hour's separation out of our lives.

Henry writes:

December 15th

On the banks of Poyna Tal. Here my love are we, perhaps the first *pair* of human beings, certainly of Europeans, who have ever trod these wilds. You are certainly a most excellent surveyor's wife and, had your husband been in the grocery line, I'm sure that you would have been all that's good, all that's sweet.

December 16th

I think, as you say, that I could have assimilated myself to any condition with a loved and loving husband, but no mode of life could fall in with my tastes better than this does. Among the hardly defined fears I had was one, that I should not suffice to you. As far as I saw of life, men always required something more than mere married companionship and, when I knew we should be thrown wholly on one another, I doubted whether it was in man not to feel *ennuyé*, hankering after some novelty. Therefore you may judge my happiness when I find you day after day contented with but one. Once some time ago I made what you called "a pretty speech" and your liking it, led me to sift the thought, which I am sure is just. It is, that a wife is to a man one of many objects, but a husband is to a woman the object. A man has his wife and his profession. A woman's profession is to be a wife.

Loojooria, December 19th

On the 17th we started two hours before sunrise, lovely moonlight ride through the forest. After getting on the plain saw several wooden wells. Man said one costs twelve rupees, lasts twelve years. Arrived here about 10 a.m. found P. Read together. Yesterday you were up 3.30 a.m., very, very busy. I wrote home letters. Today at 8 a.m. I have been journalising.

December 26th

Think of yesterday's having passed without my writing one word! Yesterday, the happiest birthday and Christmas I ever recollect, albeit you were nine hours away from me, the longest time we have yet been separated. But I had what was next best to your company, Solitude, and as I sat here I traced back the same period in each year up to 1823.

December 31st, 1837

The last day of a year that has brought to us almost unmingled good. We have just been going over each month, and tracing our several paths till they merged into one.

Who is blessed as we are? Let us begin the next year in more absolute dependence on the Almighty and set before ourselves certain definite habits to be either checked or acquired.

Henry answers:

If we can, dearest, but I have more difficulties to get over than perhaps you imagine. However I'll try.

71

Journal to a friend continued:

Camp near Gorakhpur, November 1837

Before taking you out to camp, it will be as well for you to know the nature of our business there. In explaining it I will assume that you are as ignorant of Indian affairs as I was myself before I left England.

In this country, Government may properly be called the head landlord of all the soil. The chief part of the revenue arises from a levy on the land, which may be termed rent, or tax, which is gathered in small sums by intermediate Native proprietors, and paid by them to the collector of the *zillah* or district. About fifty years ago the levy on the greater part of Bengal was adjusted on a perpetual settlement by Lord Cornwallis. This seems to have been a very hasty proceeding, though the company will not yet swerve from the Mede-and-Persian-like unchangeableness of their law. They have, however, adopted a more moderate system with the territories since acquired. And the settlement now in progress, based on the Revenue Survey is for the limited period of twenty years.

The whole country is divided into portions commonly called villages, but answering much more to our Irish term of "town-land", for the word does not necessarily imply that there are houses in the divisions. I was at first amused to hear of "villages that were all jungle".

I will quote a passage from Sir Charles Metcalfe to illustrate what has been said of the village system:

"The villages are little republics, having nearly everything they want within themselves and almost independent of any foreign relations. They seem to last where nothing else lasts. Dynasty after dynasty tumbles down, revolution succeeds revolution. Hindoo, Pathan, Mogul, Mahratta, Sikh, English, are all masters in their turn; but the village communities remain the same. In times of trouble they arm and fortify themselves. A hostile army passes through the country, the village communities collect their cattle within their walls and let the enemy pass unprovoked. If plunder and devastation be directed against themselves, and the force employed be irresistible, they flee to friendly villages at a distance. When the storm has passed over they return, and resume their occupations. If a country remain for a series of years the scene of continued pillage and massacre so that the villages cannot be inhabited, the scattered villagers nevertheless return whenever the power of peaceable possession revives. A generation may pass away, but the succeeding generation will return. The sons will take the places of their fathers. The same lands will be reoccupied by the descendants of those who were driven out when the village was de-populated. And it is not a trifling matter that will drive them out, for they will often maintain their post through times of disturbance and convulsion, and acquire strength sufficient to resist pillage and oppression with success.

"This union of the village communities, each one forming a separate little state in itself, has, I conceive, contributed more than any other cause to the preservation of the people of India through all the revolutions and changes which they have suffered. And is in a high degree conducive to their happiness, and to the enjoyment of a great portion of freedom and independence. I wish therefore, that the village constitutions may never be disturbed and I dread everything that has a tendency to break them up."

You can conceive that it is of the utmost importance to have correct maps, and accurate statistical returns that the revenue may be fairly levied. Terrible abuses have existed on this head. In confirmation I may mention having found it recorded among the official letters of the Collector of Gorakhpur that so late as 1819 a Rajah here gave in a list of twenty-six villages, the names entirely of his own invention. For these he obtained from the local authorities a settlement which was sanctioned by Government.

In order to obtain the required documents, the Revenue Survey is going on, or as I heard a gentleman (a surveyor hinself too!) remark with great naiveté, "Government have a curiosity to know the state of the country." Henry is the head of a survey establishment to which belong two or three assistants, about a dozen *crannies* or clerks, and hundreds of natives. There is a separate establishment for the settlement of boundaries. When these have been marked off, each field is separately measured with a chain and a map of the village made by the eye, accompanied by a statement of the extent, soil, crops, of every field. This is called the *Kusrah* work, and is carried on entirely by natives, who are paid according to the extent they measure. The surveyor takes by instruments a scientific map of each village and the professional total is compared with the *Kusrah* total, the correctness of which it proves. A separate map is then made of every village, accompanied by a statement of its extent, quality of cultivation and arable land, means of irrigation, number of houses and inhabitants, the castes to which they belong, and all such details. A certain number of maps form a volume, which, with the *Kusrahs* is sent to the collector for his guidance. Duplicate copies being deposited in the Surveyor General's office. There are also maps of each *Pergunnah*, or county, on a reduced scale, showing the relative position of villages, their boundaries and geographical features.

The establishment here is divided into several camps of which Henry's is the Headquarters. As the work is completed we move from point to point of the district. In such a life we see more of the country and its inhabitants than can be known to the dwellers in bungalows and "upper-roomed houses", and I willingly take the inconveniences of a wandering life in consideration of its pleasures.

You would be much amused at the people who in the course of the day visit our tent. The "potent grave and reverend seignors" of the village come with all due étiquette, turbaned and belted, leaving their shoes outside, salaaming to each of us, and according to their rank standing or sitting during the interview. I have smiled at the contrast when one of these precise and solemn gentlemen conversed with Henry in measured tone, and with the proper number of "Sahibs" and bows, while Henry sat without coat, waistcoat or jacket, his legs over the arm of the chair or his feet on the table, and rattled away. Then, there are continual references from the villagers and the camp-followers, who have frequent disagreements. There are the line-cutters and field measurers, coming in with their reports. The *moonshee* with his reed pen behind his ear, ready to read and write the Persian notes that are perpetually passing. And there is, never-to-be-forgotten, the little old *baboo*, with his broken English, his large spectacles, and his shrivelled skin, looking very much like a bit of burned rag that one could blow away. "Baboo" is applied to those writers who understand English, and are to be found in every office. They are almost all Bengalees. This little man is a complete copying machine and a tolerable mathematician. He cannot endure that his book should be found fault with. "Sir, you are my father and my mother. One, two thing I do, no mistake can make, multiply, sine, co-sine. Sir, you are my sucking father, Sir. I no mistake make."

Henry's day is generally occupied with these people, but his work does not take him much away from home. Besides all these, our camp includes a carpenter, a smith, a bookbinder, a number of grain merchants to supply the camp, the wives and children of our servants and of the other people, cattle of all kinds from elephants down to kids. In short a complete patriarchal establishment.

The cold weather has now set in, nor can there be a climate more delightful than that we now enjoy. There is seldom any wind and for months no rain. The sun is too hot to be exposed to during the day, but we can sit out of doors in the *tope* and the mornings are delightfully fresh and cool. India is the land of lands for domestic enjoyment. A lady who shrinks from driving over rough or smooth, riding through a jungle, or crossing a piece of water on the back of an elephant has no business in camp. One who cares much about visiting and parties is out of her place in the *mofussil*, and one who minds living on mutton and fowl for six months in the year had better not marry a surveyor. Our life in camp teaches us how many things we can do without. There is an exclusive (and entire) companionship between people so situated. [A wife] may learn enough of her husband's work to take an interest in it and even to give him some assistance. Those about you do not understand what you say. So there is no fear of distorted repetitions. We escape all scandal, all censure, all the deteriorating gossip which one despises, yet is led to join in. There is the fullest enjoyment of nature, perpetual change of air and scene. More like the birds of the air than human beings. If we have a chance guest it is without form or trouble. "Pitch a small tent and grill another fowl," are the only directions needed.

I wish I could vividly bring before you the increased interest with which I have read the Bible since I have been in the East, and seen daily exemplifications of expressions which before conveyed only a vague meaning. I have noted the passages that most struck me, and here they are.

We are now on the edge of a great *sal* forest, where vegetation is rank, and the climate moist. For many weeks we have been without rain, but its place is supplied by an abundant dew. Till the sun has been up for some hours, the moisture loads every leaf and spray, and falls off in showers at a touch. The heaviest dew I ever saw at home gives not the idea of that in an Eastern climate. Here it is truly what Moses calls it, Deuteronomy xxxiii 13, one of "the precious things of heaven". But, copious as is this moisture, it is wholly exhaled when the sun has been sometime up. And the arid soil bearing no trace of what loaded it a few hours before, shows more strongly than I can tell, how justly temporary penitence is illustrated by the words, Hosea vi 4, "As the early dew it goeth away".

All writers on Eastern customs tell us of "putting off the shoes", see Exodus iii 5, Joshua v 15, but no description can give the vividness felt when one actually and hourly sees this practice. Every native leaves his shoes outside when coming into the presence of a superior, and all, of every rank, take their shoes off when going into a mosque or temple.

The bedding of the Orientals has been frequently quoted in explanations of the command "Take up thy bed", Matthew xi 6. Indeed almost every man who moves about at all here takes up his bed which is generally merely a blanket, or two folds of cloth quilted together with cotton. The other bed in common use is a *charpoy*, or frame of light wood, laced across with twine, and raised on four legs, about eight inches high. This is very light, and I have repeatedly seen a man walking along with his *charpoy* on his head. One day lately, a man who had [been] hurt in a quarrel was brought into our camp on one of these beds, "borne of four", just as I suppose the sick man was carried to Jesus. The one I speak of was borne on the men's heads, but a *charpoy* is frequently made into a couch for transporting the sick by swinging it with cords from a bamboo which four men bear on the shoulders. An easier conveyance could not be devised, for it has no jolt, and I have for my own use, a sea-cot so swung, which I usually prefer to a palinquin for a long march.

In this country all the flat roofed houses, that is, those that are not tiled or thatched, are used to sit or sleep on. They are surrounded by a balustrade, showing the rationality of the injunction of Moses, Deuteronomy xxii 8, to make "a battlement round the roofs", as without this precaution life would be endangered. As I walked on the roof of the great mosque at Gorakhpur and looked down into the open squares within the houses, which from the streets are quite concealed, I thought how easily David might have seen Bathsheba from such a place.

The *mootsuddies*, or native pen-men who work in the survey, are constantly coming into the tent. They place the reed pen behind the ear, and carry a small china inkstand stuck in the girdle. Bringing exactly to mind Ezekiel's description of "a man clothed with linen, with a writer's ink-horn upon his loins".

There is a *sowar*, or horseman in attendance in Camp to go messages and carry dispatches. And when he is wanted, the order is "Tell the *sowar* to gird on his belt." When he arrives and is to wait, the order is "Tell him to loosen his belt."

One evening we were out driving, and coming to a village we got out of the buggy, and sat down to talk to the people. Some of the lads, who gathered round us, looked very athletic, and Henry set two of them to run a race. Their dresses consisted of the *cummerbund*, and a coat made somewhat like an open shirt. When they prepared for the race, they took off this upper coat and drew the cloth tightly round their loins. This trifling act said more than a hundred homilies, to explain the phrase "gird up the loins of your mind", 1 Peter i 13.

One day Henry gave a man a sum to calculate, he went outside the tent, smoothed the dust, and then wrote with his finger on the ground. John viii 6.

I have mentioned that a native in travelling always carries his *lota* and a roll of twine by which to draw water. Some of the wells are of a great depth, eighty or a hundred feet, and the water forty or fifty feet from the top. So that to a man sitting by a well without his *lota*, no address would be more natural than the Samaritan woman's "Thou hast nothing to draw with, and the well is deep. Whence then hast thou water?" John iv 11.

The passage: Ezekiel iv 9–17, wherein the prophet is commanded to use dung as fuel for preparing his food, appears to us very revolting, but in the East, it bears a very different aspect. Here, dung is the chief article of fuel. Women and children may be seen carrying on their heads baskets of it that they have collected, and then preparing it for use by kneading it up. Sometimes it is laid in cakes against the wall to dry. These cakes are afterwards built into conical stacks. Sometimes it is laid along the ground in parallel ridges a few inches apart, and when dried, another set of ridges are laid across these, so that the stack when finished, presents alternate hollow and open squares. In places where wood is scarce, one may account for any substitute being employed as fuel, [but] cow-dung is just as much used in the forest as in the bare plain. Manuring the land is a practice hardly known, except with respect to small patches of ground for opium, tobacco, or esculents.

Our camp life brings to mind the frequent mention of tents in Scripture. In narrative and illustration "Removed as a Shepherd's tent", Isaiah xxxviii 12, conveys an idea of entire sweeping away, to be estimated only by those who have moved from camp to camp. One day a spot is full of life and animation. Canvas dwellings of various shapes and sizes are pitched all round. Servants, cattle, all the etceteras of an establishment are to be seen. Return to the place in a few hours, and there is not a trace of all this, unless some broken earthen vessels strewn about. The stir that animated the spot is gone, and very often no one knows whither. Isaiah liv 2. "Enlarge the place of thy tent, lengthen the cords, strengthen the stakes" are words that often occur to me when I see the cords of our tents stretched out, and the wooden pins that secure them made fast in the ground. Nothing can present a more forlorn aspect than a tent overthrown, and one who has seen it can see the force of Jeremiah's comparison for bereaved Judah when he makes her say: Jeremiah x 20, "My cords are broken, there is none to stretch out my tents any more, or set up my curtains."

I read lately a paper in the *Meerut Magazine*, which struck me particularly, from its references to the work of the Survey. In another letter, speaking of Henry's employment, you will find mention of village boundaries. Now listen to the magazine:

"The importance of fixing village boundaries is as well known to the Eastern as to the Western Nations, and the punishment for removing land-marks has always been severe. In Deuteronomy xxvii 17 the offence comes next to murder and manslaughter. In the course of settling these disputes, the most solemn adjunctions are entered into, and it frequently happens that the decision of doubtful cases is left to the conscience of the opponent, who walks barefooted over the ground he assigns as the boundary, with his hand on his son's head, after having been sworn by a Brahmin, undergoing purification, and other equally binding ceremonies. Sometimes the man who marks the boundary carries on his head a vessel containing Ganges water."

All this seems strange to our insular notions of hedges and ditches, but the case is very different in countries where the only division between villages is a slight ridge of grass or earth, which may be washed away by the first rain. On the same subject may be quoted the passages Jeremiah xxxii 14–15, where the documents of purchase are put "into an earthen vessel, that they may continue many days". It is not uncommon to bury an earthen pot in the place which has been marked as a boundary, that "after many days" it may be dug up, and produced in evidence.

The Bible contains numerous allusions to clothing, not to be understood if we think only of our own closely fitting garments. In this country the dress of the very poor consists merely of pieces of cloth without any sewing. The young man laid hold of by those who led Christ to Calvary "left the linen cloth, and fled from them naked". It is very common here for a person who is seized to loose his garments which remain with the pursuer, while the pursued makes his escape.

FIVE

To Allahabad

Early in 1838, the survey of the Gorakhpur district being finished, Henry was transferred to continue survey work in the neighbourhood of Allahabad. Honoria writes about the change of scene to her friend. She then takes up her journal to Henry in the sixth month of her pregnancy when she had reached Papamao near Allahabad.

Journal to a friend
January 12th, 1838

We started about 4 a.m. for Azimghur. We had come to the regions of camels instead of elephants. It was apparent that we were in a more decidedly Moslem district; Mahommedan tombs and small chapels, or Eedgahs, were abundant but none looked of a recent date. After passing the Gogra we saw few Hindu temples, large or small. The Mahommedans are more a trading than an agricultural people and abound most in thickly inhabited districts. Besides, Gorakhpur, being near the hills and [in] former times chiefly forest, probably escaped the Moslem invaders. The Mahommedans are a stronger built race than the Hindoos, the complexion of both is much alike but the latter have more slender and pliant limbs.

January 14th

We reached Jaunpore, a very old city, containing much that is interesting. Thro' the midst of it flows the River Goomtee, which is as its name imparts, a wandering stream which also flows thro' Lucknow. It has steep banks and where it intersects the city, there is a fine bridge of seventeen arches. All along the bridge, at each side, are recesses which serve as shops. In one sits a tailor, working little close-fitting muslin caps for sale. In another a shoe-maker with a pile of gay embroidered slippers with turned up toes beside him. Or perhaps we see a man making *hookahs* [out of the] shell of a cocoa-nut with a tube inserted, or an old Mahommedan seated cross legged in front of his wares, his eyes closed, the sun beaming right on his face lighting up his grey beard and scarlet turban. The picture of enjoyment with his *hookah* beside him and the pipe in his mouth, he slowly inhales and exhales the perfumed tobacco undisturbed by the bustle around him. One of these old Moslem gentlemen actually had what I had hitherto supposed to exist only in story books viz. a blue beard, a fine deep blue.

Between the recesses the ground is covered with baskets of fruit, grain, and vegetables, beside which sit the vendors, men and women with heaps of *cowries* and rice before them. At one end of the bridge is the *serai*, or place for travellers. It is a square with sheds and huts round it. It was crowded with travellers; some who had just arrived were unyoking their bullocks; others who have been there longer were preparing their food or smoking or sleeping.

But the Rajah's carriage is waiting for us, his highness having graciously lent us one of his many conveyances. This was a chariot of English make, but shabby and moth-eaten; the horses, of which the Rajah has ten pairs, were in bad condition and the harness was mended with bits of rag and rope. It carried us safely however on our sight-seeing trip.

I must take you in it to the great man's house. We entered by a gateway into a court yard, where the Rajah and his son were standing, the first a large fat man about thirty-five years of age apparently, the latter a lad of sixteen. Both had a quantity of black hair which fell beneath their turbans on their shoulders, both were rather fair, especially the lad. They were dressed in wide trousers, the stripes going round, as is the invariable fashion of striped silk, vests of Kincob or flowered satin, and long outer coats of figured silk. They wore splendid Cashmere shawls round their shoulders – the father's was yellow, the son's white – and silver tissue shoes. The elder had on English white cotton stockings, which I have observed on two or three other native grandees. They both wore turbans of gold lace twisted with bright colours and round the edge many strings of jewels. In the front a feather of pearls and rubies. Both had a languid heavy expression and they were incessantly chewing *paun* and spitting it out. The lad spoke English very well, and the father understood it a little.

We were led upstairs and through the house, which had been furnished by the late Rajah. There was an endless succession of rooms, all lofty, but some large, some merely closets, some long and narrow, many almost dark. The walls of almost every room were covered from floor to ceiling with pictures. Some were native, some Chinese,

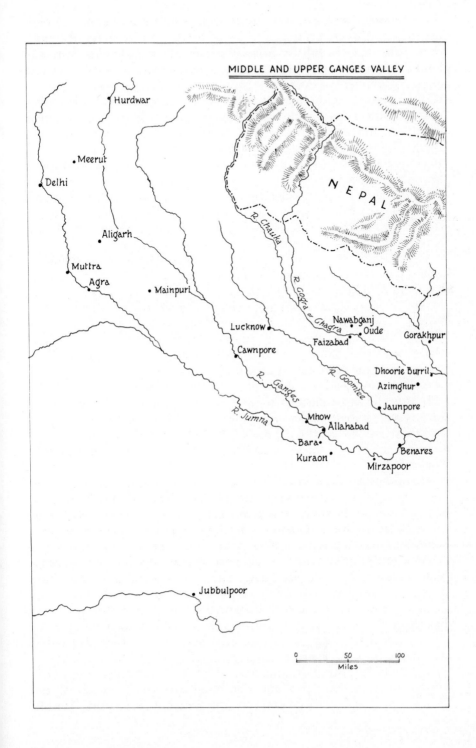

MIDDLE AND UPPER GANGES VALLEY

Hurdwar

Meerut

Delhi

Aligarh

Muttra
Agra

Mainpuri

NEPAL

R. Chauka

R. Gogra or Ghagra

Lucknow

Nawabganj
Oude

Faizabad

Gorakhpur

Cawnpore

Dhoorie Burril
Azimghur

R. Goomtee

R. Ganges

Jaunpore

R. Jumna

Mhow
Allahabad

Bara
Kuraon

Benares

Mirzapoor

Jubbulpoor

0   50   100
Miles

some French, and English engravings. And of several there were duplicates. Of one print, a likeness of Saadut Ali late king of Oude, there must have been fifty or sixty copies side by side with Siston as Paul Pry, and French opera dancers. Then there were wardrobes and chests of drawers of every description. Some that they opened for us were crammed with fineries of English chintz, others with Indian muslin, others again had curtain fringes and bordering, all crammed together, and many moth-eaten portfolios of caricatures, cases of shells. There were a great many tables with raised glass lids like what are in jewellers shops. In these were every kind of cutlery, trumpery jewellery, haberdashery.

One was filled with kaleidoscopes, another with curtain pins and steel pens. In one case were a crowd of dressed dolls, in another a lot of ladies' bonnets that seemed to have been made a dozen years ago. There was every species of cookery ware and glass. Mathematical instruments, clocks, toys and carts. From the ceiling were suspended, without any order, chandeliers of blue, green and cut glass, some very handsome. There were French and English books in abundance. Boxes of every kind, from giant English trunks to little carved ivory puzzle boxes. Beautiful alabaster chimney ornaments, mixed with coarse, grotesque clay idols, maps, globes, telescopes, couches, chairs, and beds, all crowded together with as little order as I have observed in the catalogue. In the midst of one rather handsome room was the figure-head of a ship, set up as a piece of sculpture.

It was the most curious sample of wasted money. In two of the rooms were billiard tables. The young gentleman asked Henry to play and they had two or three games. Their play was about equal. Afterwards they played chess, which his young excellency understands very well.

He told us he was a widower, but would soon marry again. We saw his son, a boy of two years old, also his younger brother, who seemed ten and was far the smartest and most intelligent of the set. I wished to visit the ladies, and after some delay I was admitted to see the Rajah's wife, his two daughters, and the wife of his youngest son. One was a very beautiful girl of thirteen. She was tall and slender, with delicate features and large soft black eyes. She wore a petticoat of dark blue gauze, flowered with silver, and a rose coloured mantle round her head and shoulders. She was disfigured by the horrid nose-ring; and her feet and ankles, hands and arms were perfectly loaded with jewels. On each finger a ring, and from each ring a string of jewels passing down the back of the hand and joining a band of jewels round the wrist, the same sort of ornaments on the feet. A treble string of jewels round the head, with pendants that hung over the forehead. All the ladies were dressed in the same way, differing only in colours. The old lady wore on her thumb a ring, in which was set instead of a stone a looking glass about the size of a half-crown and into this she very often peeped.

I was amused to see that as the completion of their finery each had a printed cotton pocket-handkerchief such as would cost about sixpence at home, and these they waved about as if wishing they should attract special attention.

The lad who spoke English accompanied me as my guide and interpreter. I entered a large room where the Ranee was seated on a couch. The girls stood round her, and there were several attendants, men and women, standing by. The old lady rose when I came in, bowed and touched her forehead with her hand. I courtsied and she took my hand and seated me beside her. They all examined my dress, seemed much amused at it, asked if I always wore gloves, if all English ladies wore combs in their hair. How old I was, how long since I left England, whether I had ever been married before, what my husband's occupation was? I asked to see their jewels, and they led me to another room, where servants brought several boxes to the lady. She seemed much delighted to show her finery and truly it was amusing to see strings of pearls and gold chains tied up in little pieces of dirty rag, and huddled together in a box secured by a clumsy padlock. The Rajah himself joined us here, and told me one necklace had cost 50,000 rupees. A pair of bracelets 500, and so on. The pearls were the largest I ever saw, and the gold chains the most massive. The other jewels were chiefly rubies, very large garnets, emeralds, and diamonds. The latter were I fancy of an inferior quality, at any rate, being not cut regularly but merely rounded, they had little brilliancy.

I must have seen twenty or thirty necklaces, as many head-bands, bracelets etc, and I could not help sighing when I thought what villages must have been plundered to supply all this finery. At last I rose to go and after many salaams and courtsies got away.

It struck me that this noble family had a remarkably plebeian look, and we afterwards found that they were mere parvenus. The present Rajah's father having done service to Government by bringing in a prisoner on whom a price had been set, was rewarded by the title.

Camp Bara, near Allahabad, January 25th
Nearly four months of total drought have baked the very fields into something like brick. And it is marvellous to see the delicate green blade of the barley thrusting itself through so ungenial a soil. You can hardly imagine the disagreeableness of the dust on this journey. The roads were five or six inches deep in a fine white powder which every breath of air sent up in clouds. Indeed the buggy passing through it was sufficient to raise a glory round us and this dust penetrated into the

eyes, nose and mouth. I felt as if saturated with it and all our clothes still smell of the enemy.

We have hardly seen a bamboo since we crossed the Gogra and these are a great loss to the landscape. But all along the road there is a great deal of *keekue*, or mimosa arabica, a slender tree somewhat like the acacia but with leaves much smaller so as almost to resemble moss, and branches more thorny. It bears a small yellow tufted blossom and is a very light, pretty shrub. It seems to rejoice in a dry soil, springing up along in the dusty roadside looking so cheerful and contented that I always like to see it.

The crops here are different from those we have left. There is little tobacco or wheat, a good deal of opium, sugar cane and barley. Nor do we here see the *michauns* prepared as retreats from wild elephants.

The dress of the natives too has a somewhat different character. The prevailing colour is a brownish olive green, and a dull reddish yellow, both very unbecoming to black forms, which look best in either white, or brilliant tints. Both men and women here wear trousers which are made very loose round the waist but fitting close from the knee to the ancle [sic]. I do not like to see females thus arrayed. Their trousers are generally made of blue and white cotton, the stripes going round. The men's are of green or yellow cloth quilted with cotton, and they have often a close jacket of the same with a small sash round the waist and a close fitting cap. Their tight figures without any flowing drapery are an odd contrast to what I have been accustomed to see lately. This dress is worn chiefly by the people of the Bundelkund.

The city of Allahabad stands on the point of land at the junction of the Ganges and Jumna. The junction of any streams forms a sacred place to Hindoos. And at the present season there is a vast concourse of pilgrims to Allahabad. It is a curious but sad spectacle, and truly the zeal of these idolaters is a reproach to us. A tax of a rupee is levied by Government on every pilgrim and a *lakh* of rupees is collected here yearly by this infamous levy. Surely a time will come when it will not be believed that a Christian nation traded in idolatry.

It was near sun-set when we approached the Ganges. Sir Charles Metcalfe and Lord Auckland had recently passed, and the relics of their train enlivened the scene, consisting of smart looking servants in the Government uniform of a scarlet robe. The different channels of the river were covered with boats, from the little light *dinghee* to the heavy flat-bottomed vessel carrying cotton. Along the beach, and on the Islands were encampments, chiefly of pilgrims, conspicuous by little scarlet flags, of which each pilgrim carries two. Here two or three Mussulmanns with their long beards and showy dresses were galloping along the sand. There a string of camels were led to a boat and all means used to get them whither they are most reluctant to go. The driver holds a long string to one end of which is fastened a hook, which is put into the camel's nose. But in vain did he pull with all his might. In vain did the people beat the poor creatures with sticks. They obstinately planted their four long legs into the ground as far as possible apart, and curving their necks and pulling back their noses yelled most pitifully. At last they were obliged to yield, and with a very bad grace were put on board. Poor things, all I have seen of them looked in miserable condition, but believe their natural appearance is rough and ragged.

After ploughing our way through the soft sand on the beach, we entered the city, which was clean and had many European-like buildings. The streets too were not Indian looking, for the houses stood side by side, instead of having gardens between them. There are beautiful roads all round the station. We drove about three miles to Mr. Montgomery's★ house. The cantonment consists of the parade ground and the ranges of huts for the *sepahis* and for two or three miles round there are bungalows, or thatched houses with sloping roofs. And *puckah* houses, or those that are built of brick, and have flat, lime roofs. Most of the dwellings stand in the midst of neat compounds, or enclosures. After rain, it must be a very pretty station, but now, there is not a blade of grass to be seen, and the trees are covered with dust. Some of the fences I have seen round the compounds in this country are exceedingly beautiful. The outer fence is often of the prickly aloe, such as we have in greenhouses at home, but here it grows to a great size and the leaves are so sharp and strong that they form an impenetrable hedge. Within this, there is generally a belt of flowering shrubs, with blossoms red, white, yellow, and of all other colours. I have also seen the outer fence of the strong tall grass with white feathery heads growing on stalks six or eight feet high. The blossoming trees raising their boughs above these white tufts have a very pretty effect.

Beetah, January 29th

On the 25th we made an excursion of sixteen miles into Bundelkund. The country is the most miserable I ever saw, far more desolate than a mere uncultivated plain, for here were the crops, but blighted. Pulse, which under the different names of *gram*, *dal*, *urra*, *mêsh* forms a large proportion of the food both for man and beast, suffers continually from frost, and the blackened fields looked the very image of famine.

We went West to Mhow, the road lying along the Jumna, of which we had occasional glimpses. We stopped a couple of hours with a custom-house officer, one whose business is to inspect the transit duties, and prevent smuggling. His house was made entirely of bamboo and matting and very cool and pleasant it was. A framework of bamboos supported walls, partitions, doors, windows, all made of mats. We returned by water, and were about five hours dropping down the Jumna. The night was soft and pleasant.

Beetah, February 3rd, 1838

The weather has for the last week been decidedly warmer, and the noon is now rather oppressive; still, the evenings and mornings are delightful.

Tilgunnah, February 9th, 1838

If I could draw you should have a series illustrating buggy *dâk* travelling in India. The roads, except immediately about the station, are of the most wretched description, being frequently more like ditches some two or three feet deep, which in the rains form regular water courses. Afterwards they become beds of slime and as they rapidly harden they retain every deep rut left by the *hackeries*, every print of the buffaloes' feet. Even on the most frequented roads we often encountered an obstacle from the mode of irrigation by which water is carried in a trench or canal from the tank to the fields. These canals often run right across the road, supported by banks of a foot high, which afterwards become baked into very respectable walls, and give us terrible jolts.

The best road is often the mere wheel-track over the plain. Only this requires good light. The general direction to the *syce* being, "Go on before and look for the road." Another variety of high way literally deserves that name, the natives call it "*bund*". Imagine a wide plain rather below the usual level of the country and therefore during the rains a lake or swamp. Across this a raised causeway from two to eight feet high, formed only of earth, without the least fence, and barely wide enough to admit the buggy wheels. And our horses are such as many a one would fear to venture on. English cattle require such care and attention as they could not receive in camp, and the country horses are very bad tempered.

Imagine us setting off from camp. There is the *tope*, and there are the tents, and the *clashies* all squatting round a fire so close together that their heads look like a circle of beads strung together. There are the *bunniahs*, or corn merchants sitting in a long row, each with a basket of grain before him, beside him a pair of rude scales, and a heap of *pice* and *cowries*. It is evening and the surveying parties, as they come in are going up to the *bunniah* to provide for their suppers. The little red and white flags on the top of long slender bamboo shafts, which are used in the work, are leaned against the trees, and look very gay. In the foregound imagine Henry and me seated in the buggy, our backs and feet well adjusted to be ready for a shock, and now we are to set off. But no, Bison-tail will not stir. Two or three men come behind and push, one or two others try to turn round the wheels and another pulls by a rope at the horse's leg. Even on three legs he maintains his ground. A few days ago eight men could not make him move. At last he rears up, quite erect, and ends by lying down. After half an hour or so, he at last condescends to go on, and trots briskly along. Coming to a *bund*, Bison-tail takes advantage of his situation, and will not stir. We are afraid of his upsetting the buggy, so in self defence we get out. This happened yesterday evening. Henry and I walking, followed by a man leading the horse and three or four more drawing the buggy. The magnates of the village having come out to meet us, were salaaming, and doing the polite to the utmost. We were surrounded by the country people who had seldom I suppose seen an English face, and thus we marched, till we came to level ground, where we were on fair terms with the horse.

On our march from Chupra sudden rain had swollen a stream, which ran across the road so much that we were carried across on a *charpoy*, borne on the heads of men who swam over, and our buggy followed in a similar way. Yet we have never met with an accident.

Here is a sample of "a letter from a lady in camp, to a lady in cantonments".

My dear Mrs. M.,

Many thanks for the *tussah*. It is very nice. But I return the cloth you sent for lining my cloak. It is too deep a yellow. Will you kindly have it made lighter. I send some flannel to be dyed for Mr. Lawrence's jackets. Will you desire your *durzee* to see them cut out and get a *tickah*-man to make them up? The *durzee* you sent me works neatly enough, but cannot cut out. Can you recommend me a good *dobee*? Ours is a very bad one. When the *boccas-wallah* comes, will you get me some Europe buttons and a thimble? I should also be obliged if you will let me have the pattern of your collar, and desire the *chiccau-wallah* to work one like it.

We have got very bad bread, will you desire your *Khitmutgar* to send us some from the baker you employ. I am really ashamed of giving you so much trouble, but I have not done yet. I want something to make a warm dress for these cold mornings and I shall be much obliged by your sending me some cloth fit for the purpse.

Yours very truly – H.L.

Camp. Tuesday. Answer
My dear Mrs. Lawrence,

I send some fine *puttoo* that I think will answer for your gown. My *durzee* shall cut out Mr. Lawrence's jacket, and I will get the buttons and thimble if I can, but the *boccas wallah* seldom comes round now.

I send out a *dollee* and hope you will find the things good, also some bread from our man. The cloth merchant fears he cannot make the lining paler, so I have given it back to him, and send you some of a different kind. I have desired our *dobee* to enquire for one for you. Can I do anything else for you?

Yours sincerely,
E.M.

You see I have a very good natured executrix of my commissions.

February 19th

I don't think I have described a tent or our mode of living in one. You have all seen tents at home, but I do not recollect ever seeing a marquee that had more than one fold of canvas in its construction. Our dwellings have two walls or rather shells, being in fact one tent within another, with an interval of five or six feet between them, forming a verandah or passage all round the tent. This adds much to the coolness. The outer fly or shell is white, lined with crimson. The inner is likewise white, lined with chintz according to taste. When the tent is pitched the first object is to choose good shade. Then the ground is levelled and covered with straw. Upon the floor are spread *sutringees*, or striped carpets of thick cotton. In the cold weather the floor is covered with rugs.

The doors are curtains – *purdahs* – that let down, and in the doorways there are likewise here, as also in every house, cheeks or screens made of reeds split very fine and painted and woven with thread, the reeds forming the woof, so that the cheek easily rolls up. The middle part is covered with coarse green gauze, so as to keep out insects and also to prevent people outside from readily seeing within. Besides these we have glass doors for the tents, and when the hot winds blow, *tatties* are hung up to the windward side, and every other opening is closed.

Do you remember how my uncle used to talk of "the preeminent [sic] of a young lady leaving his comfortable house at Madras, to marry a man with a single poled tent?" We laughed at the expression without having any very definite idea of what it meant. Little did I guess that I was myself to inhabit such a dwelling, but having tried it I can answer for its being a very comfortable habitation. So much so that, when Henry gave me my choice, I preferred it to a double pole, as being so much easier to carry about. It seems strange enough to look on a house as only a temporary abode for the rains, and to have our home as it were under a huge umbrella.

It is best to describe particularly the whole tent family, that you may understand when I speak of our travels. The smallest is a *shooldarrie*, it has but one shell, or fly, and the sides are only a foot or two high. It has two upright bamboo poles, eight or ten feet high and perhaps twelve feet apart, with another bamboo laid across them, over which the cloth is thrown. There are generally two or three *shooldarries* in camp, one for a cook house, one for a guard etc. and they are convenient if another sleeping place is wanted.

The *raotee* is larger, having higher walls, or *kunaughts* and regular doors, but it likewise has only one fly, and is not fit for either hot or blowing weather. But it is nice for travelling being very light and easily transported. A hill tent, too, has two flys. It is twelve feet square with a pole in the centre. A regular single pole is twenty-two feet square and I will describe ours as a fair specimen of one. It is lined with buff chintz and divided across the middle by a cloth screen eight feet high. One half makes our regular sitting room, the other half is subdivided into two little places, one for a bedroom and the other for a little drawingroom, to which I can go when Harry is particularly occupied. The verandah at this side is divided by curtains into two little dressing rooms, and outside is a bathing room, formed by a *kunaught*.

A double poled tent may be from twenty to forty feet long and proportionally high and wide, and when fitted up with glass doors, warm carpets, and lampshades fixed to the tent poles, it is as nice a room as anyone could desire.

Keeree, February 23rd

Another march has carried us further South towards the Reewar country. We are in the best *tope* I have yet seen in this district, and the mangoes are now in full blossom.

At this moment Henry is conversing with the native Deputy Collector. It is only of late years that natives have been appointed to official situations and it is to be hoped that by thus opening places of responsibility to them, their character will be raised and they will acquire a somewhat higher standard of honesty. When we refer to our own history and see the system of bribes and tyranny that existed in England from the Conquest to the Revolution, we see that these faults are not confined to any attitude but exist wherever ignorance and irresponsible power are found. We have only to look back half a century to our own system of control to be taught that Europeans find gold as tempting as do Indians, provided it can be taken without glaring scandal. The natural question then is how has the standard of public opinion been raised among ourselves? And the obvious remedy here is to apply the same moral remedies to the natives that have [been] so much use among ourselves.

Judging however by the progress any nation has hitherto made, generations must pass away before a healthy principle can be infused into so corrupt a mass as the Indian nations and the inflexible integrity of Europeans is one of the most likely means to improve native character. The law of the land and the ever increasing publicity of the press [and] a higher standard of morals have very much checked the acceptance of bribes by Europeans.

The half-caste population, too, are coming more into notice. They almost exclusively fill the situations of clerks (or *crannies* as they are called) in the offices. They do not bear a very high character in general and how should they? Doubtless they inherit many native dispositions from their mothers and their education must be worse than defective. However they seem as a body to be making efforts for their own advancement. They are held in great contempt by the natives, except as they may possess money or influence, and the European prejudice is strong against them, so that they are much to be pitied. They are very jealous of any reference to their birth, and those I have heard speak were emphatic in talking of the natives with contempt.

It is amusing to hear the native versions of English titles, and at first I could hardly recognise my old acquaintances as "Clector Sahib", "Dipty Sahib", "Shistan Sahib". Under our Government there is a double arrangement quite beyond my comprehension by which there is for almost every office not only the officer but one acting for him. As the judge and the acting judge, the collector and the acting collector and so forth. Our poor little *baboo* very naturally thought that every one of our titles was accompanied by one acting. One day I asked him how old he was, he replied "I have fifty-six years lived, four years and I shall die". "But why, *baboo*?" He held out his hand and shewed the line of life, which he said only reached to sixty. Henry then said, "Look at my hand, what do you read there?" Of course old *baboo* read of long life, and wealth. "Very rich will be. Resident will be." "Not a Lord?" "Acting Lord will be Sir, Acting Lord."

The complexion of the natives varies very much. I have not seen many of the higher class, but those I have met, both Hindoo and Mohammedan are fairer than the lower, as might naturally be expected. In general the Brahmins are fairer than the other castes, and almost always finer looking men, unless, as is no uncommon occurrence, they are overgrown with fat.

The children when very young go about absolutely naked with long hair, their ankles and wrists adorned with silver, tin or coloured glass.

Up to ten or twelve, they wear only a waist-cloth and a piece of cotton round their shoulders. At this age they are generally much disfigured by the collyrium which is applied within the eye lid and gives to the eyes for a long time a weak and bleared appearance. The swarms of children in every village are absolutely astounding, outdoing Ireland over and over.

There is a marvellous change of countenance between youth and maturity in the natives. It is rare to meet a man with a pleasant expression. The mature have generally a cast of cunning or a scowl. But among the lads I have seen as fine, open intelligent countenances as any can be. The chief defect in Hindoo features is the lower jaw, which generally is square, and extending far backwards. Otherwise the face is often handsome. The Mussulmen cultivate their beards but frequently shave their eyebrows so as to have only a little strip or line of hair.

February 24th

We have for coolness pitched a hill tent to sleep in, and have the whole of the single pole as a sitting room. In the centre is a table covered with papers where sits a *baboo*, busy writing the names of villages which are dictated to him by *canangoe*, a native Government servant who is standing by. It is noon and there is little sound in the camp, the *clashies* are gone out to work and most of the folks who are still here are lying under the trees asleep. A pleasant breeze is rustling through the tent, making us feel very comfortable. And we have the ceaseless sound of a bird, called I believe the kuku, though its note is but half that of our cuckoo, being an incessant cry of "cook, cook, cook, cook", continually disappointing my ear which listens for the other syllable.

It would be difficult to describe all the minutiae which makes life here so different from home, particularly to females. The total confinement to the house during the day at first irked me greatly, accustomed as I was to freedom of motion. We have here no such thing as a delightful rambling walk, no visiting of the poor in their cottages, no going out alone and unquestioned. At home we talk much of Indian luxuries, but what are so called are in general only precautions against the climate or the results of native customs which prevent a man from doing any work but his own. You would be amused to listen of an evening when we come in from driving and I say to the *syce* "*Kido balatee panee lao*", "Tell them to bring soda water." He calls out to the bearer, "*Oh Sardar balatee panee Mem Sahib ka waste*" (for the lady). The bearer replies "*bohut acha*", very well, and shouts to the *kitmutgar* "*oh khannsama gee, balatee panee lao, juldee, Mem Sahib ka Waste*," "Oh Mr. House Keeper, bring soda water for the lady." The other returns, "*Lia*," "*It is brought*," and in due time the soda water appears. But all this is not half so comfortable as it would be to have one efficient servant. The real luxury of India, and one that would well bear exportation is the cleanliness. Of course there are some innately dirty people, even in this land of *bheesties* and *dobees*, who deny themselves the indulgence of personal purity; but they are the exceptions. Everyone bathes and changes the linen at least once a day and in the hot weather oftener. This must conduce to health as it does to comfort. I find the tepid bath agrees with me better than the cold and so I fancy would everyone who is not very strong.

> Kuraon, March 2nd

Yesterday was still and sultry. We went on an elephant, lent us by a neighbouring Rajah. It was a huge creature, some eleven feet high, I think, and even when it knelt down and I stood on a table it was like climbing up a ship's side to get on its back. It was a gaily caparisoned animal too, having housings of scarlet and yellow and one tusk cut at about eighteen inches in length and bound with silver. The other tusk had been broken off accidentally. From so high a seat we had an excellent view of the neighbouring country, and a brilliant moon lighted us home.

This morning we were astir very early, and went out, I on my pony and Henry walking beside me. There is a good deal of opium cultivated here abouts, and at the early hour we were abroad, we saw many people, men and women at work collecting it. The poppy is white, and after the blossom has decayed, before the seed is ripe, the people prick the capsule carefully in many places, the milk oozes out and soon becomes congealed. In this state it is carefully scraped off with a broad flat knife, and without any other process I believe, is thus sold. The drug is entirely a Government monopoly, and must be a profitable article of commerce. The collectors receive four to ten rupees, eight to twenty shillings per *seer* (2lbs.). It is a crop however requiring much care, manure, and is liable to be destroyed by frost.

The day was truly Indian. At first perfectly still, and sultry, then strong gusts of wind blowing clouds of dust, and whirling before it the dry mango leaves with which the ground is this season strewn, and ending in a heavy fall of rain.

Soon after breakfast we had a visit from the Rajah of Mhow. I was quietly sitting at my writing, when a bearer came in in a great bustle, saying "*Rajah Sahib aza*" (the Rajah is come) and then native-like he stationed himself behind my chair with a *chowree* in his hand (a piece of attendance I am not in the habit of having) that by having been "in the presence" he might look for some *buris* from the great man. The great man however was not a very great one, having been deposed because, as he told us, of his adherence to the English cause in some late affair.

He is a quiet, heavy looking, middle-aged man who spoke little. Only two attendants were with him, one with a silver stick remained outside, another stood behind his master and seemed his mouthpiece, for to him he looked when there was anything to be said.

It was a day of visits, for about 4 p.m. came another grandee. A fine looking old Rajpoot named Dokhul Singh. He was quite an old gentleman and must in his day have been handsome, rather fair complexion, high nose, and snow white moustaches. He wore a white turban and robe of white muslin, underneath which were trousers of crimson satin embroidered with gold, embroidered shoes, scarlet stockings, white gloves, and round his shoulders a splendid white Cashmire. I do long to lay hold of the beautiful shawls some of these grandees wear. It seems to me as if men had no business with them, and they would be so nice to send home. Our visitor has lately obtained from England a decree by which he has gained some twenty villages hereabout from his nephew, the Rajah who lent us the *hatee*. The case had been for nineteen years in litigation, and after having been given against the plaintiff in all the courts on this side of the water he referred it to England.

Dokhul Singh had many attendants, and I felt as I looked at the group, as if I was looking at a picture. There sat we in our tent in patriarchal fashion receiving this old gentleman. Behind him stood two men, one who looked nearly as old as his master and who seemed a favourite by the familiar way in which he joined the conversation. Four or five other servants stood near, and outside were a couple of soldierly looking attendants each carrying a silver stick five feet long. Old Dokhul asked a great many questions about London which, as the place whence his decree came, had in his eyes vast importance. However, he hardly believed Henry's account of its size and population, and looked very incredulous on hearing that there was a road under the Thames and that carriages drawn by steam went twenty or thirty miles an hour on a road made of iron.

He asked about the crops, whether we grew much rice, and when he heard of the daily post enquired whether we had elephants. But his astonishment was greatest on hearing we were governed by a woman of eighteen, that woman not married. I fancy he thought her Majesty had better marry "*Coompanee*", a personage about whom he was very inquisitive, and who had evidently in his mind "a local habitation and a name", as some mighty individual.

Barokee, March 16th

We left the camp about five o'clock on the *hatee* and ascended the hill close by, which may be 800 feet. The side rose steeply and the winding path was rough and narrow. Before us went some men to cut away the branches and we were followed by a train of nondescripts who were of no use except to look picturesque. It was really curious to see the huge animal we were on, making his way up the path which in places was not so wide as his foot, and I confess to having felt nervous, for, as I sat pillion-wise behind, I had no way of keeping on except holding by him [sic]. However, when we reached the top we were well repaid. There was a splendid sunset and we looked down [at] one side on a succession of hills, at the other on the plain dotted with trees and *topes*.

Kuttra, March 21st

We came here a few days ago and are now in the traveller's bungalow close to the hills. We started about 3.30 a.m. Harry and Mr. M. on horseback, I on a *palkee*. There was no road and hardly a path and before we had gone a *cos* my bearer managed to lose the rest of the party, so I came alone through the mountain pass between this and Kuraon. We kept at first close under a line of hills, to the right, which were in parts on fire. Very beautiful is the rushing blaze, as it seizes patch after patch of dry jungle, sometimes running [in] a line, the form of which varies every moment, looking now like a vast snake thrusting itself on the hillside, now curving itself into a semi-circle and then separating into detached masses of flame.

Saw a leopard's tracks. We had for many days been hearing of tigers and leopards infesting these parts, and I certainly never felt so much inclined to look out for one, as in going through these ravines, recollecting too that the flames must drive the animals from the other hills. I know that, if any danger appeared, the bearers would set me down and run away. Happily we escaped any peril.

When we emerged from the pass at 8 a.m., I had the delight of seeing Harry who had been looking out for me most anxiously. Another hour brought me across the plain to this bungalow which [is] on the side of the first road I have seen in India, except near a station. This extends about three hundred miles from Mirzapoor to Jubbulpoor and was laid out by Captain Drummond. It is very skilfully carried up the hills near this, much as the Simplon I should think, and it leads with a gradual ascent up to a height of five or six hundred feet zig zag.

On this road there is something quite new to us in the way of aqueduct, namely bridges for the water to flow over. Before you smile, wait to understand the country we are in; abrupt ravines with stony bottoms frequently occur forming the beds of streams which during the rains swell suddenly into broad rivers, but at other times are nearly dry. A bridge spanning the whole ravine would be an expensive work liable also to constant injury, but a causeway is easily made and is not easily damaged.

You would be astonished at the streams of pilgrims, going and coming all bearing vessels for the Ganges water. Men and women, young and old, children and aged, all are to be seen. A few ride on miserable ponies, but by far the greater number on foot. I never before knew the meaning of "way worn pilgrim". Poor creatures, my heart is often sore for them as I see them toil along under their load. And there is something unspeakably painful in not being able to tell them of the fountain where sin may indeed be washed away. The pilgrimage is not however exclusively a religious journey, for the Ganges water is so highly esteemed that it is an excellent article of sale. And those who bring a load of it, can dispose of it at a very high price, besides the honour of their pilgrimage.

Kuraon, April 4th

Here we are in another sort of dwelling. The hot winds have set in, and in the tent we had the thermometer at 95°. At home we talk of a thermometer at 95° without any more definite idea of that temperature than we have of distance when we say the sun is ninety-five millions off. But people who feel hot, devise contrivances to be cool. And the result of this law of nature is the curious habitation we are in. Under the thickest shade of the *tope*, a hole is dug four feet deep, twenty square. The earth thrown up is formed into walls six feet high, leaving doors at the four sides. On the East and South there are glass doors. On the North and West there are *tatties*, or thick mats of fragrant grass. On the roof there is a *chopper* or thatch and within this the fly of a tent is pitched. There is but one drawback, the mosquitoes and sandflies like the coolness as much as we do. But we will have the *punkah* pulled and that will drive them away. How hot it looks outside! The air is darkened with dust, and the withered mango leaves are whirled about by the blast, but the stronger the wind blows the better for us, the cooler is the air that comes through the wetted *tatties* and you will seldom find the thermometer above 80°. Indeed you will forget to look at it, which is the surest sign of a pleasant temperature.

Last Sunday I was startled by hearing a sound so like the church-going bell that I almost thought it was magic. We soon found that it was from a party of *fakirs* who had encamped near us. We have since visited them, and a wild looking group they are. There may be fifty of them and their followers, all under one head, fit chief of such a band. He is old but erect and athletic, very tall and spare. His hair grey, thick and twisted into elf locks only confined by a fillet of red cloth. His beard is long and grey and covers half his cheeks. His face is smeared with ashes, and round his hollow eyes is a circle of reddish brown paint. His breast too is covered with grey hair, and he wears several necklaces as charms. He is naked except the *fakir*'s cord round the waist, and the slip of cloth attached to it.

Imagine this figure seated by a fire, smoking from a long pipe made of bamboo, the tobacco receptacle of which was held by one of his disciples. The *fakir* who seemed next in rank was a younger man with very long hair hanging on his shoulders, and filled with ashes. He was indolent looking, as well as filthy, and wore a large blanket wrapped round him. Several of the men had arms. Their matchlocks were regularly piled. And on the adjoining trees hung their circular shields of buffalo hide, and the bell which we had heard. It was evening when we first went to their camp and the bright moonlight and strong red blaze of the fire gave a wild unearthly look to the haggard faces and savage forms. Either to startle us, or do us honour, they suddenly struck the bell and blew a large conch shell and screamed in chorus, to which their many dogs chimed in with a long bark.

Journal to Henry

Papamao, May 25th, 1838

We are now settled in our new quarter. Your work is prospering despite its difficulties. We are both in reasonable good health and our prospect of a living infant becomes daily more hopeful.

June 4th

A week of illness has suspended the journal again, though I feel too that this reason is rather an *oosur*. Now, all will I trust go smoothly, till the crisis, and to that I look forward cheerfully.

June 15th

And now it is nine weeks since I came in from camp and during the last three of them I have hardly moved except between bed and couch and never had a night's rest. But "patience cousin, and shuffle the cards". I fully expect that the grand event will happen on Tuesday August 28th about two in the morning. We came to our kind friends the Montgomerys that I might be near the doctor.

June 19th

Within the last month I have at times had a feeling of fear and misgiving such as words cannot describe. The pain, the danger, the possible disappointment awaiting me, weighed down my soul.

I would not have you, my own Henry, suppose that I think of death only when I am in low spirits. On the contrary, when I am most steadily cheerful it is from looking to the next world.

My Henry, when we were married, I took too much on me the office of reprover. A conversation we had three or four months ago led me to see this, and that I was pulling the mote out of your eye, while a beam was in my own. But on the other hand, we surely were intended, in sympathy and faithfulness to speak to one another with perfect openness.

One word more darling, I do think you are not aware of the way in which you habitually speak to those around you. Their provokingness I fully feel, but dearest, do you recollect that you scarcely ever address a man without an abusive epithet? This you do, too, when you are not angry. Oh my husband, let not our child hear such words from its parent's lips.

July 8th

You arrived at 6 a.m. in a high fever. Dr. J. soon came, and the remedies took effect, but you have had a day of sad suffering, and so indeed have I, but the worst part of mine was the not being able to tend you my husband. This is the anniversary of my landing in Calcutta.

September 1st

Entered on another month. This time of hope deferred takes from me all heart for writing. Every day seems a month till our babe comes, and yet I grudge each hour that passes as bringing nearer that terrible day when you leave me.★

Henry writes:

6th September was the eventful morning at three o'clock. You had been ailing from daylight of the 5th and the pains came on more decidedly in the evening at sunset. I stayed with you my darling at your wish, but the sight of your sufferings is scarce repaid by our boy.

September 11th

All the fears and pains of many months overpaid by our blessedness, when I opened my eyes this morning and saw you standing beside me with the infant in your arms.

September 23rd

He is perfectly healthy and eats arrowroot two or three times in the twenty-four hours. When he was born the muscles of his neck were swollen and his head inclined to the left, but now this is nearly right, he

★Henry had received orders to join his unit at Kurnaul on October 31st for the impending First Afghan War.

97

evidently sees and hears. On the 15th I got up, feeling dreadfully exhausted but ever since I have gained strength daily.

Last evening we took our child to be christened, by Mr. Hammond, who was passing through. Nothing could be more hurried, uncomfortable and unsatisfactory than the proceeding.

The child was christened Alexander after his grandfather, but was called Alick for short and sometimes Tim as a pet name.

Having volunteered to rejoin his regiment and having received orders to join the army, Henry Lawrence rushed post haste, not understanding what a strenuous journey in hot weather so soon after the birth of her baby might do to his wife and son. But Honoria was determined to stay with her husband as long as possible, which meant that she must start by October 1st, three weeks after Alick's birth. A couple of months later she wrote to a friend "I dared not give way," but, "the whole journey seemed to me like a funeral procession, baby very ill and me sinking fast, yet obliged to push on that we might get a nurse for baby and advice for me."

One night as Henry was riding ahead, which he often did, Honoria was reduced to despair. She sent the bearer on to summon Henry and got out of the *dhooli* in which she was travelling. "Oh, the anguish of that hour!" she wrote afterwards "as I carried my babe about till I almost fainted. At last I laid him on my cloak by the roadside, but he cried so piteously that I at once took him up again. I thought he would die there and then; and I was so worn and weak that I had no self control to sustain me. Just as I got back into the *dhooli*, Henry rode up. The bearer had never gone near him. He had only turned back from surprise at my not appearing."

By the evening they reached Cawnpore, but both mother and child were so ill that Henry had to stay with them for a whole week before they were fit to move on. In another week they reached Meerut where they stayed with George Lawrence and his family.

Six

Ferozepore

At the beginning of the First Afghan War, (1839–42), Henry Lawrence had civil charge of Ferozepore on the Sutlej, at that time the boundary between British India and the rougher, wilder, independent Sikh kingdom of Ranjit Singh. All troops going to or coming from the war passed through Ferozepore. On August 2nd, 1840 Henry became Assistant to George Clerk, the Governor-General's Agent for the Affairs of the North-West Frontier and the Punjab. On November 11th, 1840 a daughter was born to Henry and Honoria. She was christened Letitia, and nicknamed Moonia. In February and March 1841 Honoria, Alick and the baby journey up the Sutlej by boat to their summer cottage at Kussowlee near Sabatoo in the Simla Hills. They disembarked at Roopur. One of Henry's letters to Honoria refers to the Rajah of this place, "talking of Bhoop Singh to an old man the other day. I said 'Is he mad?' 'No, sir, he is a *shaitan*,' meaning Satan or devil."

Ferozepore, Sunday November 24th, 1839
This year has nearly ebbed away unrecorded in any extant journal. I had kept a pretty close account until May when the book containing it was stolen with some other things I was sending to you.

Sunday December 8th
We have now got a very nice regular camp establishment and with little exception as good a set of servants as I ever expect to have. Your papers are in order and I now feel able to take my proper work in the house department. For the first time I actually know in what our property consists. We are I believe wholly out of debt, and have some arrears due to us. So that as far as outward circumstances go, we have the prospect of beginning the year most comfortably. Indeed, love, were you strong, we should have little left to desire.

At this point Henry and Honoria each writes out a plan for the twenty-four hours of the day, and Honoria also writes out a weekly plan for language study. None of these plans were followed by either Henry or Honoria.

Monday, Tuesday. French
Wednesday, Thursday. Italian
Friday, Saturday. Hindostani
Sunday. Greek

Yes darling, an excellent plan and I hope it will in a measure shape the disposal of our time though exactness is not attainable in our roving life. My little arrangements must dovetail into yours.

Sunday January 12th, 1840

I must make accurate lists of all we possess, for with our continual changings I forget. Then we are pilfered from, and perhaps I blame unjustly.

The first thing after breakfast, see that Henry's clothes etc. are right. How often are they wrong, and he is plagued and I am vexed! Then the daily accounts, ordering dinner, the *durzee*, the *dhobee*, the *mistree*. See that things are mended. Not give too many directions at once. Every evening after tea, call the *khitmutgar* and see what is wanted for the morning.

Sunday February 23rd

"Unstable as water, thou shalt not excell," [Genesis xlix 4]. Is that my sentence?

Tuesday March 10th

To our boats, and next morning dropped down to Remookee. The scene very pretty, moonlight, chairs, table, candles. There we sat, our people in groups round, stooping over their fires and our boats lying below, with the lights on board reflected in the stream, some horsemen silhouetted by standing between us and the cooking fires, their standing forms all in shade. And then seated round, the fire behind them glowing in the strong light, *moonshees*, *baboos* etc. dressed in their best of silks and shawls, loitering about and whispering in expectation of the great man.

Presently a bustle heard and a crowd of horsemen approach headed by two men bearing huge torches. The ambassador steps forward, a gentlemanly middle-aged man, with fine beard. The usual extremely graceful manners and tasteful dress and snow white turban, a delicate white shawl folded over his breast and over all a kind of pelisse of dove-coloured figured satin. On each side of him sat a friend, one a

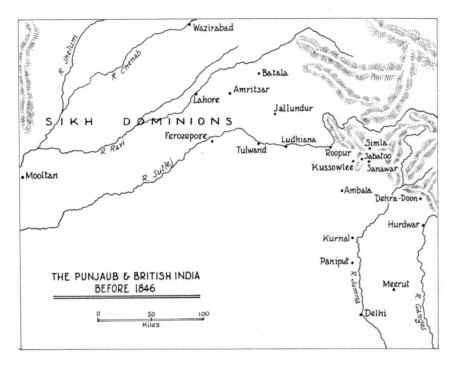

THE PUNJAUB & BRITISH INDIA
BEFORE 1846

0   50   100
Miles

young chieftain armed, less polished than the ambassador, but more warlike, much handsomer. Indeed I have seldom seen a better looking native. Brilliant eyes. He was dressed *en cavalier*, a turban of purple and gold twisted closely round his head, a purple *choga* nicely worked in gold, leather belt and sword. The other visitor was a common-place old body. After sundry politenesses they went away leaving a *nuzzer* of fifty rupees. Monday morning you went off by 4.30 a.m. How I should have liked to accompany you! But I feared the sun.

On Thursday, 19th, the snake charmer arrived, and we went down to look at him. And now unless to cantonments, I suppose our wanderings are over for some months.

Sunday April 5th

On Monday March 30th we took possession of our new house. How pleased I was with the idea of a comfortable settled abode for some months. And what trouble I took to make all snug! And during the five months we were in it I did not five times feel well enough to enjoy anything external. And then our object was to dispose of all that we had obtained.

Today darling you gladdened my heart by opening our house for the public worship of God. Thus shewing that you are not ashamed of Him.

April 11th

Yesterday we spent in the fort. It was very hot, and the first time I ever was a day absent from Alick.

April 29th

Yesterday the European lines were burned down. It was sad to see the drunkenness and hear the shocking language of the artillery.

June 9th

I am thoroughly sick of hospitality. In the little more than two months we have been in the house we have had: Mr. Laughton, Swinton, two arty girls, Mr. Ball, the Bunds, Captain Sinclair, Mr. Hawes, Mr. Dunlop, Captain Lawson, and Mr. Harlan staying, one, two, three, or four weeks each, besides several times having folks to dinner. The expense is great, but I would willingly pay the money to avoid the trouble. Do you remember darling, what pleasant evenings we often had alone? Well, now I have vented my spleen at my guests, and will make some notes.

Mr. Harlan looks about forty-five, very tall and lean and pale, with rather long black hair and beard. I should take him for a German, but he is from Philadelphia, came out eighteen years ago, got employ as a medical man in the Burmese War. Then travelled North-East till he came to the Punjaub where Runjit *purwusteekured* him. He says that, during two years he was guest at his court he got 200,000 rupees *budhies*. Then he entered Runjit's service and continued for four years. When they had a quarrel, he went over to Dost Mohammad★ who made him a general and Governor of Goozrat. He had taken a train of artillery over the Hindoo Koosh to Balkh, when our army marched to Afghanistan. On his return to Kabul Dost was afraid he would join us and imprisoned him. On the fall of Ghazni he was released, kindly treated by us, returned to these provinces as far as Ludhiana, and now proposes travelling overland through Europe and from England to America. Of course such a life has given extraordinary opportunities of seeing native character, and Mr. Harlan tells what he has seen with great perspicacity. He is a puzzling character. I think he sees no difference between right and expedience. Yet he talks exaltedly sometimes of rectitude, and a man being a law unto himself. He has a very high opinion of his own abilities and character, yet without any overbearingness or assumption. Talks as if all creeds were alike, yet is evidently well acquainted with Christianity, and well versed in prophecy, which he seems to regard as the key to all passing events. [He is] of temperate even abstemious habits, and I should think of personal

★The king of Afghanistan.

courage. After these years of barbarous life his manners are courteous, his language peculiarly correct and well chosen and he seems quite *au courant* with all the events in Europe political and scientific, as much as with the intrigue of the Durbar.

I cannot help feeling that he must at heart be a ruffian, and I am inclined to doubt much he says.

August 15th

This is the anniversary darling of your getting the order for Cabul. I was sitting on the couch after breakfast, the *ayah* brushing my hair, when you entered with the letter in your hand. Though I fancied I was prepared, it came upon me as if I had never heard of it before. That was the commencement of the four most afflictive months I ever passed. It seems as if with the birth of the child, some heavy cloud must come, for even the joy of his birth hardly cheered me at that time, thinking as I did, that but for him, I might accompany you.

1841

On the Sutlej, Tuesday February 23rd

Four months since my last entry in this book. Months of mingled pain and joy, the blessedness of the birth and health of our daughter and of the continued prosperity of our boy. The happiness of our remaining together at a time, [when] we saw so many parted. The comfort of your tender care through my illness. All through October you were generally in camp, and I could not accompany you owing to the increasing helplessness of my limbs. The beginning of November you were out, meeting Shelton's Brigade, and ferrying them over the bridge. On Saturday 14th they crossed. On Sunday afternoon came a note from Mr. Clerk, telling you to cross the bridge and see the treasure weighed. You returned on the morning of Monday 11th and that day I felt very unwell. About 3 p.m. I was in a good deal of pain, which continued increasing till 8.30 p.m. when baby was born. All connected with her birth was favourable but my limbs continued numb and useless.

February 16th

Yesterday evening we came on board the boat that is to take me and the children to Roopur.

Wednesday February 24th

Here I am once more alone, "upon the waters". You left me about seven this morning. I expect about twenty days in the boat and, if I and the children are well, hope to be busy. But during the long, long months of illness I have become insensibly what we call at home *do less* and I find myself contented to be idle. As I sit here writing my back and shoulders ache, so as almost to make me desist. Every dip of the pen into the ink is a separate pain.

February 25th

Most of the day spent in putting up *purdahs*, trying to keep out the rain and cold. Passed on our right side a village with mud walls and many trees. Then close by a hillock of sand, with the remains of buildings and then came to a bank twenty or thirty feet high, wheat growing to the verge, pure clay looking as if the river had made this channel for itself yesterday. Buffaloes swimming over. Bottom of river very uneven. One man walking ankle deep within a few feet of another who is swimming. 2 p.m. passed Tulwund, an old town on Punjaub side. The old story that I hear in answer to almost all enquiries. "It was a Mussulman *pindi*. Sikh *log* looted it."

Monday March 1st

Rainy night, wind lulled but sprang up again in the morning. Started at 8 a.m. got on slowly from the shallow water and contrary wind. In the afternoon I thought we should be thrown high and dry for the wonder of future travellers. For several hundred yards there was not a foot's depth channel. Everyone but myself disembarked. The boats were dragged through the sand.

Thursday, March 4th

But for the journal I should not know how time passes. If I were well enough to be always busy, I should get on very well, but for several hours each day weakness, headache, and sore eyes make me unfit for employment, and I really feel what *ennui* is.

March 9th

Day cool and pleasant. 1 p.m. baggage boat sprang a leak. Disembarked cargo, dead and live stock. Sent a note to Mr. Cunningham for a *mistree*. While we were waiting many people came to gaze. Picturesque *shikaree* in light skin jacket. River, very shallow, again broken into network of small streams and high sand banks. I cannot imagine how we got on at all. Alick playing with goats. Bright star light. A fortnight now without a white face or English word. But it is marvellous how well I get on. How civil all are!

March 11th

I can imagine nothing more delicious than the air just now, to my taste far pleasanter then the thin sharp rarified atmosphere of the hills. Lagaoed on Punjaub side at Barra wal Ke *ghat*. Bank high, coarse reedy dark grass, and great quantities of *buttair*, a long reed that grows in abundance on the river, used for mats and for the great spoons with which the *mullahs* ladle out the bilge water.

The boatmen, when hoisting the sails shout *"Dum Bahawal huk."* Bahawal is a *peer*, they say. Several fields of sugar cane. Great numbers of birds, flocks of wild duck and of a pretty white gull-like bird. On the shore numbers of a bird about the size of a pigeon, brown wings barred with white, very long ungainly, yellow legs. At night sleeps lying on its back with feet up and calls out *"Asman humarah ooper gheera"* ("The clouds are gathering over our heads").

The Brahminee duck goes in pairs. [They] keep together all day but take opposite banks at night. One calls *"Ao Ao Ao"* the other *"Hum aola nuheen, hum aola nuheen."* ("Come, come, come!" "we won't come, we won't come.")

March 12th

Left Barra wal at sunrise. At five I went out in the *jompon* with the children. On our side green sward and a great quantity of shamrocks, wheat, flax and sugar cane. All fields unfenced. In the distance, village and *topes*. No view of the snow today. A very happy day, both children so well and happy, and I feel better for this incomparable climate.

March 13th

Manjee picked up two stones from the bank for Alick who threw them into the river, much to the dismay of the *dhaee*, who said she meant to take them to Ferozepore to grind *musalla*. She hardly believed when I told her she would find thousands at Roopur.

2 p.m. wind increased, split the sail. The boat lay over on the larboard side, and the water poured in. All was soon righted, but for a few minutes I did not like it.

I am very glad that our voyage is safely over. In the nineteen days I have been on the river, I have never had a shade of molestation. The few people we have met have been civil. The cabin never leaked a drop. The crew have worked hard, and never given trouble. The servants have behaved well. Now and then a bit of a *dunga* among themselves. I look with unmingled satisfaction at the effect on Alick. Being continually with (him) myself I have been able to bring him into far better training. As to our ladybird, she thrives alike on land and water. I am myself much stronger and can move my limbs better. The perfect regularity of my life here has done me good. And so has the quiet though it was sometimes *ennuyant*: Rose between six and seven, breakfast eight, dinner two, tea six, bed between nine and ten. I have hardly varied ten minutes from this routine since the February 23rd. Such is the summing up of this navigation, which I anticipated with such qualms, seeing I had not you with me, dreading sickness for myself or the children or molestation from men or the elements. I do not fear the rest of the journey.

Sunday March 14th

I halted for a quiet Sunday, and spent the morning very pleasantly, reading, looking out and playing with the children. About 2 p.m. came a message from Sirdar Bhoop Singh, that he came to make his salam. In he walked, beard and ear-rings and bracelets and shawls. Looked about fifty, upright, long nose, eyes sharp, beard rather grizzled; eldest son daring figure, fair skin, good high features, three grandsons eight or ten years old, vastly polite. Begged a *chit* to notify his good treatment of me. His servants were mine. Great Dost (friend) of our Raj. Gave Alick some pomegranates. I was surprised to find myself get on so well in talking to him.

Tuesday March 16th

Bhoop Singh's father and grandfather were on the *guddee*, but beyond that I could not learn. Asked how many troops, said *"hazar sepahi, puchas sowar"* (a thousand sepoys and fifty troopers). A *pultun* was paraded for our benefit. About fifty men, two drums, a fife and a commandant. Commandant wore tight white breeches and jacket, small turban and huge boots. Marched pretty regularly, but seemed to me utter ragamuffins. "Begone brave army and don't kick up a row," thought I. Dress black pyjamas and red jackets, turban according to trade. Commandants all Moghuls. *"Pultun ke beech men Singh, Moghul, Pahari."*★ Had you been here, it would have been great fun.

This morning I sent off the last of servants and traps. Alick, Moonia and myself, *dhay* and a cold *moorghi* are all that remains. We are to start in the afternoon.

Nalaghar, March 17th

Yesterday evening set in to blow hard and was very hot. Started about four. Singh sowar, *mussalchee*, with long nose, six bearers my *jompon*. Six to share eighty-two coolies four *gharees*. Very picturesque and varied *suwarree*. Dhais red *doolie* with the wee babe in her lap. Alick in the *jompon* with me. Naked grizzled old *mussalchee*.

Amused at the politeness of all my escort. Nothing but *"Chuprassee*

★The general sense is that this is a mixed regiment of Sikhs, Moslems and hill people. Divide and rule.

Sahib" and *"Khalsajee"* and *"Dhai jee"* and so forth passing among
them.

Budge, March 18th

Here I am in another of the Rajah's country seats, but not like yesterday's. A *cutcha* bungalow of two rooms without doors. The *chopper*
very bad indeed. It seems to stand in a *cutcha* fort. Last night's road
excellent. But for a *nullah* here and there and an occasional sharp turn
you might drive a buggy over it. I was wondering who could have laid
out and made so well disguised a way, when the sepoy beside me said
that Captain Codrington had made it for the *Junghee Lord*. I wonder
how many thousand *zemindars* and their cattle might have been
swallowed up before a road would have been made for them.

"Tis a very fine thing to be father-in-law to a very magnificent three
tailed *bashaw*." And still finer to be able to claim kindred with an agent
and commissioner. "Tamas Sahib"★ had charged Rajah Ram Surrun
Nalaghari to be civil to me. Accordingly I had sentries and guards and
coolies and all I wanted. Budge belongs to him, his dominions join
those of the Patiala Rajah and of Roopur. He is a Rajput. Three of the
Rajah's sepoys were with me. All the *sowars* were with the *Burra Sahib*.
Fine looking men. Looking a thousand times better in their native
dress than the Roopur ragamuffins in their would-be European. These
men had *tulwars*, and very long spears, no matchlocks.

Today sent off my traps early, and mean to go on myself to
Sabathoo tomorrow. The few villages I have seen since leaving
Roopur, are much more civilised than ours, houses of thick mud walls
with *choppers*. People, too, comfortably dressed. I fancy we might take
some wrinkles from this wretched *cutcha* bungalow. Verandah roof
slopes down so abruptly that the outer doors are very low, not above
four feet high, consequently the sun can never strike in except when it
is near the horizon. Suppose we thus sloped the roof of our verandah,
having only one high door for Europeans to pass by. As for the natives
they are so used to low entrances that they stoop instinctively.

March 19th

I was off at sunrise. Tim sometimes in my *jompon*, sometimes on the
jomponnie's shoulder and, whenever he was allowed, stumping along
on his own little feet. Road wound among the hills, generally a
precipice to the left; in parts very steep and narrow. I should have been
nervous but had no time. So taken up was I with the enchanting
prospects. My *jompon* with eight men, four of them the Ferozeporees

---

★A son of the once famous military adventurer, George Thomas, had taken service
with Ranjit Singh.

who were telling travellers tales of Cabul and the Khyber pass and three marches without water; "Was the Khyber road like this?" "The stones there were all as big as that," pointing to a mass of rock, "and the camels and the guns had to be brought over it in a march of eight *cos*, the *Sahib log* would set off at gunfire and the followers would not get in till sunset."

About noon reached Kudlee, a large bazaar. After two or three hours halt started again, and reached Sabatoo before sunset. Halfway met the Rana to whom Kudlee belongs. A good looking young man, with about twenty followers; very polite; hoped I had got everything I wanted. At about 5 p.m. we had completed a very steep ascent, leaving behind the region of flowers and shrubs, and seeing only a few fir trees fringing the hills about. Passing through a gorge suddenly came on the view of Sabatoo with its white bungalows standing on little detached eminences. It seemed at the bottom of a basin with high blue hills all round and peeps of snow. Simla just discernible on its wooded hill. To the North-East most lovely was the scene, and the air was perfectly delicious. A very deep *khud* lay between this point and Sabatoo, the hardest pull I fancy on the whole road. Steels and Grants came out to meet me, dined at the doctor's and in the evening came to my own nice bungalow.* Enjoying the end of my wanderings, but so lonely darling without you.

April 3rd

Yesterday I called at the McCauslands and met Miss May, sister to Mrs. Laughton. She is just come out. When I meet with a new comer it strangely brings back my own griffinage. She was speaking just as I did. Three and a half years ago I was talking in the way that then seemed to me so odd. I said "What a lovely shower we had" "I don't like rain", "Oh, but this was just like an April shower at home. I stood on the verandah enjoying it." "I have only just left home. So I don't feel that."

April 6th

Time passes, beloved, and I still cling to you coming next week though "wars and rumours of wars" affright me. Weather most lovely. Yesterday I spent at Mr. Causland's. Captain McCausland knew Harlan. Said he took much opium formerly. That he was last heard of in France inciting Louis Philippe to take up Dost Mahommed's cause against us. Very probable.

*At Kussowlee, on a hill above Sabatoo.

April 9th

This is Good Friday. Last night the *jomponnies* took me a road I had not been before, and as I saw in the turn beyond me white domes I concluded the road led to a *masjid*. But on approaching I found a burying ground. It was a solemn, appropriate spot out of sight of human habitation, and bosomed among the hills. Except a glimpse at Gorakhpur, and that one tomb at Ferozepore I had not seen the mark of a burial since I quitted England. Often have I pondered on the strange way in which death hides itself in this very land of death. I have heard of cases innumerable and many awful, and among the natives I have seen a few instances but I cannot recollect any token of interment. Till here I came on the abode of silence. *Dhai* sat down and in her wild chanting voice soliloquized, "There they are young and old. No question, no answer, all silent."

SEVEN

Lettice and Alick

The First Afghan War was almost the Viet Nam of the British Empire. A "signal disaster" taught Britain the limits of her power in the Indian sub-continent. The purpose of the enterprise was to counter a new threat from Russian influence in Afghanistan. The means chosen was of doubtful morality, namely to restore by force a former ruler who had lost his throne. The undertaking was risky, since the British-Indian army would have to cross the whole of the Punjab before making contact with the enemy. This made the supply line too long. It also put the communications at risk, for the Punjab was ruled by the Sikhs who had a formidable army. Under their remarkable ruler, Ranjit Singh, they had been friendly to the British but he died during the war and it was presuming too much on friendship to send an army through the Sikh country in order to attack a neighbour with whom they were more or less at peace. The plan involved the occupation of Kabul, the capital of Afghanistan, and the officers chosen for this command were hopelessly inadequate. With a foolishness and pusillanimity that is hardly credible the British generals threw away their advantages and eventually embarked on a midwinter retreat without supplies in mountainous country surrounded by fierce, treacherous and hostile tribes. Those who survived the Afghan knives and bullets died in the snow. Out of the wholy army only one man, Dr. Brydon, staggered alive into Jelalabad, where there was a British garrison; and lived to go through the siege of Lucknow. Honoria's brother, James, was killed in the retreat. George Lawrence became a prisoner of the Afghans before the retreat and survived to become one of the triumvirate of Lawrence brothers in the Punjab and during the Mutiny. Eventually a new army forced its way through the Khyber Pass, Kabul was occupied, British prisoners were freed and the army withdrew. British honour had been more or less vindicated, but the memory of the defeat remained, and with it a memory of some disgraceful scenes.

Towards the end of 1841, just before the disaster, Henry Lawrence was sent to the front as "political officer" with the difficult task of handling relations with the Sikh army and government at a time when British fortunes were at their lowest. He succeeded in this at the price of some friction with his superiors. At one moment he was even in danger of court martial. But he acquired an unique knowledge of the Sikhs and other peoples of the Punjab and the North-West Frontier and was henceforth recognised as a man who could be relied on to overcome daunting difficulties. By the end of the war he was marked out for rapid promotion.

Honoria was left behind for many months and stayed mainly at Simla or at their summer cottage at Kussowlee in the Simla Hills, which was the only real home they ever had. She longed continually to be reunited with Henry and looked forward to the day when she would "see a long visaged, bearded, comically arrayed old man putting his head into the boat" on the Sutlej where she was waiting for him. Henry was only thirty-six but his bouts of fever and strenuous life had taken toll of him.

Honoria's letters to Henry during their separation show her as a woman with a strong grasp of public affairs and a shrewd judgement of generals and statesmen. They are good raw material for history and biography but they do not constitute a journal. They do however give some family news which would no doubt have gone into a journal, if she had been keeping one at this time. She was enthusiastic about Alick's delight at seeing some dragoons. "I wonder, if he lives, whether this martial spirit will grow up with him. Battles and babies are the two uppermost thoughts with him. When he is *pyar kuring* Mrs. Lock's baby, he says 'Dear little baby'. And when he is big he will have a gun and sword." Six months later on August 11th, 1842 Alick, aged four, underwent a more practical test of military spirit. "Mr. Steel sent him a little brass cannon. He was of course all agog to fire it off. Hill charged it, but I am sorry to say, when it came to the point, our boy hen'd, and began to cry. I was very vexed. Much worse I was angry and gave him a slap. For a little while he was sadly snobbish, crying and making excuses to get away; that he was sleepy and would go to bed etc. I was determined not to yield to his cowardice. I took him in my lap and reasoned with him and assured him of punishment if he was so foolish. At length he heard the little discharge without wincing, then he looked on while I took the match and fired it off. And at last took courage himself, and applied the match. When the nervousness was conquered he was of course delighted with the exploit, and now I intend daily, under my own eye to practise him in a small way with gunpowder. Learning to touch it himself will I hope take the white feather out of him. My boy, to have you a coward! No, no, no, that must never be!"

Twelve days later she was able to write "Tim has left off being a snob about gunpowder and, when his little gun is fired, he likes it. Today Bodee made a mine with a lot of powder, and there was a loud report, such as Tim would have roared at some months ago, but today he was quite *razee bazee*. I hope he will be a real son of a gun."

She inculcated rather a literal concern for truth, and writes "I do not often treat [Alick] to any nonsense." But she continues "The other day I told him *Cock Robin*. It was very amusing to see the effect on a little mind accustomed to a meaning in every word, and he discusses it with the utmost gravity. 'How does a sparrow hold a bow? I think that is nonsense.' 'Yes, that is right. The fly has got a little eye, so he could see.'"

The only journal which has survived from this time is what Honoria calls a "nursery journal". This includes an account of their daughter Lettice's death. Her little grave is still visited by descendants of those who loved her parents. It is tended by Indian boys and girls from the school that Henry Lawrence founded nearby at Sanawar.

Sabatoo, Sunday March 21st, 1841

My darling Alick's strong imagination makes me often tremble for his veracity. My hope is that in the same indefinable but real way, in which a child learns the use of words, he will learn to separate play from falsehood. Today he was a "Singh-jee"* who had come with Bhoop Singh to see Mamma with an air cushion for a shield and a bit of straw for a sword. He swaggered up to the door, announcing "*Rajah Bhoop Singh accar*".† They showed him in (purely fictitious), told him to sit down and came to me. "Mamma, say *bhat kurro*" I salaamed to the chair and he went out to bring the Rajah's *baba*, and one little one he put in my lap. He went through all the scene with such perfect fidelity that he must have fancied the thin air was filled with the beings he talked to.

Sunday March 28th

What is the faith I wish to inculcate, not in set sentences? The earliest element of religion is a consciousness of God's presence.

June 19th

That miserable being, Mrs. J., whom I last saw two years ago in her youth and beauty! Now an outcast, a harlot, an actress. Oh, parents ought to think of these things, and press home to their inmost souls their own tremendous responsibilities.

On June 16th, 1841 she was seven months old, our wee Lettice. Dear little thing, no child can be better in health and temper.

Tuesday August 3rd

It has pleased the Lord to put us to grief. Let me record the power and goodness of God in supporting those he sees it needful to try.

Tuesday. She was full of mirth. How she crowed and sprang almost out of my arms!

On that last Monday evening, Harry had collected all the children about him on the parade ground, and was playing at leap-frog with them.

---

*i.e. an important Sikh.
†Rajah Bhoop Singh has come.

August 4th

Our Alick has been rather out of sorts for eight or ten days, slight bowel complaint, but our Moonia was firm and plump and joyous. She was beginning to step out when set on her feet and I was daily wondering and rejoicing at her unbroken health.

On Wednesday I was playing with her, when suddenly she had a very copious motion and looked pale. I came in to Harry and said she was a little out of sorts, but it was not worth while to call in the doctor. We would take her over in the evening to have her gums lanced. I now think Doctor Steele looked grave when he saw her. The lancing seemed to relieve her, and I felt no alarm. That night she slept well. Next morning Doctor Steele came, lanced her again. I asked his candid opinion. If her illness was likely to encrease, Henry would not go. He spoke favourably. That day she looked rather pale, hardly cried and played sweetly. In the evening, when Doctor Steele came, he lanced her again and I thought looked grave. I did not much like her look. She had a restless night. On Friday doctor came and repeated that he saw nothing alarming. My Henry said after breakfast "After all I had better not go." I said, "I don't think it will rain any more." "Oh I don't mean that, I mean about the children's illness."

On Friday Alick had dysentery and all Saturday. Sunday morning he became worse. Probably anxiety for him kept me from noticing her so closely.

She had a disturbed night, and stiffened herself out in a way that frightened me. I gave her a warm bath in the night. On Saturday I think Doctor Steele came again, lanced her. Still she was fretful. When she eagerly seized my breast, she would suddenly let go. In the evening however, she seemed better. I felt much worn out yet I was astir through most of the night. She fretted and was cold. At daylight I had given her a warm bath and when Doctor came in on Sunday morning he found her looking exhausted. He stooped down and listened to her breathing. This startled me. He lanced her double teeth, looked grave and went away. At noon he returned "How is the little lady?" "Oh I hope she is going on very well, but look at Alick." He examined both. "Yes, Alick is very ill, but it is about *her* you need to be alarmed."

I have always dreaded in any affliction that excessive bodily agitation which unfits me to do or to receive good, but here I was calm. So much to do. I could think but little. Leeches were put on her head and his bowels. She appeared relieved but soon fell into a weak, heavy state. For two days she had preferred donkey's milk out of the spoon to the breast, but had been most eager after toast-water, looking at every glass and spoon. About four her eyes became fixed and her breathing oppressed. I do not think she had any consciousness. Three times a slight convulsion passed over her face, but all else was peace. She lay in my lap as I sat on the couch one hand holding her, the other holding our boy.

Soon after eight, just at the hour she had been born, my treasure left me. Mrs. Craven took her out of my arms and I took my poor boy in my lap. I did not shed a tear. Then with a strength that astonished myself I carried him in and laid him on the bed while I went over to that which a few minutes before had been my daughter.

When my darling ceased breathing I thought she said to me "Mother, you are often afraid of this dark valley. See how easily I have passed through it."

I felt that indescribable crushing of my bodily frame under the blow, that made me think I too was dying. When my darling was gone I longed to be able to tell the poor natives around me of all that comforted me. I think it was Thursday night I awoke in tears, yet I felt very happy. When Doctor Steele on the noon of Sunday told me she was in danger it was like a thunder clap, but when he said that nothing more could be done and I took her in my lap to die, a holy calm came over me. And when my beauteous babe was stretched out in her last sleep her waxen form not the least emaciated her lovely hair parted on her high forehead, dressed in the very clothes I had so often delighted to deck out for her, she never looked so lovely.

Now the worms are spread under her and the worms over her, sown in corruption to be raised in incorruption. When I can think of her as all dissolved to dust it will be less bitter, but now only the decay and horror of death rise in my mind.

Sunday August 8th

A week today since her departure. Oh, what may she in that time have learned! All that we are darkly striving to know may be unfolding itself to her unclouded faculties.

August 27th

Tiger shooting and suchlike I think manly and right. If our boy lives to be a man, I hope to see him take a part in all manly exercises, but the pursuit of a hare or deer I abhor. Shooting is not so bad, inasmuch as it spares the bird the previous agony of terror and pursuit.

1842

When we came from the hills, we were for a month in camp, in a continual whirl of people coming and going and such a pressure of interesting and absorbing events, that I attended little to my boy. During that time he was well, and tolerably good, but occasionally fretful, and speaking more Hindustani than before. Then for two or three weeks Alick had dysentery off and on, and was frequently very peevish and passionate. For the complaint he had the usual treatment. Mercurial chalk, ipecacuanha, sulphur, warm baths, careful diet, but these did not act, and at last he was relieved by leeches on the anus. Four were twice applied, and checked the complaint.

In December I went to Captain Thomson's and staid [sic] for six weeks. The children of Captain Thomson were Lizzy, nearly six, Jessie nearly three years old, and Charles nearly eight months. No mother I suppose altogether approves the way in which any other mother manages her children, but their mother had somehow compassed the rare achievement of making the children happy with her, and yet not troublesomely dependent on her for everything. I have never seen children anywhere more independent of servants. I do not recollect hearing either of them speak a word of Hindustani, and they did not say much even to the European women. On the whole Alick was much benefited by his residence with them, though from his illness and his being unaccustomed to other children, his occasional fracas with them were very annoying.

I meant to sketch what my boy now is, but one week's regular detail of his doings, will be the best way of drawing his character. This morning when he awoke and I bid him get up he said, "Not yet. First I have my *doodh panee*." "No my boy, you do what I bid you." He did get up but reluctantly. This dilatory reluctant compliance is not obedience, and I am often perplexed. Not that he eventually refuses to do what I bid him but he often first tries how far he can disobey. How am I to accomplish ready cheerful acquiescence in what I tell him? I got up and went out with him. He was merrily riding his pony when his cap fell off and he began to cry. There seemed to me that general peevishness about him which I think is best brought to a head, I therefore gave him two or three smart slaps on the hand, sent away the pony and took him in. He seemed subdued and I let him come out with me again while I gathered some flowers. He then bathed and dressed and brought his little chair and sat down while I told him the story of Stephen, and said his little prayer. At family prayers he fidgeted about. I do not know what is right to do, it is not well to allow him to show disrespect to religious worship, yet I do not like connecting it in his mind with irksome restraint.

April 30th

I must beware of teaching my child deception by showing pleasure at his intelligence. I took out a microscope lately and he begged to see. He expressed great delight at seeing the fly "look so big". I hardly thought he really saw it, but said nothing. Today I put in a small flower he asked to see and expressed great delight. While he was looking and describing the flower I removed it and said "Now look what do you see?" "I see such a pretty flower so big." I showed him there was none, and tried to make him understand how wrong he was. He is so imitative and I am so delighted with all he says and does that if I do not watch us both he will get into that poisonous way of streaming off in borrowed phrases of affectation and self deception. Here is the importance of having the child always with the mother. If I knew less intimately the workings of his mind, I could not tell the real from the assumed.

Sunday May 1st, 1842

My darling boy I committed a sin today against you and against God which I record for my own humiliation. I got into a passion and struck you. When Alick came in this morning I told him to try and take off his own clothes before bathing. He began good humouredly, but in taking off his pantaloons there was some difficulty. He began to whine. I bid him try. "No Mamma, you take it off." "Try first and then I will help you." He began to cry, I was angry and gave him a box on the ear.

May 2nd

For several months I have begun regular lessons with him. But not caring much about the matter, I let other things interrupt. Now since I came here I have been quite regular and he makes progress. Alick is now rarely ten minutes out of my sight, and wholly under my own influence. A matter I have often desired, and of which I must now be mindful.

Saturday May 28th, 1842

The jungle all round us is burning rapidly and Mrs. Lock and I ready for a flight to Sabathoo. Meantime I will note an experiment I have been making with Alick. In his lesson for some weeks past, he has always had the counting frame and he can reckon as far as eight readily, adding and subtracting, by rote. He has been able to count nearly to thirty for a year past.

Last Monday when he began as usual, I put eight balls aside on the frame, telling him they were Noah and his family and we would reckon how many people had been in the ark. He demurred and I was not quite sure he understood me, I therefore reckoned for him, "Noah one, his wife two," etc. Still he shook his head and said he could not. I therefore put the frame away, saying that till he counted he should not have a new knife I had got for him. Several times on Monday and Tuesday he asked for the knife, and always got the same answer. "Bring the frame and count eight", he always shook his head and ran away, and I did not make the point one of obedience. On Wednesday Dr. Steel was here, and asked to see the knife. I told how matters stood, he bid Alick bring the frame, and the wee fellow always counted "One, two, seven, one, two, nine," and so on. I did not want to make a battle, and merely said "You may put the frame away now, but you cannot have the knife till you count properly." This was right, but I was wrong in bringing the matter in any way before a stranger, or allowing it to be made a jest of.

Next day at lessons the same scene was repeated. I had not made it a point of obedience. So I did not feel obliged to enforce compliance. Mrs. Lock and I had some conversation about the matter and I began to doubt whether I was doing right. After dinner Alick came running into me for some water for his garden. "Why my boy you have had a great deal, how many times have you had water?" His back was up instantly. "Tell me," I repeated quietly "how often do you think?" "No, I won't say." Frequently he has just gone so far in obstinacy, and yielded when he saw me resolute. I took him to the bathing room and said, "Now my boy just reckon how many times I have given you water, one, two, three, four." "No, I can't, Mamma." Thinking that being flurried he might really forget I repeated for him one, two, three, etc. on to eight bidding him say it after me. "No." I whipped him with a little slip of whalebone, but with no effect. While smarting he called out "Yes, yes Mamma, I will be good, I will reckon," but the next moment returned the same resolute look, and "No, I will not reckon."

After about half an hour spent thus, I did not know what to do, feeling I had got into a contest which I must win. As he stood resolutely before me he saw me rest my head on my hand. "Mamma are you praying to God?" "Yes, my boy, I am asking Him to make you good." He immediately knelt at my knee and said earnestly, "Oh God make me good, take away this naughty and make me good." I was in hopes the evil was subdued, but the next moment the case seemed as hopeless as ever. I tied his hands behind him and left him for a little while, from five to ten minutes, in the bathing room. But I returned too soon. I had no patience. Half an hour might have done the work. I found Alick as firm as ever, whipped him again and tied him to the bed post. I was glad to see such resolution in his character and afraid to break his spirit. Yet I could not give up. I lifted up my heart in prayer and was composed and calm through all, but I hardly felt such pain when I thought him dying. I think if I had had more patience all would have been well, but the moments seemed as long to me as to him. Several times I left the room for a few minutes and returned finding him the same. "Will you now reckon one, two, three etc?" "No, I will not." "Then I must whip you again." "Yes, do," and with a sore heart I again whipped him. Once or twice he said "Mamma, I'm afraid of the rod."

Then I feared I had gone too far. I immediately laid it down saying "My boy, I don't wish to touch the rod again, only count as I bid you." "I will not." Then at other times he would yield, "I will Mamma, I will count," and then he would begin "One, two," the evil seeming to rise up again. "No, I can't, Mamma." "Then say it after me." "No, I won't." Sometimes he took the stripes like a Spartan, sometimes cried out "Dear, dear Mamma, you hurt me, kiss and make better?" Several times too he said, "Just pray to God once more," but I thought it dangerous to let him make religion a pretext for dis-obedience and replied, "No, my boy, God will not listen to you while you are obstinate. You must try now to be good, or He will not help you." Then he would say, "Just give me one more whipping and then I will say it." This went on for three hours, from four, till seven and I was deeply grieved. He seemed to have made up his mind to pass the night tied to the bed post and I could do no more.

At last, when the servant announced tea was ready and I was going away, he yielded, and in a different tone said, "Yes, Mamma, I will be good, I will make you glad." "Then my boy reckon as I bid you." He did so, reckoned to eight several times without hesitation. With a glad heart I released him, but then felt puzzled what to do, I longed to take him in my lap, and make up with caresses for all the punishment I had inflicted. But this would have been only self-indulgence. I merely told him I was glad he was good.

I was rather disappointed at seeing him in one moment as merry as ever, seeming not to remember what had passed, but I avoided saying anything that might lead him to affect feeling. When we went to bed I spoke seriously to him, told him of God's displeasure and prayed with him. Through the night he was restless, starting from his sleep. "Yes, yes, Mamma, I will be good, I will reckon," and frequently wakening saying he was thirsty. Darling child, with what costs to myself I punished him! I think he was subdued, not merely exhausted, but I am by no means sure I took the right method. Perhaps, had I left him for a longer time in the first instance, I might have avoided the conflict. Perhaps had I prayed more fervently God would have made him yield. For one thing I am most thankful, that he was not the slightest estranged from me, but on the contrary clings more than ever to his "Own, dear Mamma". I hope the remembrance will be enough now and that we shall never again have such a conflict.

Sunday June 5th

"The sure way to make your child miserable is to give him everything he desires." Children must be taught self denial. True, but how? Will he learn it by seeing his parents eat buttered toast while he gets dry bread? But, you say, would you pamper children with giving them whatever they fancy? No certainly, but I would not require a child of four years old to shew more philosophy and self command than we practise ourselves.

EIGHT

Delhi, Agra, Lucknow

After the end of the First Afghan War Henry Lawrence was reassigned to new work three times in a year, before finally being appointed Resident in Nepal. This put him in the top rank of the Indian Civil Service and gave him a salary that was far beyond his modest needs. He gave most of it away and started planning a hill school for the children of other ranks in the British army, where they could be brought up in a healthy climate. The spot eventually chosen was Sanawar on a hill opposite the Lawrence's own cottage at Kussowlee. This school was sometimes referred to as the Lawrence Asylum.

In the following chapter Honoria describes her journey with Alick through British India and the still independent native state of Oude up to the border of Nepal, where Henry was waiting for her.

This chapter consists of extracts from a letter to a friend and from "a journal for ourselves". In order to make the combined text read smoothly we have taken a few editorial liberties with the wording.

Kurnal, November 1843

It is now nearly two months since Henry was ordered to be at Kathmandoo by December 11th. When Henry first got the appointment we had many fears and misgivings that he might not be allowed to take his wife to a country where no white-faced woman had ever been seen.

All the intelligence we have since received has however been favourable, and accordingly here I am on my way to join him, he having sped on a fortnight ago. Still, I am not altogether happy, dreading that I may yet be prohibited. Another month will decide.

How many packings have we had in the last year! It is just twelve months since I left our sweet hill dwelling at Kussowlee for the dusty plain of Ferozepore, there to meet Henry on his return from Afghanistan. Then came the two exciting months, when the prisoners came

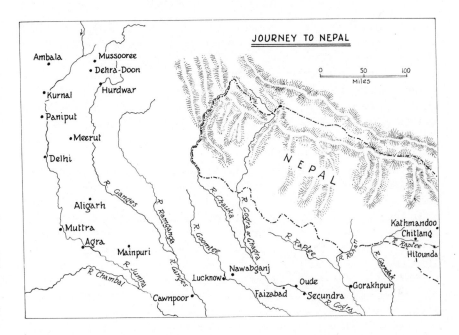

back with the Kabul force, when the Army of Reserve was assembled, the Governor-General and the Commander-in-Chief on the spot, and a whirl of reviews parades, festivities and lamentations. For all the show and glitter could not in many a lonely heart fill up the place of those who were never to return. Having shared in all this for a while we gladly on January 2nd turned our backs on the whole wilderness of tents, camels, elephants and horses, Lords, Ladies and Aides-de-Camp and set out for our new appointment at Dehra-Dhoon, that beautiful track stretching at the foot of the hills between the Ganges and the Jumna. We visited the hill station of Mussooree, and traversed the Dhoon from Hopetown to Hurdwar. When lo! we were ordered to Ambala, where we arrived on February 3rd. Then we visited the greater part of that district, "dwelling in tabernacles" till the heat drove me to Kussowlee in March. There I remained till October, Henry now and then giving me a week or two.

Two years ago, when we appeared certain of remaining at Feroze-pore, we were building a house there which is not yet sold. At the same time we built and furnished a cottage at Kussowlee for the hot weather. This dwelling we sold last year, expecting to live at Mussourie. Luckily we did not build either there or at Ambala, but we this season once more fancied ourselves settled and built another house at Kussowlee. Now we are again absurd enough to believe that we are going to remain at Kathmandoo and have accordingly got rid of all our worldly goods except our wearing apparel. "Three removes are as bad as a fire, as poor Richard says." So have we found to our cost, buying things dear because we must have them, selling them cheap because we must get rid of them. And then trying to carry about some few household goods, the vexation of their arriving smashed, cracked, rubbed, bruised, drenched after jolting on miserable *hackeries* over unutterably bad roads, being dragged through streams of all imaginable depths and regaled with alternate showers of dust and rain. Such are the "luxuries of Indian life".

It was on the 10th of last October I left Kussowlee and proceeded to Ambala, to join Henry. Then came a month of hurry skurry, bustle bustle. *This* we must take, *that* nobody would buy. What *shall we do* with these? While Henry was daily besieged by crowds who were in attendance while he completed the settlement of the assessment of Khytul, a district that lapsed to our government in March last. Besides, this is the season for travellers in India. Regiments are moving, people who have spent the hot weather in the hills are going to their respective headquarters – home is a word rarely heard in India, except speaking of Europe – and hardly a day passes that did not bring us wayfarers. At length after one night's travelling we reached Kurnal, this place, on November 6th.

Kurnal was formerly one of the largest stations in India. For some seasons it has been so unhealthy* that it is now abandoned, and most dismal does it look. Having been suddenly deserted the buildings are scarcely impaired and you pass long lines of barracks, hospitals, and stables, flag staff, racket-court, church, bells of arms, bungalows, gardens, out offices, all empty, looking as if a plague had devastated it in a night.

Delhi, November 24th, 1843

However, I passed a very pleasant fortnight with John and Harriet at Kurnal. At this season every place is healthy and it was delightful to meet our own kith and kin.

Oh dear, how pleasant it would be to go home, and only have to step into a coach and then be whisked to one's destination!

Henry left me on the 10th instant to hurry on to Nepal and I am going on more leisurely with no companion but Alick. Have you got money for your journey? You must not carry many rupees in your *palkee*, lest you should be robbed. There are no bank notes. Well you must get a draft upon the treasury of each station you pass through. But at some places there is no treasury. Then you must got a *houndie* or bill upon some native merchant there. You will have to pay high

*Owing to the opening of an irrigation canal that bred anopheles mosquitos, while in other respects doing much good.

discount but it can't be helped. Now you may lay your *dak*: there is such a run on the road just now that you must bespeak bearers several days (ahead). Once all this is done there is no changing your mind, unless you wish to forfeit the money laid out and half as much more as demurrage. Consequently when you sometimes meet people who for some reason wish to put off their journey, great is their anxiety to get someone to take up their *dak*.

Is your *palkee* well provided? – Yes – here is a flat tin box on the roof; let us look at the contents; here is a change of clothes with all dressing apparatus and there we find a box of tea, canister of sugar, ditto sago, teapot, plate, cup, saucer, knife, fork and spoon. A loaf of bread, cold fowl, pepper and salt, two pints of beer, a cork screw and metal tumbler, a candlestick and some wax candles. Pretty well. Some charitable person on the road will replenish your stock as it gets exhausted. Take care you have the medicine chest inside. Oh and don't forget to tie on the pole your little tin kettle, your brass *chilumchee* or large basin to wash in, a *lota*, or small brass cup, and, as you are not strong, you had better add a small *mora*, or light bamboo stool. Now are the *banghies* ready? Those tin boxes with pyramid shaped lids and wax cloth covers, which are slung in pairs at each end of a long bamboo that the man carries across his shoulders. Yes, all right. And have you written to the civilian of each district you will pass through, to give you *sowars*, a mounted guard? And have you got the post master's paper about the demurrage? And have you got some *pice* (small copper coin) in case you want to buy milk? Yes, yes, everything. Then just tie that roll of string to the *palkee* in case you want it, and now goodbye. But stop! you have left behind your little writing case. Well put it under the pillow, and now you are ready for a start.

On November 22nd I left Kurnal at 1 p.m. with Alick, who being now five years old is a very pleasant companion. He talks English and has always done so, a rare accomplishment for children of his age brought up in the country.

We came in the Nawab's carriage, as far as Paniput, passing over the ground on which the Empire of Hindostan has been so often lost and won. The trip was a good specimen of the comfortless luxuries we sometimes have in India. I was to go twenty miles in the carriage. And four pair of horses were laid on the road. There were two armed horsemen riding alongside, two grooms running with the horses besides the coachman and a *Jemadar*, to wit literally a Lieutenant applied to a sort of Major Domo, or, as I recollect hearing the wife of a general officer translate the word, " our *sanctum sanctorum*". Possibly she meant factotum.

The conveyance was a rickety, uneasy barouche, and as we started in the day to go in a south direction there was the sun blazing into every corner of the carriage. Fancy yourself sitting inside a spoon held opposite the fire with a piercing cold wind blowing about your ears, and raising clouds of dust in your face as you go bump, jolt, grind, grate and bump again over a vile road. I was glad to reach Paniput and get into the *palkee*, much as I dislike that overgrown coffin.

About eight in the evening I stopped and got the bearers to boil the kettle and dispatched a *sowar* with my *lota* to the nearest village for milk. Very consolatory is a good cup of hot tea prepared under such circumstances. While I squatted with my boy on the ground, the scantily clothed bearers squatting round and smoking their *hooka* turn and turn about, and the *musalchee* holding his flaming torch to light us. The old man who had come to be paid for his milk said, "I have a boy of that size who is dying." On enquiring and finding the child had fever, I produced the medicine chest, and gave a dose of calomel and antimonial powder with some castor oil. Just afterwards another man brought his son, with enlarged spleen, here my medical skill was at fault, but I thought a dose of rhubarb and magnesia could do no harm. One of the bearers then begged for a similar dose for his little brother, and I was glad to get into the *palkee* again before my stock was spent.

On we jogged, Alick sleeping soundly and myself sometimes waking sometimes dozing till daylight, when the bearers put down the *palkee*, saying there were no fresh men at the station to take it up. I got out and saw we were in an utterly bare and desolate place. A piercing wind was then whistling, but I knew in a few hours the sun would be scorching us there. Looking round, I perceived a mile or so in advance, a clump of trees. If there are trees, there must be water; if water, there is probably a well; if a well, there is some dwelling. Besides there were some kites hovering about, a sure sign of life. So I promised the bearers a present if they would take me on to the trees, and there I found shade with a *bania*'s (corn chandler's) shop and felt quite at home. I gave the men money to buy meal to make themselves *chapatees* (thin cakes), and sent off for some milk, took out my eatables and, having the *mora* with me, sat down to breakfast.

The *bania* would not let my kettle pollute his *choola* (fire place); but a few sticks were soon lighted elsewhere and I made myself very snug sitting to wait till the bearers had eaten and smoked, when they promised to take me on. Just as I had finished breakfast, I saw a carriage drive up. All my troubles were at end, we got into the carriage and about eleven were safe in R.'s house. Then came a good washing and clean clothes.

Delhi, November 27th

And now I may say with the natives, "*Ankh-bhur geya*," (My eyes are crammed), for I have seen in these days what I should like to feed on for a month. First Delhi itself. The *Chandni Chouk* or main street would anywhere be admired for its length and width. Down the centre flows the canal bordered with trees, under the shade of which at this season most of the business of the shops seems carried on. Native shops never make much show, but there must be many wealthy merchants here, if only in shawls and jewels. About halfway up the street is the *Sona Masjid*, the golden mosque, a square building mounted by three cupolas, where Nadir Shah sat to enjoy the promiscuous massacre that went on for three days after he had taken possession of the city, and near this is the *Khoonal Darwaza*, the bloody gate, commemorating the same dreadful slaughter. We visited the palace, a melancholy place, where the present puppet king subsists on the pension given by John Company. But there is enough left to show what it must have been in the days of Aurungzeb and Shah Jehan. The king, I believe, does not much distress himself about bygone glories, but employs himself in making confectionary, at which he is adept.*

One beautiful little *Masjid* is in good repair. This *Motee Masjid*, or pearl chapel, is on a small scale, the enclosed area paved with black and white marble, the sides chiefly of marble fretwork. All was chaste and beautiful except the gilt dome which marred the effect.

The grand Lion of Delhi is the *Kootub Minar*. We set off at sunrise and drove twelve miles, a good part of the way through a perfect wilderness of tombs, more or less decayed. Halfway we stopped at one that was in good repair and worth seeing, the tomb of Sufdar Jung, the Vuzeer, or prime minister, of one of the Emperors. Our ciceroni in the various places had for all Mussulmen transactions only "the time of the Emperors, two hundred years ago", and for all events in Hindoo history, "seven hundred years ago, when Prithvi Raj reigned". Whoever built Sufder Jung's tomb, it is a very beautiful object, and is in thorough repair, quite a refreshment after the ruins of the palace. There is a lofty domed building with an arched colonnade in front and *minars* at the corners, forming one side of a hollow square containing garden, canal and tank. Immediately under the dome is a carved sarcophagus of white marble. The walls are of this beautiful red granite with which I am so delighted.

About ten o'clock we reached the *Kootub*, which had been standing before us all the way. We went past it half a mile to Maraolee, to look at the tombs. Tombs indeed! On every side they stand as close as cells in a honey comb. Some are very beautiful. One was in its way quite perfect, a square about fourteen feet each way of pure white marble rising with four or five steps all round. Surrounding the slab at the top was a balustrade four or five feet high of spotless marble carved into

*He was also a distinguished poet in Urdu.

125

openwork like lace. In the centre was a marble sarcophagus. How I should love to raise such a tomb over my children!

In all these buildings ancient and modern, there is the same absence of all apparent fastening. No cement, no rivets. It seems as if the separate stones were all accurately squared and then hold together merely from being exquisitely fitted and balanced together.

We went to see a curious, but not very agreeable sight, a huge well into which men dive for exhibition. The well is circular. The people there told us it was 120 feet to the surface of the water, and as much more from the surface to the bottom of the well. I should have guessed the height above the water at sixty or seventy feet. Pretty well for a jump. A number of divers were standing round. We bespoke four men to leap, and in a moment down they shot one after another, arms and legs outspread striking against the water apparently with the force of a cannon ball and diving as if they never would come up. Up they came, however, and in a minute were standing dripping beside us, having come out by a side opening in the wall. We gave them four *annas*, about sixpence each. Alick was delighted with the sight, but it made me sick.

The *Kootub* itself is a vast circular obelisk, tapering from the base and crowned by a cupola supported on pillars. The outline of this vast shaft is broken and I think injured by four projecting galleries that encircle it at about equal distances, like rings on a finger. These galleries are supported by brackets of very rich carving and tapering to a point like a fishing rod, so that at a distance you expect to see it droop from its own weight.

At this season, when the air is cool and we only want shelter from the sun, it was delightful to sit under the shadow of the *Kootub* looking up at its vast proportion. The side that was in shade shewing a rich sober tint, while the extreme verge on which the sunlight rested glowed almost with a glory.

The *Kootub* stands in the midst of a chaos of ruins, evidently of very different dates and styles. The dilapidation of all around makes it the more marvellous that this one pillar remains absolutely perfect, not a scratch or crack or crumble.

Agra, December 9th, 1843

One ought to be at least six months at Agra, to take it thoroughly in. My ideas are so sadly barbarized by the only great towns I have seen in Ireland and England that I cannot yet realise the profusion of white marble. The first impulse is to think of stucco or Roman cement or plaster of Paris, and not till I have touched, examined, tasted as it were particular parts, can I believe that the structures before me are as massive as they are exquisite. Bishop Heber used exactly the right words when he said "these Moslems designed like giants and finished like jewellers." Marble seems to have been as abundant and easily managed by the architects as pie-crust is by a pastry cook. The Taj! All I can say of it is, that if I had commanded a magician's wand, I would not have altered one item in the design or details. Such a tomb would have been worthy of Isabella of Castile.

Went out one morning at gunfire. Folks start at gunfire, but seldom talking of setting out at daylight. These phrases smack of the camp and other wanderings. You rarely hear a distance given in miles: "How far is it to Delhi?" "It is ten marches, or two night's easy run", or perhaps, "I laid horses on the road, and did it in three days."

At gunfire then, we started to visit the fort, one of the marvellous monuments left by Akbar. He we are again in a wilderness of sandstone and white marble. The place is quite strong enough for all picturesque purposes, and I suppose is really able to resist anything but artillery. I do not affect military knowledge, but the fort wall gave me the same idea as that round the town of Delhi, of being the enclosure of a park, rather than a fortification. Long unbroken lines of wall stretching from turret to turret, and bastion to bastion. One hall the *Dewan Am*, or hall of public audience, as *Dewan Khass* means the place of private audience, is a splendid room now used as an arsenal. Here Lord Ellenborough gave his grand entertainments last year, and here stand the much talked of *Somnath* gates with their drapery of scarlet and gold, the flags taken in China, and other trophies. The gates are in a much less crumbled and shattered state than I expected to see, the carving is very fine and the upper part and frame are in good repair. All was again fitting up for the Governor-General's reception, and all was stir in preparing the large force now assembled here to march on Gwalior. The old story in India, feasting and fighting.

What beautiful names these Orientals give to things. Here too is a *Motee Musjud* all marble and carving and fretwork, another pearl. And there is the *Jasmine Burj*, the Jessmine tower, a lovely little arched chamber, marble of course, overhanging the Jumna on the side where that river washes the fort. Looking across the river eastward the rising sun lighted up the most delicate mist, which was harmonising and beautifying every object on the banks. A wilderness of domes and turrets, mosques, palaces and tombs with Taj like a presiding spirit rising among them all. And in strange contrast to these airy proportions and exquisite executions, the great heavy lumbering boats of the river heaped up with bags of cotton, all clumsy and half civilised. Beneath the palace are a curious set of caverns, or rather catacombs, which open to the river, but are interiorly a complication of cells and passages. One called the *Fansee ghur*, or place of hanging, is a dark little chamber, within which is a pit, very deep and wide crossed by a beam.

The entrance to this had been walled up and has only been known to comparatively recent time. And very fit for the *Mysteries of Udolpho* was the discovery, namely that the remains of human skeletons were found hanging from the beam and it is asserted, of female skeletons. This *phansee ghur* is supposed to be the place where obnoxious ladies were disposed of. A plan less liable to detection than sewing them up in a sack, near as the Jumna is. 'Twere vain to attempt to lead you up and down and round about, pavements, pillars, lace-like screens, massive walls, pointed arches, and round galleries, steps, gardens, fountains, canals. Seeing them hastily has left on my mind but a confused idea of grandeur and beauty. And oh! it was cruel to see wooden door frames fitted into these lovely marble arches to fit up the rooms for the Governor-General.

Overlooking the river is the noble elevated platform where stands the throne of Akbar, a huge block of black marble, carved in Persian characters. It was an unbroken block till its sanctity was violated. Once Doorjun Mull sat down on it, and it split, once Lord Ellenborough stood upon it and it bled. You may be incredulous, but seeing is believing, and there I saw undoubted reddish stains on the black marble.

You must accompany me to Futtehpoor Sikri, about twenty miles from Agra, where Akbar held his court. Another family had promised to join our party and Mrs. T. sent out tents. The Governor-General was in camp there. Wherefore tents and carriage were in abundance. Three double poled tents, and sundry smaller ones were therefore sent out by his Lordship's Commissariat. General Avitabile, the hyena-like Italian who governed Peshawar, on his departure from India, made over to Lord Ellenborough a mule carriage which his Lordship handed over to the Commander-in-Chief, and Sir Hugh Gough kindly lent it for this expedition.

General Avitabile's carriage is an old barouche sort of thing, large and easy, but with its worn out red cushions, battered outside and clumsy Punjaubee wheels, very unpromising looking. To this were harnessed four mules, the harness being a most ingenious complication of broken straps, toothless buckles and knotted cord. On the sad stump that remained of a coach-box, sat a wild Punjaubee. A long-nosed, very bony black man with long, black hair and beard, a queer wisp of a turban twisted round but not covering his head and sundry pieces of blue check cloth hovering about his shoulders and hips. How these people keep on their floating drapery is always a puzzle to me. This man held the reins, but had no whip and the work of making the mules go on was performed by an equally "Salvage man" running alongside, whose office was to talk to the mules. Once our running footman fell behind, and the mules stood still in the midst

The miniature shows Honoria Marshall, with the inscription on the reverse reading:

Honoria Marshall
1808 – 1854

Miniature worn by
her husband
Sir Henry M Lawrence
see paper att.

Honoria Marshall before her marriage. She brought this miniature with her to India. Henry had it made into a locket by an Indian silversmith and wore it always. A dent on the back appears to have been caused when Henry was mortally wounded at Lucknow.

Henry Lawrence at the time when he first met Honoria.

Henry, about 1848, holding the miniature of his sons reproduced overleaf.

Henry's sister Letitia, Mrs. Hayes.

Honoria, about 1847, by James Fisher who painted miniatures in Bristol in the 1840s.

Honoria (Honey), daughter of Henry and Honoria. A miniature painted at Mount Abu about 1854.

Their sons, Alick (Tim) and Harry (Moggie). A miniature, probably painted in 1848.

queerest garb in which the lords of cre-
-ation ever arrayed themselves.

I flatter myself this
is a tolerably
correct picture,
for I im imme-
-diately recog-
-nized it as
the Durzee.
A cap of
this shape
is worn
by all
ranks,
materials
varying
from
dirty rag
to velvet.

A Nipal Tailor.

This is a comfortable, well-to-do
man; the very poorest here, as
elsewhere, have little clothing
of any kind — I have not observed
the men addicted to ornaments
like Hindustanis.

A page from Honoria's Nepal journal.

Silhouettes of Harry, Henry and Honoria, made in Lahore by Mrs. Kate Hill about 1852.

"Is this the way
Papa fights?"

Harry, in his hot weather
undress. Sketched by
Major Edwardes

Henry and Honoria's son, Harry, drawn by Sir Herbert Edwardes in 1849.
The toy cannon is probably the one referred to in the introduction to
Chapter Seven.

Sanawar, the Lawrences' school, in 1848.

A portion of the Lawrence Asylum
Sketched in 1848 by
Printed at the Lahore Chronicle Press

A print of Henry, about 1850, from a
miniature by an Indian artist.

Honoria on her death bed in 1853,
her face swollen with illness. From a
Daguerreotype.

of some deep sand. The coachman did not attempt to make them move, but shouted out, "Oh! *bolna wala*! Ao!" being "come here, oh you whose work is to speak!" and accordingly the *bolna wala* came up and expostulated very effectually with the mules, and off once more they scampered over rough and smooth.

Next morning we were up before daylight and back to Agra for breakfast. Lady Gough gave a ball that evening which most of the party wished to attend. I did not go, for I saw no necessity why I should victimise myself by dressing at the time I wished to go to bed. But, for those who like such, it must have been a great sight with the numbers of military now assembled at Agra. Nothing but uniforms and decorations at every turn. "Who is the gentleman in plain clothes?" is the question, when any stray civilian is seen. For my part I had enough of military spectacle last cold weather at Ferozepore. Forty-five thousand troops at a review were more than I shall ever see assembled again probably. And between ourselves I do not think the effect imposing at all in proportion to their number. No review that I have seen has given me half such grand ideas as the sight of one regiment marching up Shipquay Street.

The weather is now delightful, clear, still and bracing. The climate of our cold weather with an English-built house to live in would be perfection. But here, where everything is arranged with reference to the scorching season, the cold weather has many discomforts.

This great house has more rooms than I could count, but not one that is thoroughly comfortable. The number and size of the doors are alone sufficient ever to prevent one's feeling snug. My bedroom is about ten feet by eighteen feet and has six pair of lofty folding doors, not any of which fits closely. Some will only stay shut when kept in order by a table or box; others will not open beyond a certain angle. Oh for locks and hinges and bolts like those at home! Here it is a serious undertaking to stretch up to the great stiff bolts that fasten the doors and, when you have after infinite pulling and twisting and shaking effected an opening and sat down to read or write, open it must stay till you choose to get up and close it. Servants cannot shut the doors after them, even if such an idea ever occurred to them, for the fastening is inside. If you wish for privacy, you must be prepared to get up and remove the barricades every time you call "*Qui hi!*" unless you have immured a servant along with yourself. Folks who have been long in India are no more incommoded by servants sitting in the room than by so many chairs or footstools. I began too late. These black forms gliding about with bare feet and coming unexpectedly into one's presence still worry me unspeakably. Then the noises of an Indian house! The echoing of every sound through the gaping, yawning, staring dark rooms and corridors! The reverberation of "*Qui hi!*" in every direction and the annoyance of servants sitting all about to shout out "*hasir*", ready, or the still greater annoyance of their having gone outside to smoke and talk, so that you may "*Qui hi*" till you are black in the face without getting an answer.

I hope patent stoves will not have superseded coals and turf before we go home. How delicious would be a wide polished grate with all appendages, a nice fender, shining fire-irons, and a blazing fire to poke! Here in the upper provinces most rooms have fire places, but such comfortless incomplete things, and the wood we get for fuel is of a smouldering unsatisfactory sort that leaves off blazing the moment it is not puffed. And there it sulks itself into a sort of charcoal, the look of which is enough to chill anybody. In the hills the beautiful pinewood makes a most comfortable fire.

Have just seen a notice in the newspapers of the sickness that has prevailed in Agra, in consequence of which the demand for wood for the funeral piles of the Hindoos has raised the price of fuel enormously. We talk of it as an annoyance but its scarcity and indifferent quality are a serious grievance to the poor. Their chief fuel is formed from dung. It is kneaded into flat cakes. The fire they yield is hot and not offensive. I am astonished where people find enough for the large consumption we daily witness. I have seen boat loads brought for sale.

From this you will judge how abundant are cattle. And so they are, milk and *ghee* from cows and buffaloes being a main article of diet, bullocks being used for the plough, for cleaning grain and drawing water, for carts and panniers. Asses, too, abound but are used only by two classes, washermen and bricklayers. Camels and elephants are the usual public carriage, at least from Allahabad upwards. Sheep are kept by the natives chiefly for wool, few among the flesh-eating Mussulmans being able to afford meat. Flocks of goats too are kept for milk and for slaughter. Pigs maintain themselves on the offal of the villages and, as scavengers, are tolerated in large numbers. They are eaten by the very lowest and poorest class, reckoned almost as impure as the swine themselves. Troops of half starved dogs infest every village; if you saw these you would understand the tone in which dogs are spoken of in Scripture.

Lucknow, December 20th, 1842

Here I am one stage further on my journey, and very happy at finding there is no obstacle to my journey to Nepal where Henry arrived on November 30th. I was detained at Agra a week beyond my original plan by the approach of the Governor-General, whose cortège like a whirlpool sucked in all around. All bearers being engaged for his Lordship, no private *daks* could be laid. At length the great man arrived, and little folks could stir abroad. Great was the bustle after the temporary stagnation at Delhi, Agra and Cawnpore, all famous places of merchandise especially for European goods. I in vain tried to make purchases. "The Lord Sahib is coming, no carriage is to be had. All our goods have been stopped on the road," were the universal replies.

On December 13th I once more got into my *palkee* with Alick about sunset and jogged on till sunrise, when I stopped and made tea, offering a four *anna* piece, about sixpence reward to whomsoever would get some fresh milk in my *lota*. It was soon filled and having plenty of biscuits and sandwiches we made a comfortable breakfast. Filling a bottle with tea, I set out again.

I could not use half the nice fresh milk brought, and handed the *lota* to a *palkee*–bearer to empty. He threw away the milk he would so glady have drank, it was polluted by my touch. Not perhaps after all that the pure fresh beverage would have been agreeable to him, for I never saw a native Hindoo or Mussulman enjoy the milk till it had been in some way cooked. Thus it is often in camp provokingly difficult to get a little fresh milk for tea close to a village with abundant flocks. I believe that as soon as the milk is drawn off, it is put in *gurrahs* those earthen jars of such endless use, which have been previously smoked. Then it is cooked in some way that gives it a mingled flavour of earth and smoke, with oil floating on the top. Consequently if in travelling you wish for the luxury of a good cup of tea, you must look out at milking time, morning or evening, just before the cattle go out to graze at sunrise or after they come in at sunset. An hour afterwards there is not a drop of unsophiscated milk to be had.

We did not reach Mainpuri till 2 p.m. and I was greatly exhausted. The bearers vary much in their mode of carriage, some keeping step and running smooth; others have a dreadful pace. Fancy yourself in a sieve shaken to try to send you through it, and occasionally receiving a smart jog to facilitate the process. Had it been possible to be ground small enough first, I am sure I should have been sifted out on the road the first stage. Some bearers make me quite sea sick. Altogether it is a most amazing conveyance, and I have not yet got reconciled to being thus hoisted on men's shoulders. Not that they have any feeling of degradation from the employment; it is what they are born and brought up to and the labour is not greater than most other bodily employments. Eight men run with a *palkee*, four at a time carrying it. They are relieved at stages of about ten miles, which distance they go in about three hours, and then their work is done. It is very pleasant to see the natives in any joint labour of this kind, their good humour and willingness to help one another. Often when I have looked at a set of bearers or boatmen, each taking his turn at the work, without shirking or grumbling, I have thought how differently our own country folk would behave. Fancy too a lady who, if she have a servant in another *palkee* with her, is travelling with twenty men or upwards at night through a country where for hours no habitation is seen, she very likely unable to speak a sentence of Hindustani intelligently, and with still less hope of understanding a word the bearers say. Remember too her property, perhaps shawls and jewels, all travel in the *petaras* slung to the ends of a bamboo borne on a man's shoulders, and that she and her possessions are in the power of a score of stout fellows, or double that number when the old and new sets of bearers meet. All this too on the very ground where *thugs* are slaying scores, ay hundreds of travellers, strangling a man for half a crown's worth of silver ornaments he may happen to have, or not unfrequently without any purpose of plunder, merely to keep their hands in. Yet in this way an unprotected woman travels safely from one end of India to the other. Thus I have come from Kurnal hither.

This same *palkee* is a long box, about six foot long, three foot wide and a trifle higher, lined and stuffed with a mattress and pillows. Sliding doors open at each side, and at the ends are little windows. At each end projects a stoutish flattish pole, that behind being straight, that in front slightly curved upwards, the whole is supported on low feet. Four men take this up, two in front, two behind; they have small cushions to relieve the pressure of the pole which rests on the alternate shoulders of the men; that is if the first has it on his right shoulder, the next takes it on his left. When tired they all change shoulders together. Off they trot thus loaded, and keeping up a grunting song, "huh-huh-huh-huh," or sometimes "heek-heek, hah-hah,". They rarely set down the *palkee* till the end of the stage. Good bearers even relieve one another, without setting down, when you feel the jog suddenly cease, and the *palkee* soused down. Then comes the cry of "*baksheesh, baksheesh!*" and the traveller gives a trifle, about sixpence, for the men to smoke.

Jaded, sick, hungry, dusty, how pleasant it is to reach a house, lie down on a couch and enjoy a thorough cleansing and a cup of tea. At Mainpuri I halted for a few hours and then proceeded to Cawnpore and on to Lucknow. I am very glad to have this opportunity of seeing a town and court still kept up in native style. There is a cantonment some miles off but my friends live in the city where there are no Europeans save the Resident and his train, and some officers in the King's service. Very amusing is the étiquette of a native court and very showy are the cavalcades.

Lucknow, December 28th, 1843

I have just returned from witnessing the grand procession in honour of the arrival of a new Resident, Sir George Pollock. Parks and villas adorn the neighbourhood up to the very walls of the city, being the country seat of the royal family and nobles. Lucknow with its white stucco, gilding, and red paint has a very upstart look after the "melancholy and gentlemanlike" marble and desolation of Agra. Nevertheless this is a curious and even splendid city. The quarter in which I am staying is that of the palace and Residency and here the streets are wide, and among the buildings there are trees and gardens. There is a curious dash of European architecture among the oriental buildings. Travellers have likened the place to Moscow or Constantinople. Gilded domes surmounted by the crescent, tall slender pillars, lofty colonnades, half Grecian looking houses of several stories high with pillars, verandahs, and windows, iron railings and balustrades entirely foreign in this country, cages of wild beasts and brilliant birds, gardens fountains and cypress trees, the winding river Goomtee, with its bridges and boats, elephants, camels, horses, *palkees* and *doolies* all make a confused and very dazzling picture. And to these are added a very strange accompaniment for a Mussulman city, to wit, statues innumerable of every imaginable design, from a gigantic soldier, painted to the life and presenting his arms with a most valliant air, to Jupiter, Venus and all other personages entitled by prescriptive right to stand up in every material from Parian marble to plaster of Paris. On one side Hercules flourishes his club at you, on the other stands a shepherd in a tie-wig and three cornered hat making love to a shepherdess in hoop and ruffles. The material is stucco and these figures must be a sore abomination to "true believers". They were introduced about half a century ago by a certain General Martin.

The suburbs of Lucknow are unlike any I have seen in India, for here there are buildings and gardens and a look of habitation, instead of the bleak desolate barren waste or wilderness of tombs around Delhi and Agra. Here too all the principle thoroughfares are watered and the absence of dust is quite marvellous to those who have been used to other towns of the East.

We went out one morning to drive through the City. Our road first led through a fine wide street with clean looking shops. In a native bazaar of the better sort the shops occupy the open front of the lower story, generally raised a step from the street, and screened by an awning of cloth or a mat supported by slanting poles. Doors are seldom seen and indeed could seldom be used for the shop is open like a shed and the goods are stowed inside at night. Near the threshold sits the owner, very much at his ease amusing himself with his *hookah* till a customer calls. First the *bania*, most important of all. His counter is generally elevated a foot or two and neatly covered with coarse red cotton cloth, ornamented with flowers cut out of white cloth and sewed on. Ranged round are large open baskets and small sacks neatly rolled down round the top containing *atta*, coarse wheaten meal. But though *atta* is for sale at a *bania*'s there is little demand for the prepared article. Each family grind their own and the work is solely that of women. The *chukee* or mill consists of two circular stones, twelve or fourteen inches in diameter laid one on another. Near the edge of the uppermost is a wooden peg inserted as a handle to turn round the stone by, and in the centre is a hole where the grain is poured in. The only preparation is to spread a clean cloth on the ground for the *chukee* and then down sits a woman alone or with a companion to relieve her, and "the sound of the grindstone" is thus heard in every village almost in every house during the greater part of the night. This reminds me that when the army of the Indus was marching through Scinde in the beginning of 1839 they were in danger of starving, not for want of grain – of that there was plenty – but for want of women to grind it. No man ever dreamed of such an occupation. And when the Commissariat officer indented at each stage for so much grass, grain, etc., there was likewise an item of so many women to grind.

The list of wares in the *bania's* shop continues:

Dal [split pease], *oojie* a preparation of wheat, like coarsely granulated flour, very white and nice, *mida* flour and other varieties of grain, salt, sugar and spices, large globular jars made of skin holding oil and *ghee*, clarified butter, heaps of tobacco looking like a black paste from the way it is done up. These are the chief ingredients for housekeeping. On the other side there are piles of cooking vessels, brass for the Hindoos and for the Mussulman copper which is tinned over before it is used. These are first the *degchee*, like an orange slightly flattened at the bottom with a wide mouth and a lid that serves as a plate. *Degchees* of every size from a quart to several gallons are the grand utensil in our kitchen. Then the *talee*, a flat plate with a narrow, standing up rim, the *lota* that most useful of vessels, the smallest holding half a pint, the largest a quart. The *kotura* shaped somewhat like a deep saucer, the *tavah* a convex iron plate on which are baked the thin unleavened bread of the people, and large iron spoons. These various utensils are piled up pyramidically according to their sizes and when you have some of each, your kitchen is finished. At least it wants but the grooved stone and long rolling pin for bruising and mixing the multitudinous ingredients of a curry.

The front of the *bania*'s shop is festooned with strings of *chillums*, those cups of red earthenware which are used to hold the fire and tobacco on the top of the *hookah*. Here too are to be had the indispensable variety of vessels formed of baked red earth without which we should be badly off. The most useful are *guraks* and *soorhais*, the first are globular vessels with a small mouth and short neck the second are like tall-necked squat-bodied bottles and are used to hold drinking water. All these being unglazed are porous and keep their contents cool. Being cheap they are unceremoniously broken and thrown away when they have met with any legal defilement. I have sometimes when travelling got a nice curry and rice served in dishes of this earthenware, when I might have starved had I waited for a dinner out of my hosts' own metal vessels. Fragments of these broken earthenware pots are very abundant and are used for many purposes.

When I have observed a man taking a broken piece to carry a little water or fire to light his *choolah* with, I saw what is meant by the desolation of Israel when "as in the breaking of a potters' vessel, there shall not be found in the bursting of it a sherd to take fire from the hearth, or to take water withal out of the pit." (Isaiah xxx 14).

Next in number to the *bania*'s come the *hulwai*'s or confectioners. In their shops is a sunken fire place on the top of which is placed the iron stew pan in which most of the good things are cooked. The common cheap confectionery is composed chiefly of sugar and butter but the more delicately prepared sweetmeats of the natives are delicious. Eggs and milk are I believe rarely used. Eggs certainly never come into use among Hindoos who count them unclean, but somehow they make a great variety of very nice confectionery, generally flavoured with rose water. You cannot imagine the swarms of flies and hornets that buzz round the *hulwai*, who seems quite unannoyed by his visitors, and only takes a *punkah* to drive them away when they carry off an unreasonable share of his sweets. The various *meetais* are ranged very prettily on large metal trays which are set on neat circular stands formed of reed or bamboo. The itinerant confectioners run about the streets carrying on the head a tray of sweetmeat covered with a cloth, in one hand the stand to set it upon, in the other a clumsy pair of scales, made of twine and coarse basketwork, weights made of rough stones, and a heap of *cowries* and *pice* to give in change.

The cloth merchant sits among his heaps of cloth, chintz, white calico, muslin, silks and broadcloths, and generally those exposed are of a coarse kind. Here and there a Kashmiri shawl merchant may be seen surrounded by balls of every coloured thread, mending or finishing a shawl. The *durzee* or tailor with a troop of workmen under him [is] generally busiest at the beginning of the hot and cold seasons, preparing the light muslin garments or quickly wadded chintz jackets in common wear.

The jeweller with a tiny portable furnace and a few rude tools doing marvellously delicate work in gold and silver. Often have I seen an old white bearded man with his nose pinched in by a pair of uncouth spectacles poring over his alembic in a most alchemist like style. His fire is charcoal, kept glowing generally by fanning it with a *punkah* or blowing it with bellows. The *punkah*, literally wing, is never shaped like our fans. The large one suspended from the ceiling is merely an oblong frame of light wood covered with cloth and slung edgewise, pulled back and forward by a rope. The hand *punkah* is of various shapes, sizes and materials but is always set on by one side to the handle. The common sort are formed by a date leaf, split and neatly plaited. The bellows are two leather bags meeting at one end, where they are joined to a sort of nozzle. A man sitting on the ground holds a bag in each hand and alternately [dilates] and contracts them.

Among the tradesfolks one in great request is the *barmooja*, or grain parcher. He or she, for women often do this work, sits over a stove with baskets of various grains and an iron pot on the fire, half full of coarse sand. A handful of grain thrown into this hot sand and stirred about with a sort of broom made of split bamboo becomes in a few seconds *chabenee*, the grain cracks down the sides and turns almost inside out, swelling and curling. The best I think is from rice, but it is likewise made from Indian corn, wheat, pease, etc. *chabenee* is much used by travellers and is eaten to stay the stomach during the daytime until the evening meal is ready.

All these you must imagine sitting on the ground cross legged and their knees stretched out so far and so flat that the thighs form nearly a right angle with the body while the heels almost touch it. Each religion and sect distinguished by their dress. Properly speaking, no Hindoo ought to wear anything that has been defiled by scissors or needles. His garb is made of three pieces of cloth, one for the turban, one to gird round his loins and another to wear round the shoulders, but very few adhere to this original law except at the time of cooking and eating.

Not that all are rigidly secluded, for well dressed women are to be met in the country drawing water and otherwise occupied, but in towns they seem to have scarcely any work abroad. The men appear in every variety of costume, the very poorest, as elsewhere, with only a cloth round the middle, gay youths with a rakishly put on turban, curled beard, close fitting vest with sleeves open nearly to the elbow, the waist girdled tightly in by the *kumerbund*, wide drawers or else a nicely folded drapery of cloth, confined above the hips by the *kumerbund* and hanging to the knees.

The most brilliant colours are used by the people, shawls of every variety from the coarse cheap shaped *jamawar* to the most costly kashmirs and every shade of red, yellow and blue. Many wear a light sort of blanket called a *looee* dyed scarlet. Others have a quilted jacket of gay chintz. Shoes with curled toes of gay colours and shewy embroidery, turbans generally white, but sometimes very showy.

Here you meet a *shooter sowar* or camel rider seated on a peaked saddle with gay red and yellow harnessings, jingling bells round the neck of the camel, which the rider guides by a string fastened by a hook in the animal's nose. In riding the string is generally held short and the long neck of the camel is turned from side to side just like the tiller of a rudder.

Alongside of this tall slender creature you may see a huge elephant waddling on, his face painted all imaginable colours, the points of his tusks sawn off which are tipped with silver and, if he is a favourite, his ears pierced and absolutely fringed with silver rings. On he heads, apparently very slowly and without an effort, but you find what a rate he is going at, when you see one of his keepers run alongside carrying the ladder. First there is a huge pad put on the elephant's back and girded round with strong cords. Over this is thrown a *jhool*, or saddle cloth, generally of scarlet broadcloth, but sometimes very splendidly embroidered and fringed. Above all comes the *howdah* which if belonging to anyone of rank is covered with plates of silver and the ends fashioned into lions' or tigers' heads. The *howdah* is pleasant enough when once you are fairly in it but for a lady it is rather a troublesome ascent. The huge leviathan-like creature stands winking very dreamily with his queer little piggish eyes, twitching the muscles of his wrinkled face to shake off the flies, or switching himself with his bare lank tail. The *mohout* sits on the neck, his knees just behind the ears. On the signal being given he touches the elephant with the *ankoos*, or the steel crook he holds in his hand, saying "*Baiat*" (Sit down). Down go the hind legs first and then the forelegs, not kneeling – for the joint at the knee turns inwards and throws the foot out. Now the elephant is down, a man in attendance opens the *howdah* door and places a ladder. Make haste, for the mountain you are ascending begins to move. It is just like climbing up the side of a ship which has a strong inclination to stand up on her bow ends. There you are seated safely. "Ooth", quoth the *mohout* and gives another knock on the creature's head with the *ankoos*, now be prepared, for he will first straighten his forelegs, and you may sway backwards almost over the *howdah* if you are not prepared. Then the hind legs are raised and the vast creature waddles off without seeming to feel the people on his back more than the flies on his nose. The front of the *howdah* holds two people, with a seat behind for your servant who generally climbs up by laying hold of the tail.

The elephant sweeps past, very often with a deep toned bell hanging round his neck, and if he carries anyone of rank, preceded by men bearing silver sticks and followed by horsemen with swords, shields, matchlocks and spears. Next perhaps creaks a huge clumsy wagon drawn by oxen. Then a *dhoolie*, or litter containing a lady and carefully curtained up. There you see a *bheestie* carrying on the right hip a skin of water. Perhaps he is going to water the street, and it is very pretty in the level light of the morning to see the showers of water which he dexterously feathers off from the neck of his *mushk*. Here we meet some stylish native looking very uncomfortable in an English buggy. Anon comes a bundle of shawls and brocades sitting cross legged in a *palkee*. Today there was in addition the long procession going to give the *istikbal* ceremonious meeting to the new Resident. Much importance is attached to this *istikbal*, it is one of the grand definers of rank, respect being indicated by the rank of the person who goes out, and the distance he goes.

Sir George Pollock arrived within two or three miles of Lucknow yesterday. But the astrologers pronounced it not a lucky day for the king to go out, and His Excellency therefore halted a night at Dil Khooshgar, heart's delight, a very pretty park of His Majesty's. Today all being auspicious, the whole town was in a stir before day, guns firing, drums beating, troops mustering. We were in an open room above the gateway through which the whole procession passed. I was particularly pleased with a carriage nearly covered with gold and drawn by eight richly caparisoned elephants. Another carriage was drawn by twelve fine horses. There were carts of light bamboo filled with pigeons, which being let loose in flocks and flying about in the morning sun had a very pretty effect. And I am sorry to say there were men bearing hooded falcons which were to be let loose among the pretty pigeons, but this I did not see. We sat for some time looking up the street, down which His Majesty was to come, and down the road where the Resident was to meet him, when a discharge of artillery announced that the king had left the palace. Presently we heard the *dunkah*, a kettle drum borne on a camel and used only for royal personages and there was a stir among the crowd.

There were camel riders, jingling along, running footmen in long, loose, scarlet robes bearing silver staves, cavalry dressed like our lancers, men in complete armour, bands of music and sundry other militaries, behind all which came a gayly dressed elephant bearing kettle drums, another with a man holding peacock feather *chowries*, bundles of feathers something like hearse plumes, and other *chowries* formed of the huge white tail of the yak or Thibetian cow, another gay elephant with another man bearing a golden *chatha*, or umbrella and then another elephant abundantly smothered in jewels and embroidery bearing a *howdah* of gold and silver, wherein squatted His cross-legged Majesty of Oude, so turbaned and shawled and jewelled that it was difficult to discern in the mass of finery whereabouts the speck of man was. He looked straight before him with vast oriental dignity, seeming as if he would not have turned his eyes right or left had the moon dropped down at one side and the sun at the other. And as if he was perfectly unconscious of the surrounding multitudes. I could scarcely believe the creature was alive.

The *dunkah*, the *chowrie*, and the *chatha*, are the special prerogatives of royalty and woe be to the subject who in the royal presence ventured to assume any one of them. Once, when the king was passing, a European maidservant of Mrs. L.'s stood looking with a parasol to shade her from the sun. The king sent an orderly to rebuke the offender and afterwards represented the grievance to the British Agent. After the royal elephant came scores of others, more or less adorned, with the royal family, the nobles of the court, sundry English officers in their staff uniforms, and a glittering jumble of I hardly know what.

We looked down upon the gay crowd as it swept through the gateway and just saw in the distance another glittering cortège as the Resident approached. Another discharge of artillery announced that His Excellency had received the royal king and had got into the *howdah* with the king. Both parties now joined and marched slowly back together through the town and up to the palace, where there was a grand breakfast. We did not attend this part of the show, but I had been amused for days before at receiving "His Majesty the King of Oude's compliments" inviting me.

My stay at Lucknow has been too brief for me to pick up more than generalities. If you want particulars, and those most amusingly given, read an account of the Mussulmans of Upper India, by Mrs. Meer Hassan Ali. It is a most strange and interesting work and makes one long to know how it came to pass that a woman with her cultivated mind and seemingly right principles, came to wed the Meer. She lived for many years at Lucknow much respected by both natives and Europeans, and is now I understand the matron of a boys' school in England, having left her husband, not being able to stomach his large establishment of wives. He is still living here and from his residence at the British capital goes by the name of "Meer Londonee".

Doctor Login, at whose house I am staying, is allowed professionally to enter the royal *zenana*, the favourite queen being just now ill. Her Majesty sits behind a curtain and puts her hand through a slit that her pulse may be felt. When she feels better she sends a *ziafut* of fruits and sweetmeats and ready cooked provisions. These royal gifts come on platters of the red earthenware I have so often noticed and which is in use from the palace to the hovel.

One of the prettiest sights at Lucknow is the royal garden, the ground is beautifully laid out with walks, shrubberies and fountains. In the midst is a summer house gorgeously fitted up in an Indo European style. All the comfortable couches, pillows, curtains and baths of the east with the chairs, tables and glass chandeliers of the west. In front of this building is a canal of exquisitely pure water, alive with gold and silver fishes, and a fairy ship with crimson cushions into which I got with Alick. We glided between hedges of roses, throwing parched rice to the fish which assembled for it in troops.

The grand palace is built close to the Goomtee and looks very picturesque outside. Within it is like the other fine houses, shrines and tombs, a vast toy shop. Enormous sums must have been lavished on the decoration of the palace, of the large Imambara, of Ghazee-oo-den Hyder's tomb, and other public places. The great object seems to have been to cram in as much as possible. There is no judging the height or size of a building for the huge glass chandeliers suspended as thickly as possible from the ceiling; blue, green, yellow, black, red. Very gay and very senseless looking.

There are the religious insignia of the Shiahs in every shape. The spread hand of Ali in solid gold stands up in all directions with embroidered banners hung up as thickly as whips in a saddler's shop. In solid silver half as large as life are various statues of Dhul-dhul, the horse of Hossain with two fat angels keeping guard over him. Silver candlesticks five or six feet high supporting red or green wax candles as big as the mast of a boat. The fish which is the Oude crest, two or three feet long, and made of gold and silver. Vast mirrors, models of tombs in silver and ivory, gilding, paint and tinsel make you fancy that you are going into an auction room. And all is so different from the pure, solid, melancholy looking remnants of Delhi and Agra. Here the sight-worthiness of the place consists not in any one building, but in the architectural groups, the long vistas of arches, domes and minarets, the glittering crowds, the whole bewildering mixture of Europe and Asia and the air of wealth which despite bad taste and inconsistency altogether go nearer than anything I have seen to realise my early dreams of the Arabian Nights and Lala [Rookh].

I left Lucknow on January 2nd [1844] and crossed the Goomtee by a bridge of boats. As on quitting Delhi and Agra the last view was the most interesting and beautiful. The palaces and finest buildings being on the riverside they form a fine panorama reflected in the stream, of different size and materials but all of one general character. Domes and minarets, gilded pinnacles and snowy walls. As we crossed the Goomtee we saw a troop of the royal elephants very much enjoying themselves in the water. Some were lying down completely immersed, except a few inches of the trunk by which to breathe and the convex side rising above the water. Others were standing amusing themselves with sucking their trunks full, and then squirting out the contents in shower baths over their own backs. With each elephant there were several keepers and these men were scrubbing, rubbing, squeezing and kneading the animals, jumping on and off them, every now and then rewarded for their exertions by a grunt of infinite satisfaction. The elephants whose bath was completed marched off with sleek black skins and every appearance of comfort. While others were walking incrusted with mud and dust seeming to long for their turn. Not to be forgotten however that the elephants, like children, enjoy begriming themselves with mud just as much as the scrub and bath.

An easy *dak* of eighteen miles brought me to Nawabgunge. The moon shone brightly on the pretty grove where a tent was pitched for me by the *nawab*, not like the tents used by Europeans which are universally white externally, but striped white and scarlet. Next morning I was off before daylight. And very glad I was when the sun rose, for the road was merely one out of many indistinct foot-tracks over a country but thinly cultivated.

My next halting place was Faizabad whither servants had been sent on to be ready, and had fitted up quarters for me in a native house. It was a large square room with an open arched verandah in front and a gallery running round three sides. The walls had a very pretty effect from the whitewash being mixed with pounded *mica* which gave exactly the appearance of dead silver. In front was a square pond with gold and silver fishes. And still better there was a table, a chair and a pair of candlesticks, articles rarely found in a native establishment. To be sure there were no doors and I still preserve a home prejudice against sleeping among the crowd of followers who one way or other always gather round a European traveller. But I discovered a recess in the wall that would hold the bed and got curtains hung up in front and slept very comfortably. Next evening I went out on an elephant to look round the ancient capital of Oude, but saw little beyond the native sights of a native town. One of the residency *Chobdars* (bearers of silver maces) was sitting behind me on the elephant and half a dozen ragamuffin soldiery ran in front to clear the way.

Next morning I started early and at sunrise crossed the Gogra, a wide and beautiful stream. Here I was once more in the company's territories and felt more comfortable thereat, not that I ever met incivility in a foreign state, but it is a great satisfaction to be able in any disaster to refer to a European authority. I now perceived that I had got into an indigo district. The clothes of the country folks were almost universally blue, of different shades. On the banks of the Sutlej the prevalent colour is dusky red, more becoming to the native complexion.

As far as Lucknow I travelled by night and could not observe much of the country or people, but here I was greatly struck by the improved appearances of comfort. The men were larger, fairer and seemed better fed. The abundant tanks gave opportunities of ablution such as we dreamt not of in the sandy soil to the North-West. A cotton and sugar growing country affords many comforts and the moist soil yields a rich vegetation of both trees and fields. I cannot tell you the delight it was after the stunted growth and burnt up soil to see the shadows of large trees on the fresh green grass. But withal, we cannot help in this climate connecting these beauties with the idea of fever and ague. At this season every place is healthy, but for eight months of the year the moisture that yields this rich vegetation acted upon by a burning sun is always prejudicial, often deadly. I would not therefore exchange the scorching winds and arid sands of our late residence for all the luxuriant beauty of Bengal, or Gorakhpur which closely resembles it.

Comparing old and new impressions, telling stories to Alick, trying occasionally to doze, I jogged along, stopping about noon under a tree to cook some sago. It was about 3 p.m. when I saw a nice looking house standing among well cultivated fields and was rejoiced at the prospect of a comfortable resting place. It is a rare thing to meet the house of a European anywhere out of a cantonment. No officials reside in the district except indigo or sugar planters and opium or customs officers, or in a very few places where one may find a squatter or grantee of government lands. The dwelling I had now reached had every appearance of comfort and even luxury, and I must confess that I greatly enjoyed the sight of flocks of poultry, ducks and geese, promising a good dinner, for both Alick and I were very hungry.

At the door a servant met me to say his master was absent. "But you expect me?" "Certainly, everything is ready for the cherisher of the poor." "Is there any dinner?" "Of course. It is ready." "What is there?" "Everything." "I only want one dish. Let me have it quickly." "Your Excellency's orders are obeyed, it is brought." Here the *malee* (gardener) appeared with a basket of vegetables. "Let those," said I "be dressed for dinner." "What is the use? Has not the cook already got everything?" and thereupon I made over the vegetables to the *ayah* for her own use. I lay down on a sofa, Alick playing about but every now and then coming up "Mamma, I'm so hungry." "Never mind, my boy, we shall have dinner immediately." But when an hour had so passed I again summoned the servant. "When will dinner be ready?" "It is ready; it is brought." "Bring it quickly, we are hungry." "Of course." Another hour passed, again I summoned the servant and in short after several similar questions and answers the man appeared about eight o'clock, with his hands joined in supplication. "Will the slave's fault be forgiven?" "Why, what's the matter?" "To tell the truth there is no dinner". "No dinner! Then why did you go on saying it was ready." "The slave was afraid your Excellency would be angry." "I am angry now, why did you not tell me at first, when I could have got dinner elsewhere?" "What can I say? What could I do?" "Bring me some eggs then." "The fowls here do not lay eggs." "Make some *chapatees*." "There is no meal." "Get me some fresh milk. I have tea." "At this hour there is no milk that is not boiled." Luckily, the absurdity now was so great that I was more inclined to be amused than angry. At length we got some tea and *chapatees* and went to sleep.

Next morning we were again astir before day and about sunset crossed the river Raptee. It was exactly six years since Henry and I had before crossed that stream leaving Gorakhpur, and I hailed it as an old friend. I recognised the canoes formed from one hollowed stem, the bamboos used as oars and rudders, the clear placid stream; and in another hour we were comfortably housed with old friends.

Gorakhpur was the first part of India I became acquainted with after our voyage up the Ganges from Calcutta, and then appeared to me quite fairy land. After six years wandering among the plains and hills of upper India I returned to Gorakhpur, and thought it more beautiful than ever. The highest part of the snowy range was standing out as of old. The huge tamarind trees, the clear tanks reflecting the old mango trees where the monkeys skipped about as merrily as ever. All the peculiar characteristics of that most beautiful country came upon me with the fresh delight of novelty and the charm of recollection. We left Gorakhpur on January 9th and the first few miles after quitting the cantonment, lay through the *sal* forest, that vast girdle of vegetation that surrounds all the eastern part of the Himalayas. When we traversed it last, there was no road but the track formed by the line cutters who were with us on the survey.

NINE

The First White Woman in Nepal

Nepal, where Henry Lawrence was now the British Resident, was, and is, a fiercely independent state. It maintained its independence by keeping foreigners out, even as tourists until 1951. It suited the British Government to have a friendly neighbour for whose affairs they had no responsibility. So Nepalese independence was respected, the only contact with the British being through a Resident at the capital, Kathmandoo. The Resident was only allowed to travel a few miles round Kathmandoo, and up to his summer cottage at Koulia. He was allowed to have with him a British doctor and a small escort of Indian troops under a British officer. No other Europeans were allowed into the country and, until the rule was relaxed for Honoria, no white woman had set foot in Nepal. Before that, the Resident left his wife behind, if he was married; and the same rule applied to the two European members of his staff.

The Resident's duties were to watch over British interests, while keeping out of Nepalese politics. These duties were important but not onerous. The intrigues of the court at Kathmandoo were bizarre and murderous, but the common people were not oppressed. Their two years in Nepal were the only period when the Lawrences had time to restore their health, to read, to write and to survey the scene before them. During this time a high ranking foreign visitor was admitted to this hermit kingdom, Prince Waldemar of Prussia, a noted traveller and explorer, who became godfather to Honoria's second son, Henry Waldemar Lawrence, the first white baby born in Nepal.

Bheem Phedi, Nepal, January 18th, 1844
Here I am, fairly in this land of which I have been thinking and hearing so much and dreading, wondering whether I should ever be allowed to enter it. I reached Bessoulia, within the Nepal frontier on the afternoon of Saturday 14th, and there found Henry encamped on the verge of a dark line of forest with a background of brown and blue mountains. In camp were the tents of two native gentlemen who were

bearing him company, Sirdar Bowaney Singh and Kajee Jung Bahadoor, the soldiers of a part of the Nepal escort who had attended him, and a band of Ghurka troops dressed after the fashion of their country, dark jackets, wide white *pajamas* and small turbans, ornamented in front by a crescent of silver. Our camp was pitched upon a level, where the high, dry, reedy grass had been cleared by burning. We rested Sunday and on Monday after breakfast set out. Our cavalcade was about a dozen elephants, some with pads some with *howdahs*, looking very much in their element as they made their way through the rank grass which reached up to their shoulders. The ponies from Nepal are the nicest I ever saw, they come from Bhootan, stout built, shaggy little creatures, good tempered and sure footed with an ambling pace that gets over the ground surprisingly fast. Henry, Dr. Christie and Alick were each thus mounted. Our aforesaid troops with about one hundred coolies carrying our baggage.

This day I made my first trial of the *dandee*, a very uncouth but most comfortable conveyance. It is a hammock slung upon a pole, carried by two men. At first I felt rather as if I had been sewed up in a sack to be thrown into the Bosphorus but I soon found how very easy a conveyance I was in. But the *dandee* would be very trying in hot weather. The pole comes within a few inches of one's face, so that the curtain when thrown across almost touches one.

Our road after travelling through a mile or two of grass ran through a forest to Bichakoh, eleven miles, where we found our tents pitched close to the dry bed of a stream. The place was pretty – how could it be otherwise in the heart of an almost untrodden forest with undulating ground? But it was nothing to the beauty of our march of Tuesday and today. This difficult path, a mere foot track over ascents and descents and along the beds of torrents is the only pass entering their country which the jealousy of the Nepalese has hitherto allowed strangers to see. And this one road is rendered apparently as difficult as possible to deter travellers. In numberless places large trees had fallen across the paths and the path forthwith wound round them. Some had thus lain undisturbed till perfectly decayed, retaining the original form of the trunk. Transmuted into fine mould covered with sward, they looked like gigantic graves. Nature indeed establishes an effectual barrier for more than half the year, this jungle through which we are passing being deadly except in the cold weather. Deadly that is to all except the tribe of Aolias, a race who defy the malaria, traversing the jungle all the year round and even residing at the *choukies* at each stage. To these men we are indebted for the keeping of our intercourse with the world beyond the valley of Nepal. They carry our letters up and down. A few that we met on the road reminded me of the Dangurs, colonies of whom were settled in the newly cleared lands of the

Gorakhpur forest. A race on whom climate seems to take no effect, hard-working, merry and very fond of strong drink, as ready as an English sailor to do extra work for an extra dram.

Our second march to Hitounda led us over the lower range of hills into a nearly level *dhoon*. Forest thick as before, *sal*, *seemur*, shrubs, ferns, creepers. Middle of the march an abrupt ascent and descent brought us over the crest of the Chira Ghatee, a narrow pass with perpendicular sides, just wide enough to admit one elephant. Very grand the noble creatures looked, filing through the pass which they completely filled up. The road lay principally through a water course with a small thread of clear water traversing it. At length a path through a dense jungle brought us to Hitounda, where our tents were pitched on a pretty level sward by the banks of a rapid stream, the Raptee.

The village of Hitounda stands on a bank above the river. There is a *patee* raised on piles, and a very filthy straggling bazaar. The people were very uncivilized looking, but showed us no sort of rudeness. Here Henry went fishing. We halted one day at Hitounda and took our journey again at sunrise today. Our road, except the last two or three miles, lay through the bed of the Raptee which we crossed nineteen times, in some places ancle deep, in others much above the knee.

Chitlang, one march from Kathmandoo, January 20th, 1844
Our baggage was sent off at sunrise yesterday, all except our breakfast which we ate in the open air. Very cold the air was but we had a fine glowing fire, round which we sat under the shade of a lofty cliff above our camp, which was pitched on a little level where the hills receded so as to form a winding valley, through which flowed a stream. We were still in a region of wood and jungle but the vegetation had assumed a more mountainous character. Our road led first up a bare precipitous hill, a zig zag path with such short turns that in places there was barely room for the *dandee*. There were ponies but the gentlemen walked most of the way, helping themselves along occasionally by laying hold of the ponies' tails. Alick sometimes rode, sometimes was carried astride on a man's shoulder.

In the *dandee* I was carried head foremost up the ascents and this I think made me more nervous than if I had seen the road before me. But by degrees the perfectly secure footing of the bearers gave me confidence and I could enjoy the beautiful scenery and vegetation.

We saw a good deal of cultivation in the valleys below us, and the first traces of regular inhabitants since we left Hitounda. The houses are altogether unlike anything I have ever seen in Hindostan and reminded me of some at home – Caramullion, Mr. David Hamilton's abode – built of brick two or three stories high, with tiled roofs and projecting carved balconies. Some squalid enough but others have a substantial almost comfortable look. This is a bleak hillside, the highest point on the road to Nepal. We had been travelling for about ten hours and were very hungry, albeit we had halted halfway to lunch on some cold meat and a bottle of beer. We had sent on a tent which ought to have been ready pitched, but on our arrival we found it had not yet arrived. Luckily some of the servants were up. They had made a good fire and were dressing dinner. Moreover, a table and some chairs had arrived. So we might have been worse off. The night was clear and very cold with piping winds that seemed calling one hill to another. The gentlemen soon kindled another fire, near where the cooking went on, and we sat round it, wrapped in our *bukoos* watching the stars set behind the western hills and speculating whether the tents would arrive before another constellation set.

At length dinner was ready and even laid on the table. At first we were rather in the dark when I luckily remembered having with me a folding lantern of wax cloth, made by a pattern Major Pottinger had brought from Herat. Alick's lance was there too. We stuck it in the ground and suspended the lantern from its point, and enjoyed our dinner not a little. Afterwards we gathered round the fire, heaped on more wood and made some whisky punch. In the midst of this we saw torches approaching from the other side. And up ran Jung Bahadoor, quite *au désespoir*, that we should have had such *tukleef* without his knowledge. That the lady should be sitting in the open air, while he was lying in his tent! Dreadful! He never could recover from the shock. And now he had brought his own tent to be pitched for us. We had all along known that the Kajee Sahib was snug on the other side of the hill and now we could not help suspecting that he came with his offers of aid because our own baggage was close at hand. However we accepted of his tent, and he sat with us round the fire while his servants pitched it. And never did I more gladly lay myself down than on this occasion.

Kathmandoo, March, 1844

I resume this narrative after two months, but the last march to this place is still fresh in my mind. We left Chitlang on January 20th after breakfast, and after two or three hours march over the hills we came to a crest of a range, and below us lay the valley of Nepal. It was unlike anything I ever saw, more like an artificial model than any actual scenery and suggested a crowd of new and strange ideas. How did we ever get here? How shall we ever get away? How could this "emerald set in the ring of the hills" have been first discovered and inhabited? And being known at all how comes it to be so little known? What sort of a world shall we find when we descend?

The first irresistible impression given by the valley is that we are looking at the basin of a lake, and such tradition asserts it to have been. I must refer to books for the name of the hero, who with his sword cleft a passage for the waters. From Chandagiri we descended towards Kathmandoo by a winding ravine so steep and rocky that I am afraid of seeming to exaggerate if I describe it, at the same time saying that this gorge is the sole road by which goods and travellers have admittance into the kingdom.

At length we reached the level and found a good road leading to Kathmandoo, the capital of Nepal and the residence of the king and court. The town is pretty nearly in the centre of the valley and about half a mile further on stands the Residency, a large substantial home, the property of government. The grounds are about half a mile in circuit and include the houses belonging to the doctor and the officer commanding the escort. The ground is undulating and varied and planted with a great variety of trees.

Spring has now burst forth in the valley, more like home than aught I have seen in my wanderings. When we came here it was quite refreshing to see the genuinely wintery aspect of all without. Except the evergreens, the trees were bare, the fields were fallow and in the morning our gravel walks had a delightful crackling frost. How pleasant to watch the budding of leafless branches once more! Below, the crops follow each other so closely that the ground rarely has the comfortable look of reposing itself that the winter gives at home. The crowds of wild duck that come here for the winter have taken their flight towards the snow and have been succeeded by flights of swallows and by the dear cuckoo. In the garden the hedges of wild rose are covered with blossoms and the silver rod, more luxuriant than I ever saw it, is completely wreathed with blossoms of dazzling white. And let me not forget the special delight of a green turfy lawn, such as I have never seen in India. At Simla and the other North-West stations I suppose the vegetation would be as beautiful as here, but there, there is hardly a level as big as a curl paper that is not seized as a building site. And there, too, the scarcity of water and its position at the bottom of the ravine almost preclude gardening. Here the abundance of water is one of the pleasantest and most striking features to anyone from Hindustan.

The population of Nepal consists almost entirely of three classes, Nawars, Ghurkas and Bootias.* The first are the aborigines and now constitute the labouring class. In former days the valley was divided into four or five principalities, and judging by the remains of their towns they must have been comparatively civilized. Towards the end

*"Bootias" are people from the neighbouring state of Bhutan.

of the last century Nepal was seized by the Ghurkas who issued from their native hills and conquered a wide range of country. To the Nawars they were unsparing tyrants. We went a few days ago to a town some five miles from Kathmandoo called "the place of cut noses". The inhabitants were the last to stand out against the Ghurkas, and when eventually subdued, great numbers were massacred; and the survivors were every one deprived of their noses. The place is now in ruins, but has remains of Buddist temples of richly carved wood. They seem to have exterminated all the upper class of Nawars. I believe there are none extant above the class of cultivators, and diligent cultivators they must be.

All the husbandry is carried on by the hand; ploughs and cattle for the yoke are unknown. So narrow are the cultivated terraces that from below only the perpendicular sides are seen and from above, the horizontal surfaces appear continuous. The Nawars, whose handiwork all this culture is, are a hardy looking race. They cannot be very severely tasked, for one half of the days seem holidays. Those whom we employ here as carpenters, masons, labourers, tailors, come to their work late and go early and absent themselves for days together. Not I should think the conduct of men to whom their wages were a matter of much moment.

Nepal being certain of the periodical rains is exempt from the famine that so often desolates the plains. It has little traffic and is not over populated. The Nawars are markedly different from other tribes. Muscular and square-built, broad Tartar face, high cheek bones and narrow eyes, complexion of dingy white brown, but some of the women absolutely rosy. The men have no beard, and scarcely a vestige of moustache or whiskers. The women's heads are bare, a most marked difference from the Hindustanis who are exceedingly particular about keeping the sheet over the head. It would be extremely disrespectful in a woman servant to appear before her mistress bare-headed. So apt are we to be influenced by those around us that I have felt very awkward in [the] presence of natives with my uncovered head, much as St. Paul says in 1 Corinthians ii 5–6.

April 10th

But while writing all this I feel the more strongly how absolutely ignorant we are of the minds, thoughts, motives, domestic habits of those around us. We get accustomed to look at this people merely in their relations to ourselves and are apt to forget that they have any existence beyond. No stone or iron ever formed such a division between people as caste does. And as it was the intention of the Almighty to separate "a peculiar people" we see here practically the aptness for the intended object of numberless institutions of the

Mosaic law that read at home appear frivolous and unmeaning. Separation of food goes further to keep people apart than difference of colour or language. 'Tis like a screen of glass that always keeps you at a certain distance and prevents contact, though at first you may not see anything to prevent approach.

April 12th

I am sitting in the verandah this lovely morning which is like a spring morning at home. But here we want what makes spring at home so lovely, the music of the woods.

Our precious boy Alick has now completed his fifth year. In appearance he is very little changed from infancy, except in size. Still delicately fair, very thin and tall for his age, red hair, grey eyes deeply sunken in his head, a high forehead larger than the average and well formed. His intellect is in some things quick, in others very slow. I think he is remarkably slow in any combining of numbers, and he seems to me very dull about learning to read. But he reasons more than most children of his age and learns *viva voce* very rapidly. I think his observing and intellectual powers are well cultivated.

Lawrence Pemberton arrived in February. A fine sturdy child aged four years. At first his arrival showed our own boy in a very unamiable light. He was recovering from a feverish attack, was weak and dumbfounded by the stranger, and for several days he was more whining, captious and selfish than I ever saw him. Now he is much improved and very much happier with his playfellow. Your own son has totally lost the strangeness and turning away from you that many a time made my heart sore. For ten days he has said his lessons to you and you have cut me out in my own department, for with half the trouble to either him or yourself that I gave and took, you get on twice as well.

We rise at six, breakfast at nine, dine two, tea seven, bed before ten. We are much happier since we left off the evening dinner, better every way, for we only overfed and lost the dear delightful *tête-à-tête* evening. Of late we have been reading aloud and enjoying ourselves to the utmost. We have too got into the Bala Khana which with its nice verandah cheerful prospect and perfect privacy is a nice place. I did not think India could give such happiness as we feel here. Last week Alick and Lawrence were detected by you pilfering some sugar, you whipped them both and kept them till the afternoon seated separately in the large room. Both took the chastisement submissively. 'Tis impossible to judge of their penitence till we see what they do next. The two are constituted as differently as possible, and could they be mingled would balance each other's defects.

Our small society here is not the best. Captain Smith, no doubt plucky, rough and ready when there is anything to be done, but bullying and over bearing and crouching, with a zig zag up and down notion of truth that makes it hard to believe a word he says. Dr. Christie harmless and inoffensive in general, but ignorant on most general subjects, and without wit to make the most of what he does know, puzzleheaded and mystified and undecided. We rarely see the suite save at meals and then are glad how soon we can get away from them. I see no glimmer of principle in either, of any motive higher or broader or deeper than "my own advantage" or "what the world expects".

Two days ago came a *ziafat* from the king in honour of his second son having attained manhood. A few days ago he was solemnly invested with a thread round his neck, the badge of manhood and of his tribe. And now the next question is to get him a wife. The royal family here, having a blot on their scutcheon, their alliance is degrading and is spurned by all Hindoos of good birth. When therefore a bride is wanted, messengers go to Gorakhpur to seek out a likely girl among the Zemindars. Large sums are given which induce some poor family to yield a daughter, but the family who consent to the alliance are always in bad odour among their brethren. A mission is at present gone to the plains in search of a lady or ladies.

The *ziafat* sent here consisted of a long train of servants carrying on their heads trays and baskets covered with coloured cloths, containing dried fruits, spices, sweet meat, and various preparations of milk, raisins, almonds, pistach nuts, *neoza*, walnuts, *sooparee*, dates, cloves, cinnamon, mace, pepper, sugar candy etc., with a flock of goats. We went out to receive the present, took some spice and sugar, divided the rest among the servants and gave fifty rupees to the people who brought it.

A subject of great interest here just now is the arrival of some English cattle imported by the king, four cows and a bull. Messengers have been sent to Bessoulia to meet them, and litters prepared to carry them up the hills. Unfortunately the poor cattle were detained in Calcutta to exhibit at the Agricultural Show, and two cows and the bull have died from heat. Old Sirdar Bowanay Singh called bringing long rods that had been sent from Bessoulia, shewing the height and length of the cows and exciting great astonishment.

April 22nd

Ten days ago was one of the tragedies that thank God have ceased in our own dominions. A *sirdar* of some note, absent on frontier duty, died, the news arrived accompanied by some of his dress. And four of his wives burned themselves in company with this relic of their husband. As the corpse was not here, we did not hear of it till it was over, nor did we see any token of what went on, as the sacrifice took place about four miles from hence at Paspatnath. *Satis* are not practised by the Nawars, but appear frightfully common among the Rajpoots and Sikhs.

May 5th, 1844

The soils are poor and light, in many places not seeming worth the labour given to them. However the people shew no symptoms of want, and nothing can be more beautiful than the mantle of cultivation spread over the valley, of every tint from the springing blade to the nearly ripe corn, broken here and there by small hills rising like islands from the level, covered with dark dense foliage, and generally crowned by a little temple. Each field too, has its little shed for the watchman; here generally a low straw hut on the ground, shewing the greater security here from wild beasts than they have in the plains, where the watchman's hut is always raised on a scaffolding of branches out of reach of a tiger.

Yesterday evening we crossed a green level which once was a parade ground. There still are barrack for a few soldiers, who I fancy stay there to watch us. Although there is no sensible interference with our proceedings, yet on every side men are loitering about, soldiers and others, to see who enters our gate and who goes out. In fact I believe not a common coolie would venture to come without the Durbars sanction. So jealous are the Nepalese of foreigners gaining any influence or intelligence.

Leaving the parade we crossed a very good road, leading from the city to a country house of the king, Balajee. This road is bordered on either side with trees, chiefly willow, very shady and picturesque. Then we passed through the outskirts of the town. Here we found a merry party of Nawars assembled, men, women and children, all well clothed, many with silver and even gold ornaments. The women almost all comely, their hair combed off the forehead into a knot at the back, where were stuck sprigs of bright flowers, pomegranate, larkspur and others. There was a great look of contentedness in the whole group. When we approached they begged we would not come too near to defile their food, and we stood at a little distance. There was a plate made of oval leaves as big as my hand, pinned together with short slender twigs. On each plate was a large thin unleavened cake and some "savory meat, such as their soul loveth", probably flesh of the buffalo or goat stewed with onions and oil. A woman went round with a large brazen ewer pouring a little water on the hands of each. All looked patriachal and pleasant, except that in front of the feasters was a little image daubed with vermillion and with a canopy of cut paper and tinsel, and ranged in front numerous little lamps and nosegays.

Leaving this group we descended into a richly cultivated level, which might easily be made a lake, by embankments and turning in the mountain streams. We had on the left the hill of Swamboonath, one of the holiest places here. The hill is thickly wooded and is ascended by stone steps, at the summit stands a temple with a slender gilded cupola, the approach on either side is studded with small images. "On every high hill and under every green tree" these are to be seen. We could just hear in the evening breeze the sweet sound of the small bells with which the base of the cupola is fringed.

Passing through the cultivation we went on a high causeway, such as intersects all the low fields, leaving the crop in no danger of injury. To the right lay the wide valley. More in front was the residency compound. The large house and two smaller ones, standing on a gentle acclivity and peeping out from the plantations around, looked more like a gentleman's place at home than any thing I have seen. In the plains a house however spacious and comfortable, must always have a bare, glaring, staring aspect, for it must stand clear of trees both to catch every wind that can fill the *tatties* and for fear of insects. But here we have fine *toon* trees, which in size and growth somewhat remind me of the chestnut, close to the house actually shading one end of it.

We soon entered a shady road skirting another detached hill planted with bamboos and willows and then found ourselves at Balajee, not a very regal looking residence but pretty. It consists of two sides of a square. The building [is] two or three stories high, the upper story having balconies of carved wood. The walls are white and the sloping roof is tiled. From the Residency we see this palace two or three miles distant embosomed as it is in trees. Its clean white walls and fresh red roof look very like a comfortable inn or farmhouse at home. The two other sides of the square are completed by trees and walls and small buildings. In the centre are two large tanks, one a little lower than the other, the upper one swarming with fish. Just now work people are very busy all in and about the square constructing booths and grass screens, putting up little earthen lamps and making the preparations for the marriage of the king's second son, the bride for whom lately arrived from Gorakhpur.

Sunday May 11th

This place in a peculiar manner brought Scripture to mind; the thick population, the carefully cultivated terraces, the frequent feasts, all are of Canaan. There is a large class of household slaves whose work is "hewing of wood and drawing of water". Every evening we meet troops of them returning from the neighbouring hills with burthens of faggots, men and women often singing and generally looking well fed and clothed. Water drawing is not so laborious an occupation here.

The firewood grows some miles off but water runs by every man's door.

Goitre is frightfully prevalent and is attributed to the water. Certain springs supposed free from the taint are in great request. Every day our Hindoo bearer brings a jar from one special well, to which the Mussulman *bheestie* cannot go as it would be defiled both by his act and his leather *mushk*.

A few evenings ago we were out late, and saw a pretty sight. This is the season for the home bringing of the brides who have been betrothed some months before. We fell in with several processions. The bride and bridegroom were each carried in a covered litter preceded by a band of most discordant music and followed by as large a following as the friends could muster, footmen, soldiers, horsemen, elephants. Though [it was] after sunset, a large umbrella was held in front of each litter as a badge of rank. What particularly struck me were the attendants with lights, not lamps but torches, otherwise like the parable. Matthew xxv 1–3. At intervals along the road the procession was to pass, we saw groups who loitered about waiting for its arrival, each holding a torch ready to kindle, some provided with an earthen bottle of oil, some without. As the evening advanced and the procession gathered these groups into its ranks winding along the road with its uncouth music, which at a distance was endurable, enlivened by the occasional letting off of fireworks and matchlocks the scene was very pretty. The *barats* are still prettier at Kussowlee where the party are obliged to go almost singe file, thus making a long string threading the ups and downs, the ins and outs of the narrow mountain paths. I speak of Kussowlee as it was when myself and one other lady were its only inhabitants and the hill people had no interference with their customs. I know not what is now.

Henry and the other gentlemen went yesterday to a small house★ ten miles off, 1600 hundred feet higher than this, and I am perfectly alone except the children. I have therefore plenty of time to think of this, our singular position and its absolute seclusion from the rest of the world. If a small party were out on the wide sea with carrier pigeons in attendance to carry the letter bag, it would be much like our position.

May 29th

The wheat crop is cut or rather pulled, for it seems all to be rooted up and tied in bundles. Instead of "the cattle treading out the corn" as in the plains, the grain is beaten out by a very puny sort of flail or more frequently the sheaf is held by the roots and beaten against a stone.

★At Koulia.

On the 26th and 27th of this month were great *galas* here, being the marriage of the king's second son. Although the one road open to us is impassable for many months there are divers other entrances to the country never closed by malaria. It is difficult to believe the efficiency of that jealous policy by which strangers are excluded. Various entrances to Nepal touch upon our own frontier, yet rarely has a European or British subject ever attempted them and the police are so vigilant that no Nepal subject can pass without express order. I suppose all this will crumble away in time like the wall of China. And it is amusing to observe the polite way in which these people maintain their own way. You propose visiting Tibet. "Certainly," say the court, "we shall be delighted. You shall have all possible assistance." But, if you made your preparations and set out, the first march half your coolies would run off. The next the remainder would fall sick and, the court all the while protesting their sorrow for your disappointment, back you would have to come. When we were coming here in January, Henry proposed taking a detour a little out of the usual course. Futteh Jung was delighted. "Oh, yes, all should be ready, it was a nice road, there was no difficulty." But when we got to the stage from whence we were to branch off, Futteh Jung came to our tent. "He was grieved but it was not his fault. He had just received accounts of dreadful sickness on that road. Forty men had died in one day, he could not suffer his friends to run such a risk."

Unfortunately, on the 26th, Henry was too ill to move. He had got fever I think from staying out too late a few evenings before among the moist rice fields. When his apology reached the king, great regret was expressed and there was immediately a visit from Matabur Singh, General, Prime Minister and Commander-in-Chief. Matabur is a very agreeable old gentleman, albeit we know he never speaks a word of truth. Under fifty, very tall and portly, with strongly marked features, more like an Afghan than a Ghurka; his chin is shaved, as no Hindoo wears a beard, but his whiskers and moustache are large and bushy, twisted ferociously upwards. His long intercourse with Europeans* has given him easy manners with us and he shakes hands, a fashion adopted by all who affect European politeness but which does not supersede the orthodox hug wherewith all visitors of rank are greeted. Henry and the General put their hands on each other's shoulders and then touch right shoulders and left shoulders alternately.

Henry was too ill to move, so Dr. Christie was summoned to give the accolade. Matabar looked very well on this occasion. He wore simple drawers and vest of white mohair with a shawl round his waist,

*He had lived for four years in British India.

a curiously shaped cape of crimson velvet embroidered with gold.
Fancy a gourd, the skin split into five or six divisions from one cut to
the centre, each division turned back and fastened by a button, and
you may have some idea of the general's head in its cap. He likewise
wore over the left shoulder a sword glittering with jewels. A splendid
buckle on his waist and rows of diamonds encircling his throat and
wrists. He sat down and expressed great sorrow at Henry's illness,
declared he should eat nothing that night, that his liver was melted and
his heart dried and that if we could but open him we should see it was
so. He then asked me very courteously how I liked Nepal and how my
temper was. I answered that my temper was very happy and Nepal
was a fine country, where through his prosperity I got on very well.
"But are you not very lonely? You have no lady to say how do you do?
At Simla the ladies and gentlemen meet on the road and talk." "No, I
read and write and have my husband and child." "Wonderful."

On the 27th Henry was still too ill to go but I went in my *jampan* to
the near parade by the edge of which the cortège was to return and
there sat with the children. here was a large concourse of people chiefly
Nawars all with the thriving peaceable air that distinguishes this place.
The men generally dressed in a dressing-gown-shaped dress, very
short waist and very long skirt, like what is worn by the women in the
western hills, with a roll of cloth round the waist and a close bonnet on
the head, every part composed of a coarse white, home-spun cloth.
The women wear full petticoats white in colour and a long sleeved
chintz jacket. They do not cover themselves with ornaments like those
of the plains, where everyone has ear-rings or bracelets though only
made of brass and copper or sealing wax, and the nose-ring is worn by
every girl and woman from the day she is betrothed till she is left a
widow. The only ornament I observe here is an ear-rim wedge. The
bottom and top of the ear is bored, and in each hole is put a piece of
metal about an inch long and thicker than a quill, with a top like a
stopper at each end.

The Nawar men are sturdy limbed and short necked, flat faced and
generally heavy looking. Here the women carry the water pot resting
on the right hip, with the arm round it. The never failing baby, instead
of being astride on the mother's left hip supported by the left arm,
while the right hand is left at liberty to adjust the water pot on the head,
is carried on its mother's back tucked up in a sheet, just after the
fashion of our own Irish beggars. The women are not handsome; flat
faces and small eyes, and generally squat figures, but they have a
comely good tempered look, good teeth and a ready smile. So that
they are to my taste among the pleasantest favoured people I have
seen. Such were the ingredients of the crowd that I entered. Men,
women, children, all civil and good tempered. They immediately

opened their ranks and made a wide lane between where my *jampan*
would go down and the side of the road. Not one in a hundred had
ever before seen a white face. Not one had ever seen a lady, yet there
was no crowding or pushing round me, though I had not above half a
dozen servants with me, none of them armed.

First came the Hindoo band, that assemblage of all most discordant
sounds, kettle drums, droning pipes, cymbals made like a pair of
broad brimmed brass hats knocked together. Next came some of the
cortège, sometimes a fat elderly gentleman sitting cross legged in a
litter, a running footman carrying an umbrella. Then a young cavalier
mounted on a strong little Chinese pony – if white, with the legs and
tail dyed red – and ambling briskly along; the groom holding by the
tail and a ragamuffin troop of followers coming along at a kind of
trotting pace. Now and then somebody of more pretension on a bony
raw-boned horse. The rider dressed in the comical travesty of our
uniform adopted by the Ghurka officers, to wit a low turban twisted
with gold and silver chain, white muslin drawers and a scarlet jacket
embroidered like our infantry but with as much lace behind as before,
the sleeves cut off at the elbow and a great patch of fur below the
epaulettes and the loose sleeves of the white undervest hanging from
under all.

After a while came the king's bodyguards, a most slovenly looking
set; turbans like those I have described, very wide white drawers, and a
loose red jacket more like a shirt. These gentlemen seemed as proud as
schoolboys of their musquets and gunpowder. Every now and then
firing volleys and continually popping off shots. By the time they
came opposite where I was sitting they seemed tired, and down they
all squatted on the road, till the music of the royal band roused them.
Up they got and pop, pop, went the musket again.

Presently came about a dozen elephants, the *jhools* of which were all
fringed with small silver bells, making a very sweet sound at every
step. On these sat the king, princes, generals and other grandees. On
one sat our two gents, with old Matabur's eldest son, a heavy, squinting, uncouth young man in all the glory of a cocked hat and feather,
with a general's coat.

In a litter covered with gold brocade was the bride and I saw a little
wee bit of a curtain that opened on the other side like a lid lifted up to
peep at me. His Majesty bowed and stopped the elephants while he
sent Captain Dulee Singh to ask how I was. I mention all this to show
the politeness with which a lady is treated by people who were
supposed to hold us in abhorrence.

The procession was escorted by torches, though still broad daylight. After the elephants came the troops. There was some three
thousand of them coming at a funeral pace, and every now and then

halting to fire a volley. I was not disposed to wait till they passed and turned back to the Residency. Before I reached the door, came Kajee Futteh Jung galloping after me with the king's compliments, to hope I had no inconvenience.

Compared with Lucknow this was but a shabby sort of procession, but it was very pleasant, shewing the prosperous state of this little kingdom. There was not in the crowd a beggar, not one who looked scantily clothed or ill fed. Indeed, whatever personal faults and absurdities the king and his family may have, the government must be a good one. There is no appearance of absolute penury in any quarter, no complaint of injustice and exaction.

One evening as we were riding a few miles from the capital we came where some workmen were repairing a bridge and the superintendent was paying the labourers their wages. You can hardly imagine how strange each particular appears in a native government, first that a bridge should be built at all anywhere beyond the royal precincts; a bridge only for the use of subjects! Then having been built that it should ever be repaired; the usual plan being to let the original of anything go to decay and begin a new one, probably to be never finished. But most wonderful of all to pay the labourers instead of making them work for nothing, and to pay them daily, instead of keeping them months in arrears. All these were symptoms of a healthy government such as I have seen in no other native state.

Koulia, Sunday June 9th

The weather continues hazy; the temperature is 60°. The hill we are on has no other habitation, but we see villages nestled into the valleys around us. There is not only the prevalent vivid green of the young rice but large patches of a deeper tint, where the potatoes grow. From Herat and Kabul to Thibet and Burma have the English bestowed this boon. And by this will our name be remembered when governors, generals and commanders-in-chief, Sudder Boards and members of Council are forgotten.

Dr. Christie has just come in; he met a Bhutia funeral. The body was accompanied by about fifty people. The son going first, carrying a flag. When the spot was reached, they set down the corpse on a pile of wood, and walked round it three times. A fowl was then killed by twisting off its head and the head thrown on the corpse. Then everyone broke some branches off the neighbouring trees and threw them on the pile, which was set fire to. He did not wait to see what was done with the ashes. In the valley I have seen bodies burning close to the river and wondered at the unceremonious manner it was performed. A pile of wood by no means sufficient to consume the corpse and one man in attendance with a long stick to stir up the fire. From this there came volumes of smoke of a most offensive smell. When half burnt the body is thrown into the river, at this season a shallow stream. But happily kites and jackals abound.

I have written about the beauties of Koulia, but, but, but it has one drawback and that is the leeches. Every bush, every branch absolutely bristles with these odious creatures. I grasp at a beautiful fern, and I find I have laid hold of leeches. We descend to a beautiful dell, and presently are crawling over with leeches. The ponies kick and plunge, for the leeches are biting them. The cows and sheep grow lean, for the leeches devour them. When we come in from walking, we make a careful search all over our clothes and bodies for leeches. Henry wakened in the morning with the pillow all bloody, the leeches had been grazing on his luxuriant locks. At dinner we say, just wait a moment, allow me to take that leech off you. To the servants these vermin are a sad infliction, our rooms are upstairs and comparatively safe, but the natives sleeping on the ground are cruelly bitten and their clothes are by no means an agreeable sight. As to the *jampanees*, whose garments "in longtitude are sorely scanty", their stout legs are absolutely fringed with the leeches, which are in general smaller than the medicinal leech, but infinitely more vivacious and vicious. How the natives manage about the pollution I know not. They esteem leeches, most unclean beasts. When they have been brought for me from hospital, I have seen the bearer refuse to touch the jar they were in, and when they dropped off me the *ayah* would not pick them up. They are kept by people of very low caste, who bring them, apply them and take them away.

Well, every place has its evils. At Simla the conversation is "Have you many fleas in your house?" "No, I haven't so many fleas but I'm devoured by bugs." F sharps and B flats as the more fastidious call them. Or in the plains, it is "I feel the heat dreadfully because I perspire very little." "Oh, I perspire enough, but then I have the prickly heat to such a degree." There are not many mosquitoes here, but the sand flies keep me from sleeping.

Wednesday August 1st, 1844

The last sad day of your earthly existence, my sweet daughter. I can recall the anguish of that time only too vividly, but I cannot thus bring back to mind the comfort, the mighty consolation that then upheld my soul. I am afraid to dwell on the memory of that time, lest the agitation should injure my unborn treasure. Yet I wish to think of the faithfulness God then shewed to his own promise, and thence to strengthen my faith in his supporting power in whatever maybe to come. Once more I have the hopes and fears of expecting another confinement. So far my health has been better than in any former pregnancy, for which I am most thankful. God alone knows how my heart yearns for an infant and he alone can give me one.

Sunday August 4th, 1844

The Baghmati and Vishnumati are now very much swollen. There are good bridges over both supported by wooden posts, with road way and parapets of mason work. They are narrow, barely admitting our little carriage, and the people do not seem to reckon them very strong, as elephants are not taken over them.

There are now, I don't remember whether there were in the cold weather, numbers of white long legged paddy birds. Every evening these may be seen flocking from the moist pastures and the shallows of the river to lodge in the willow trees for the night, and about sunset their snowy plumage ruffles the dark green foliage. This is the greatest place I ever saw for ducks. Towards the Loondee Kel there are many pools most unseemly and unsavoury where myriads of young ones quack and dabble under the care of a man, who stalks about up to his knees in mud and with a long bamboo keeping the little fry in order. In the evening they are gathered into large light canister shaped baskets slung one [on] each end of a pole across the shoulder and carried home. Pigs too seem to be eaten by others besides the *chumars* and sweepers to whom they are restricted in the plains. I have seen a comely looking Nawar lass of an evening summon the grunties to the door of a comfortable looking house, and pour out for them some savoury looking broo.

August 6th

Eating and drinking seems as much the business of life among the Nawars as with more civilised people. Just now the weather is unfavourable to meetings in the open air, and the cultivators are busy, but of an evening we often see the leaf plates and dishes lying as if just used and thrown away; and frequently I see little earthen vessels containing some sort of food, left on the road with the dogs and the crows feasting thereon. Sometimes these offerings with a little oil and a wick burning, some flowers and a dab of vermillion, which seems indispensable in all religious affairs, are placed opposite one of the hideous mis-shapen idols that in little arched stone shrines are to be met every few yards. Sometimes they are placed on the road without any apparent object.

These Nawars are the most cheerful race of people I ever beheld. There was little labour, I fancy, for the husbandman from the time the wheat and other cold weather crops were gathered in about April till the rain descended in good earnest at the end of June. As soon as the low ground was fairly soaked the work began in earnest. In each field there was a small patch of rice sown as thickly as possible from which the whole field was to be planted. When the land was reduced to mud by the heavy rains, the whole population turned out, men, women, and children. Ancle deep or knee deep as it might be, they carefully pulled up little tufts of the young rice four or five inches high, and dibbled it in root by root over the field. I have seen them wading about the low swamps, their clothes quilted well above the knee, rain pouring from the clouds, while they stooped and dibbled in their plants, often up to the elbows in mud, in short seeming to me performing the most laborious and irksome work I ever saw. Yet these people were singing and laughing from sheer light heartedness. And strange to say they seem very healthy. They drink large quantities of *rukshee*, a spirit distilled from rice.

The Nawars are a prolific race and the look of the infants and young children is very different from the aspect of those to the North-West. There it was painful to see them and marvellous how so many lived and grew into stalwart men. Far the greater number of infants had large abdomens, sore eyes, scald head, eruptions over the body and were altogether deplorable objects. Here they look healthy and thriving, notwithstanding their exposure to the weather. The labourers go out early in the morning, the whole family. I suppose they take some food with them, for they do not return till sunset when we generally meet flocks of them frequently singing and always looking contented. A woman with two children upon her back, a man with two children of two or three years old, one sitting in each of the baskets suspended from the pole over his shoulder, or perhaps one basket with a child, the other with his tools. A half grown lad carrying his *banghy* of fuel or vegetables. In short every woman has a baby and every man a *banghy*, except the coolies, slaves I believe, who carry, both men and women, great loads of wood, grain, fodder etc. put up in a pack on the back and partly supported by a leather strap which passes across the forehead.

Fuel and grazing are the two great wants of the poor here. Grain can hardly fail in a basin surrounded by hills and intersected by streams. Fish, I fancy, is abundant though we rarely see it. Vegetables of a coarse kind there are plenty of. As I have said, ducks, fowls and pigs, to which I may add buffaloes, form a part of the food for all. But where every inch is cultivated there is scarcely any grazing ground, and we seldom see milch cows or goats. The want of milk and *ghee* must be severely felt. In the valley there are few trees, none of any size, or fit for firewood. The surrounding hills belong to certain chiefs who there cut the timber. Even were it public property, the labour of cutting and bringing it such a distance would make it inaccessible to the poor. Small branches, chaff, dried leaves, the sugar cane from which juice has been squeezed, straw and such like insufficient substances are the firing on which the poor people depend.

August 9th

The evening before last we had a visit from the eldest son of General Mahtabur Sing, a heavy, squinting young man. He brought his father's carriage for us and requested we might pay the old man a visit. We went accordingly, tag rag and bob tail. Henry and I in our own little carriage. Dr. Christie and the children in the old rattle trap barouche of the Colonel's, and a ragamuffin assemblage of followers clinging to the horses and carriage and running alongside. It is about a mile to the General's house, a half European place, I fancy like some of the old châteaux in France. A garden surrounded by a battlemented wall, laid out in straight walks, flowerbeds and fountains, the water spouting from the musquets of soldiers and the mouths of tigers. There are few varieties of flowers; the everlasting balsams, marigolds and chrysanthemums that fill all native gardens, and a few dahlias. Great varieties of fruits, grapes, apples, pears, pineapples, peaches, nectarines, apricots, quinces, plums, pomegranates and others. But these are all wretched tasteless things. In this valley the rain begins with the warm weather. There is no dry heat to ripen the fruit or give it a flavour. One side is hard while the other begins to decay. Sometimes we get a tolerable pineapple, but nothing else worth eating grows here. Last month we got good mangoes from the Betiah Raja. That is, mangoes that must be good on the spot, but they have been plucked half ripe and are packed between layers of straw to ripen on their journey. They are thus wrinkled and stringy. Good plantains we get occasionally from Segoulee but the best plantain is far inferior to an English pear. Altogether Indian fruits, though bearing attractive names, are no more to be compared to those at home, than the pomp of the king of Oude is to an English nobleman's establishment.

The General received us at his gate and Henry and Dr. Christie had to undergo the usual ceremonies of embracing. I was let off with a salam and shake of the hand and then the General very gallantly, placing my hand within his, led me to see his horses and elephants. Among other sights there was a noble tiger, kept in the same cage with a buffalo, and apparently on the best terms. A man poked between the bars with a stick and the tiger gave a roar and sprang which made me start outside, but did not seem to affect the buffalo. Of course the tiger must be kept well crammed with other food. Were he hungry, I would not give much for the life of his companion. There was likewise a beautiful miniature deer from Sincapoor, an exquisite, graceful creature not larger than a rabbit.

After walking about a long time Mahtabur wanted us to go into his house, a large mass of buildings, with a paved court in the centre, but on the usual Nepal plan of having the lower story mere stables and storehouses, and the upper rooms inhabited. I felt too tired to go upstairs and we sat down in a little summer house in the garden, a fountain in the middle and cushioned seats to repose on. Here as usual Mahtabur began to talk politics and to tell of the discussions among the king, queen and heir apparent, with the difficulty of pleasing all parties. "One says 'come'. Another says 'go'. Another says, 'sit still'." But this is not talk for an ambassador to listen to. So we left the place, having first received the parting politeness of *uttur* and *pan*, a man in attendance brought two little gold salvoes. On one was a small gold cup with *uttur* which our host sprinkled on us, on the other little packets of *sooparee* and *chuna*, *betel*-nut and lime, put up neatly in a *pan* leaf. We each took one. This is one of the most indispensible of Oriental courtesies. More hugging and salaming and we drove away.

During the hour we stayed, our conversation was by no means very interesting. Indeed after mutual good wishes, and praises there is little left to say on such an occasion. Henry told Mahtabur that Mr. C.★ was to come out to be in Council, whereupon he stroked his stomach and said "I am very happy. I shall eat a large dinner tonight."

Nepal, April 28th, 1844

It is difficult to give an idea to those who live at home of our peculiar position here and its perfect seclusion. I feel very like Jock Mumbles "When he was up, he was up, and all the world knew he was up and he knew he was up himself. But how he was to get down I don't know, nor he didn't know himself." We can see about twenty miles in every direction, our panorama framed in by hills of varied outline and hue. The snowy peaks ought to peep at us, but two months ago they put on their veils and we have not had a glimpse of them since. Here we are completed secluded, not only by the jealous policy of the Nepal government, but for eight months of the year by the miasma afloat in the belt of forest that surrounds the lower hills.

★Probably George Clerk, Henry's old chief in Ferozepore, and a future Governor of Bombay.

TEN

A Quiet Nepalese Interlude

Some of this journal is addressed to Alick now aged six but expected to read it when he is older. And some is addressed to Henry. Honoria is ailing and then becomes pregnant. She is irritated by the three other Europeans in Nepal, Dr. Christie and Captain and Mrs. Ottley, but greatly enjoying the beauties of Nepal. Mr. Hodgson was Henry Lawrence's predecessor as Resident in Nepal. The precise location of Koulia, where the Residents had their summer cottage, is uncertain but it appears to be on the road from Kathmandoo to Trisuli near a village still called on maps Kauli Thana.

Kathmandoo, Sunday August 10th, 1845

It is somewhat with a feeling as if I had been buried for twelve months that I now resume my wonted employments, and open one after another the channels of thought that had been closed. Last August, I was obliged to confine myself to the couch to which with little intermission I was a prisoner till this last month.

Many times during 1831, I have been unable to walk, but never did I feel such continued mental prostration as during the last year. Everything I tried to understand was like writing on blotting paper. Alick's dangerous illness in November and December roused me in some measure, but I thought the time was passed for my ever being of use to anyone and that, if I lived, it would only be as a burden, a sorrow, even to him who loves me best.

On January 24th, our darling Moggy* was born. After an easy confinement I had a fearful illness of which I have little distinct recollection excepting intense bodily suffering, gleams of peace and thankfulness, especially when I thought I had not many hours to live, and sad, sad relapses into peevish, fretful murmurs. After a partial recovery, I was again very ill during May and June. Once more, I am in great measure restored, still feeble in my limbs and confused most

---

*Sir Henry Waldemar Lawrence, 1845–1908, called Harry for short and Moggy as a pet name when he was a baby.

painfully by even a slight mental effort, but free from any acute pain and generally able to occupy myself.

Tuesday August 12th, a.m.

An hour ago I saw you off, Alick and Lawrie in the little *dhooli*, on your march to Koulia. I cannot describe the strange feeling it is to send away my Tim (Alick), though under Papa's guidance and only a few miles off. Never since his birth has he been one night away from me, or more than a few hours of any day. I have been most desirous for you to take this little trip, to become more acquainted with Papa, more independent of Mama, more of the man I want you to be. Yet even this small separation makes me feel that we have come to one of life's turning points. I have watched over you through sickness when I did not expect you to live many hours. I have looked in the chasm there would be in my own heart were you taken from me. And with all this now vividly before my mind I record to you my deliberate judgement that your death would be a slight evil to your parents, compared to seeing you grow up selfish, cowardly, untrue, forgetful of your Maker, Redeemer, Sanctifier.

We now have Dr. Christie to dine every day. This is a sad annoyance. Almost every topic local and general we are afraid to introduce. Either it is personal to himself or he does not understand what one says. Literally, there is but one path clear to us and that is the comparative flavour of viands of India and Europe. It is very bad for ourselves to be in constant intercourse with a mind that we cannot help despising.

Thursday August 14th

A dramatic sketch, Mrs. Lawrence and Dr. Christie.

Dr. Christie: Good morning, Mrs. Lawrence. I'm sorry to hear you are ill.

Mrs. Lawrence: I have been kept awake by toothache.

D.: Toothache. Ah. That is awful pain. Better take a good dose of laudanum.

L.: That would keep me awake.

D.: Keep you awake. That's funny. Why I had the toothache, you know, the most awful pain that possibly could be. Well, I took a large dose of laudanum you know and then I slept like anything, and next morning, I declare if I wasn't as well as ever I was in my life.

L.: But unfortunately opium in any shape keeps me awake.

D.: Well, that is funny.

L.: I believe it has the same effect on many people.

D.: Oh yes, it's the commonest thing in the world. A great many people can't touch it. But it's a great pity you can't take it. It's a splendid medicine.

L.: I find that hyoscyamus agrees better with me, if you will let me have some, and some tincture of camphor to rinse my mouth.

D.: Camphor is but a poor sort of thing, after all. Better wait till the pain goes away of itself. It's a great chance it won't trouble you again.

L.: Perhaps not but, in case it should, I wish to be prepared. I have not slept for two nights from the pain.

D.: Two nights. Pooh, that's nothing. Why Hodgson when he was here, no, not Hodgson, bye the bye let me see, it must have been Tucker at Azamghar or perhaps it was Taylor at Allahabad. At any rate it was a civilian, I'm sure. No, I believe after all it was Colonel Smith. Well, you know, this man had the most dreadful pain that possibly could be. He was quite mad with it. I believe he hadn't slept for a month, you know. Well, what does he do, but mounts his horse one very cold morning, takes a cheroot in his mouth and gallops like the very mischief right across the country, you know, till he's as tired as he possibly could be. Then he takes a mutton chop and a bottle of beer for breakfast and falls asleep. Why he told me he slept for twenty-four hours right on end.

L.: A very good remedy, but unfortunately not within my power.

D.: No, of course. I didn't mean that, but let me see. You can't take laudanum you say?

L.: No, it keeps me awake.

D.: Well, I'll tell you what. I'll send you some hyoscyamus. That sometimes agrees with people that can't take laudanum. Did you ever try it?

L.: Yes, that was what I asked you for just now.

D.: By the powers! So it was, well I'll send you some. And I'll tell you what, Mrs. Lawrence. Camphor, though it's such a simple thing, sometimes very often has a very wonderful effect on the nerves. And toothache you know is quite an affection of the nerves.

L.: So I have heard.

D.: Well, you know, any of these gentle sedatives sometimes generally has the most wonderful effect. By the powers, it is sometimes quite ludicrous to see how they act. I'll send you over a little tincture of camphor, you know, and just when you feel the pain come on, take a little and you'll feel as well as possible in no time at all.

L.: I hope so. Thank you.

D.: Well, good morning, Mrs. Lawrence.

L.: Good morning, Dr. Christie.

This imaginary sketch is a sample of one of our most satisfactory conferences, because the complaint was not very serious, and he ended by giving me the medicines I wanted.

Thursday August 21st, 1845

After nine days absence you returned yesterday, my darling, bringing with you an atmosphere of light and joy and our son, our Alick, came rushing in, bright and loving, looking much better and altogether gladdening my inmost soul. Lawrie too is much improved, more alert and intelligent. And here you found our Moggy beaming with health and infantine joy and now I am so much stronger and better as to be able fully to enter into and value all there is to make us happy.

Friday August 22nd

The weather is sultry and oppressive before the breaking up of the rains. We are daily expecting something and that makes time pass slowly, expecting the cold weather, expecting the relief of the troops, expecting a war with the Punjaub,* expecting to go into camp. And for my own part I have been more than half my Indian life expecting my confinement.

Saturday August 24th

We sorely feel the want of some society, to hear somewhat the clash of opinions, to learn that there are other aspects or other objects besides those belonging to our own minds. There are some to whom I would refer as authority were it only regarding the day of the month, others whose judgement I respect on matters of everyday life or on abstract questions. Some few that we reverence for their integrity and largeness of heart, others that have a good taste. In short, people who at least on one subject we feel to be superior to ourselves. But I do confess that in the trio who form our sole society I find no one such point. Inanity, prejudice, apathy, selfishness, and falsehood are all I discern. Yet this is the stuff that respectable, worthy, excellent people are made of.

Koulia, Saturday August 29th

On Wednesday morning we were up at 4 a.m., took a cup of tea and brought with us a bottle of milk, ditto tea, some cold meat, biscuits and toast, two metal mugs and a few napkins. We then set off, a long array, I in my Simla *jompon* with eight Nepal men, *dhaee* in a little *dhoolee* with Moggy, you on the Kabulee horse, Tim on a Tartar *tanghan* or pony, Lawrie on a Punjaubee mule, *ayah* in our *dandee*, Luckmina in another. Altogether twenty-two carriers besides a *kitmutgar*, the *dhaee*'s husband, three *syces*, twelve bearers, a *chobdar* and two of the Maharaja's soldiers running along side. Altogether a party of thirty-five attendants and three quadrupeds, to transport you, me

---

*The First Sikh War was impending.

and three children a distance of fourteen miles, which we accomplished in ten hours. Besides fully as many more people dispatched the day before, coolies carrying clothes, food, bedding, everything in short except air, fire, earth and water. Three *kitmutgars*, two cows, a cow keeper, sundry fowls, a side of mutton, a *bheestie*, a tailor, a sweeper.

To Koulia from the Residency the distance is fourteen miles, the height about 1800 feet. I felt a strange delight in once more observing the morning lights and shades on the hill side. For eighteen months I had never been out of a morning, except my journey to and from Koulia last year when we were enveloped in rain and I was suffering too much to enjoy it.

Sunday August 30th

I rarely if ever write up my journal to the current day. I wish I could condense, or rather select, but I am somewhat like an Irish house builder who begins with a Grecian portico and ends with a clay floor bedroom.

On Wednesday then we reached the *patee* at a quarter past eight in the morning. As there was neither sun nor wind to molest us, we preferred remaining outside. There was a *peepul* tree with seats built round its roots, and here we spread our table cloth and enjoyed our cold breakfast, while the servants solaced themselves with *chabenee* and *hookah*, and, I fancy, more substantial fare. We made *extempore* couches out of the cushions of the litters and lay down under the tree while the old Brahmin who has charge of the *patee* came to look for his wonted *bakshish*.

At Dhaimtala where we had put down for a short halt an hour previously, we were besieged by gazers to whom we are a curiosity, especially Mog. We got two rupees worth of *pice* from the *bania* and divided the *pice* among the swarm of thriving looking children round us. And there was none of the brawling and scuffling that generally makes this rather an undesirable piece of kindness. At ten thirty we were again in motion taking the upper road. "The grand military road that traverses Nepal", as Mr. Hodgson says in the Journal of The Asian Society. It was like the dry steep bed of a torrent that had brought down stones large enough for Plymouth breakwater, and in the *jompon* I felt very nervous. Quite without reason, as I now think, for the bearers never once made a false step, but the *jompon*, some three or four feet wide and the seat hanging very low and with shafts ten or more feet long, is an awkward machine to navigate round abrupt corners and over slippery rocks. I was more at ease in the *dandy* where I lay down, leaving *aya* who is very light to sit in the *jompon*.

The last hour of our journey was foggy with occasional showers, and when we got to Koulia, there was a thick white mist hiding everything external and entering the house very unceremoniously, whenever a window chanced to be left open. After a careful picking off of the leeches that had stuck to us, though few had bitten, lighting a fire and changing our clothes we were all merry and hungry as we sat down to dinner. Next day we found that we all had more or less caught cold, except Moggy.

Koulia, Monday September 1st

Last evening cleared up soberly. No bright light, and the tops of the hills still clouded, but a fresh pleasant feeling all around. At night much rain. Drip, drip, drip, from most parts of the roof, but not over our beds. What would folks at home say to these same beds I wonder? The old couple have a comparably grand shake down. One corner about ten feet square of the house is fenced off by a *kanat* and here we have our four rupee *charpoy* of Segoulee build. But then we have our delightful English blankets, worth a hundred coolies and *puttoos* and *resais*. Beside us Tim is littered down on a rug, with sheet, *resai* and pillow, while Moggy is cuddled snugly in a blanket on the other side of the *kanat* where he is flanked by *ayah* and *dhaee* stretched on the floor. Lawrie is stowed very comfortably into the little *dhooli*. 'Tis a vast emancipation to require no mosquito curtains. The mosquitoes at Nepal are as numerous as in Bengal and ten times more troublesome from there being no *punkahs*. Towards morning there rose a strong east wind. I liked its whistling, moaning sound sweeping up the ravines. It sounded like a winter night at home. Even the smoke that followed every attempt to make the fire burn, and the clouds of ashes that came over the floor brought an Ennishowen November feeling with them. But I was particularly delighted to see the rain drops blister the window pains. In India there are always verandahs or *jillmills* or something that prevents the rain from dashing right against the glass.

Wednesday September 3rd, 8 a.m.

We are trying to get the house mended, but Nepal gives the best possible illustration of the chapter we were reading last night in Paley about the state the world would be in if no one kept his word. For a month you have been trying to get work people to accomplish what half a dozen men could easily do in two days viz. to put a door which we brought up here instead of one of the windows and to move the step ladder by which we get into this room outside. At present there is a huge trapdoor gaping at one side of the room threatening to crush the fingers of anyone who may lay hold of the edge in ascending or descending. By no possibility could materials have been turned to less account than they were when this house was built, but I fancy comfort was as little known in Mr. Hodgson's vocabulary as in the king's. Filth and delapidation pervaded everything. It appeared to me that nothing had ever been mended.

The very poorest here as elsewhere have little clothing of any kind. I have not observed the men addicted to ornaments like Hindustanis. But be their clothing more or less, they have a cheerful contented air that has many a time put me to shame. When leaning back in the carriage feeling absolutely as if it was a labour to smell the eau de Cologne on my handkerchief, I have met troops of these men and women coming back at sunset from the labour to which they had gone forth at morning.

I wonder leprosy is not even more common among them than it is. It and goitre are the only two prevalent complaints I have noticed. The latter is frightfully common. Dr. Christie says that, when taken in time, he finds iodine infallible for it. If unchecked, the tumor becomes hard and bony and the person, he says, becomes [an] imbecile. It is frightfully disfiguring, but does not appear to interfere with the usual labours.

Friday September 5th, 1845

The last day of your seventh year my own darling boy. Let me now state what to my apprehension Alick at present is. His constitution is extremely weak. He has grown very rapidly, is exceedingly thin and of a very nervous irritable temperament. Habitually, he is merry and often full of droll quaint speeches, but he is painfully timid. If he is reading and cannot readily spell or pronounce a word his eyes fill with tears, and he has all the air of a poor cowed child. Were I accidentally to see another child look in the same way, I should pity it as having been most severely dealt with. It is the same with every little difficulty. If he cannot button his sleeve at once he looks up with an expression of dismay. And asks for anything he wants in a hesitating timorous manner of a boy who had been accustomed to harshness. Whence is this? I do not think he ever tells a deliberate untruth, he has not the clear, ingenuous look and manner of a boy who is conscious of deserving and receiving confidence. The only intellectual point in which I perceive him decidedly deficient is numbers. "How many fingers have you?" He reckons and says "Ten". "Well now, reckon one, two, three, four, five, six, seven, eight, and how many more make ten?" He immediately looks bewildered. "If I cut off two of your fingers, how many would be left?" The chances are he answers two or seems ready to cry.

The worst of our present position is that we have no creature to consult with, on any matter, large or small. Or perhaps worse still that we are never roused by hearing conversation or observing what other people do. We read a good deal and we talk to each other, but this, though both good and pleasant, is not the way to burnish up our minds, to stir up our own resources or detect our own errors. We are too much one for that.

Sunday September 7th

5 p.m. A heavy storm of rain and thunder has just past [sic] by. The rains have I fancy lasted longer this year than usual. At any rate we never were so long without a *dak*. The suspension bridge at Tamba Khana is reported broken and when it may be mended is hard to say. We have not had a bit of bread for a week. The *atta* for *chapatees* is not very good, and the biscuits we got from Calcutta last cold weather were sent off before Christmas. So they are a good deal older than Moggy, and have not improved as much as he has by keeping. A baker would be a greater treasure than civilised people can imagine.

Thursday September 9th

Today there has been nothing but fog and rain but yet there must have been some fine gleams, for Tim and Lawrie have been diligently digging in the wee gardens they have made under the bank in front of the house. It is pleasant to see how heartily they both work at this, Lawrie just like a young Buffalo, Alick, alas! with intervals of langour and peevishness. His pale, small face and lean, lanky form make me very sad.

An amusing letter from Major Troup anent Captain Smith. Captain Smith says he "has been brutally used by Major Lawrence".*

Wednesday September 10th

On Saturday you sent *onseeree* to tell of the roof having fallen and on Monday arrived a train of coolies, bringing, I suppose, timbers because we wanted tiles. Yesterday came a *subadar* from Durbar to express the royal grief that we were eating such *tukleef* here but not a workman has come to our aid. Last evening you were catching the rain with four *chathas* and seventeen *bustons* of sorts. We all get on wonderfully well and are determined not to be bullied by Durbar into returning sooner than we intended. Indeed, with the present rain, it would be more difficult to travel than to remain even in the leaky house. None of us suffer except Papa whose rheumatism in the face is very little better. It is a strange turning of the tables, dearest, when I wake from a night of sound repose to ask you how you are and you

---

*Captain Smith (see Chapter Nine) had been succeeded by Captain Ottley as Commandant of the Resident's escort.

answer that you have hardly slept. This used to be my customary reply and now for two or three months I have seldom had a wakeful hour at night.

Thursday September 18th

Another lovely day. In the night my Alick was purged three times. He seems alert and playful this morning. My darling boy, ought we to send you home? I think it would be most desirable for him to have the sea voyage and good medical advice. But sending our boy away from us both involves much that I cannot bear to think of.

Wrote yesterday to my brother Henry and his wife. They were married at Madras on our wedding day. I feel great pleasure in contemplating the marriage. Their regard has been tested by a long engagement, and I hope her disposition and principles are what they ought to be. Of Henry I think favourably, though I know but little. He, William, Hill and I – the four survivors of fifteen children – wholly separated one from the other, and except William and myself, know little of each other.

Kathmandoo, Wednesday September 26th

On Monday we left Koulia. When we were more than halfway down, this valley opened before us, a sheet of such unbroken teeming abundance as I never saw. "The vallies stand so thick with corn that they laugh and sing." A small part was ripe but most of the crops were of the full mature green that one day's sun sometimes turns to brown. The harvest not having actually begun, there was an air of luxuriant tranquillity in the unfenced fields, which seemed ripening unnoticed.

When we got in, I was too tired even to run over and see the baby until after *tiffin*. Then I did go and saw Mrs. Ottley and her sweet healthy, very small daughter. Except the unconscious little infant whose small helplessness goes straight to my heart, I saw nothing to interest me. The new made mother seemed to look with the same eyes on the baby and on the pillow.

Sunday September 28th

The last week appears a very long time. We have now not only decided about my taking Alick but have resolved to leave Nepal in November, and probably to embark before I am confined. Since I am to go, I desire to lose no time about it, that the terrible time of separation may be the sooner over and that Alick may sooner try the change of climate from which we hope for such beneficial effects. I think too it will be less trying to leave my darling Moggy now than if he were a year older. I am glad there is such a little sunbeam to remain with Papa.

Friday October 3rd

Last evening we went to Pusputnath. We enter the town by the remains of a gateway, and pass through some narrow streets paved with brick. All the old streets and many of the old roads in those parts of Nepal that I have seen are thus paved, proving that wheel conveyances were as little known in former times as they are now. The few carriages and buggies belonging to the Residency and Durbar are the only vehicles on wheels. Even pack bullocks and horses are unknown. Nor have I seen a plough, although I hear that ploughs are used in some parts of the valley. Human labour does everything here that cattle and machinery effect in other places.

Saturday October 4th

One Sunday one of our beggars who had been absent several weeks sent a message that he was unable to come. We went in the evening to see him, as we did last month to another of our poor people, and found each very comfortably lodged in *patees*. It is pleasant to see any redeeming good in these sanctuaries of heathenism. I fancy it is peculiar to Nepal to have alms houses around their temples. The *patee* is a large hollow square of brickwork. A verandah supported on wooden pillars runs round two or three of the outer sides. These seem to be for shelter to passers by and cattle. Entering the court by a handsome arched gateway, we are in a quadrangle all round which there are small rooms, neat and clean so far as we saw. Each room is inhabited by some infirm or aged person, man or woman. In the centre of the square stands a temple, and the space between this and the surrounding buildings is neatly paved.

Cleanliness is a prevailing feature of many Nepal customs. Others are unspeakably filthy. Even the cleanest and most luxurious native here, or I fancy anywhere in India, has no idea of cleanliness in the clothes that touch the skin. And bed-linen is a thing unknown. Once in a bed made up for me at the Patiala Raja's garden house at Pinjaur there was a sheet tied with silk cord and tassels to the four legs of the *charpoy* for me to lie on. But at Lucknow I saw his Oude Majesty's bed which seemed just as he had left it that morning with nothing but silk mattress pillows and *resai*. This I believe is the usual way from the bearer, who rolls round the coarse chintz wadded coverlid, to the king, whose *resai* is of Benares *kincob*. So with underclothes. During the hot season all classes wear white and "the muslined millions" look elegantly clean. But during the cold season I never saw a symptom of anything washable under the wadded woollen or silken warm clothes. Mahtabar Singh used to wear a brocade vest. Our servants wear their wadded *chupkuns* sometimes putting a white muslin over, by way of being clean. Luckily the majority of natives crop or shave their heads and in the plains they bathe when they can. But I dare not even imagine what may dwell within the long flowing locks of the Pathans and Sikhs. As to the hill people, they never wash I believe and when they become the happy possessors of any piece of dress they wear it till it drops off. Yet these people have their cooking vessels polished and scrubbed in a way that few gentlemen's kitchens at home could match, clean their teeth diligently every morning and never eat or smoke without washing hands and mouth, before and after.

We went through a good part of the town of Kathmandoo last Friday afternoon. It must be a good deal like some of the old Spanish cities. Narrow paved or rather flagged streets, impassable for wheel carriages, houses tall and gloomy looking with lattice windows and projecting balconies of carved wood; filth and squalor, with a great outlay on elaborate carving and gilded pinnacles. We entered the town by a way I had not been before, a road at right angles with Mahtabar Singh's house, his monument of folly poor fellow.* In the suburbs we passed a *serai*, a long open shed where a man from the plains who had come up with horses was lying ill. Strange how people will for the slightest temptation or from sheer recklessness persevere in coming through the Terai during the unhealthy season. You desired the *mookhia* in attendance to have the sick man taken to the hospital in our Lines.

You estimate Kathmandoo at about four miles round and holding from forty to fifty thousand inhabitants. In the town, as all over the country, a plentiful sprinkling of small *patees*, a term applied to these public buildings, from the grandest of them down to a mere shed. Those I speak of as so numerous are merely sheds. In these travellers stop to eat and rest and when there are no other occupants, the Brahminee bulls seem to consider themselves the rightful inhabitants. These pampered useless creatures always give me the idea of sleek and well fed sinecurist churchmen, canon-residentiaries or prebendaries. To do justice however to these gentlemen, they appear satisfied with their priviledges and rarely turn rampant. They eat the best of every thing, no one interferes with them and they wander where they will. Indeed, last year they established a visiting acquaintance with our grounds, and we had not a little trouble in fencing them out. The grazing we have is all too little for our own cows and sheep and we grudge a share to these trespassers, who used to make a most indecorous bellowing and roaring, especially at night. Near the house are some clumps of Chinese bamboo, a much smaller growth than the common bamboo of Hindostan. It is the reed of which rattan is made. Sometimes two of the bulls when fighting would try to charge each other through the bamboo clump and get their horns entangled among the reeds. Great

*The Maharajah had had him killed.

then was the roaring and bellowing and crashing of bamboos. Last year, when I passed miserably sleepless nights, these encounters were no small annoyance to me. This year I think we have got rid of the visitors.

Just now opposite each [*patee*], great and small, there is a scaffolding put up to receive an image. One I noticed quite unlike anything Hindoo and very like the head of an Egyptian sphinx. Some of the images in Kathmandoo have decidedly African features, especially one hideous one near the Durbar, perfectly black with a grinning mouth, set with white teeth and the eyes set off with vermillion.

Thursday October 9th

In Kathmandoo, as in every other town I have seen in India, there are many birds kept in cages, even by the very poorest. *Mynahs*, parrots and a beautiful small speckled dove called *pudoo*. Except the *mynah*, which trains to speak like a starling, none of these can be kept for their notes. I have somewhere read that Hindoos keep birds from some superstitution about transmigration. But Musulmans appear just as fond of these pets. Often I have seen a tailor as he sat in the verandah put his *tota* or mynah in a cage beside him.

Friday October 11th

How I love the sound of running water. Sir Thomas Munro says, it is the only sound that is the same at home and abroad. Not the only one. There is likewise the "Am-Am ma" of an infant beginning to articulate. Passing through an Indian village or town, wondering whether the people around me could really be of the same race with myself, I have been startled by an infant's voice just the same as my own child's. At this place it is difficult to ascertain anything, first the difficulty of language, for the Nawaree and Parbutia tongues are unintelligible to those who know Hindustani. Then there is the indifference of the people we ask as to the truth or falsehood of what they say. Perhaps they don't know, perhaps they don't care, but in either case the easiest plan of getting rid of a troublesomely inquisitive Sahib is either to profess entire ignorance or to give the first answer that occurs. And further there is the mortal fear that every question we ask is political, that we cannot ask the price of a piece of cloth without some *arrière pensée* about seizing the country. I should rather say such is the feeling at Durbar. This strange government has the knack of keeping its subjects under a sort of control that shames the police arrangements of Vidocq and Col. Rowan. I heard before I came here a story which may be true. It is at least very like truth. One of the gentlemen of the Residency asked a Nawar the road to some place. The Nawar took no notice and the question was repeated. Still no reply, when the Sahib waxed angry and asked the man why he did not answer. The questionee looked up, put his hand to his mouth then pointed to the Durbar and then drew his hand across his own throat signifying the consequences of being too communicative. We must therefore gain our information regarding Nepal as we would about a swarm of bees. By observing, comparing, noting down.

Bamboo is put to an incredible variety of uses, sticks, poles, scaffolding etc. A single joint cut off forms a common cup for milk or oil. Before now bamboos with gunpowder and charge rammed down into them have proved useful artillery. The bamboo when fresh cut and moist are heated, split and laid under a heavy weight, and out of the thin plates thus formed the natives make most useful *piangs*, much like our bandboxes sewn together by slips of the same; they are strong, light and most useful.

Saturday October 11th

Here as everywhere else from Ferozepore, I believe, to China and perhaps to Cape Comorin there are Kashmiris. There is a little settlement of them outside the town, just by the Rani Kitalao where they have a few houses, a garden, a *masjid* and a burying ground. In features and costume they are exactly like their brethren to the north-west. The same peculiar and Jewish countenance, flowing garments, and bushy beards. Here, too, they deal in shawls and beads, making cords, tassels and such like ornaments, and pursue their trade as dyers of all bright colours.

Flowers are in good demand, they are woven into garlands and necklaces sometimes very pretty, though the object seems to be to lose all trace of the natural aspect of flowers. A native never thinks of offering you a flower without breaking off every vestige about the cup and stem, probably cutting off the blossom by the head and sticking it on a reed. Almost every man has a flower stuck behind his ear or in his turban and there is not a female, from the little girl, whose hair is just long enough to roll into a knot behind, to the old wrinkled grandmother, who feeds the pigs, that has not a flower or two stuck in her head. The bunches of young rice plants just ready for harvesting seemed among the favourite "ladies fashions for June." Dahlias which are grown here in great numbers seem exceedingly prized. Indeed, it is quite a flower for the natives, stiff, regular, scentless, gaudy, unmeaning. Men and women who have been at work all day pause on their way back of an evening, often too while carrying heavy loads, to pluck a bunch of wild flowers. The flowers however are an article of profit, everyone requiring them to offer at the shrines and temples. Some months ago when our garden was very rich in blossoms *dhai* used often to ask for some, saying she would get three handfuls for a nosegay.

In Kathmandoo as well as Patan and Pusputee there are a few wells, but the great supply of water is from deep, square paved ponds, with spouts for carrying in the stream always carved into some grotesque form and decorated with a graven image daubed with vermilion. Looking at the pools and tanks here, it strikes me that the general level of water in the valley must have shrunk greatly since they were built. Some are very deep with steps raised inside all round to a height twice as high as the water rises even in the rains.

About the centre of the town is an open space where stands the palace and the great temple from which the town derives its name. Much elaborate carving, much penurious shabbiness, much cleanliness, much filth. There is a long row of sheds with musquets and bayonets, all looking dirty. Sometimes the sentry on guard gives his musquets to a man to hold while he takes a smoke. The Durbar and some other houses here have adopted *jillmills*. There is a tall shaft of stone on the top of which is a group of statuary, something like one we saw at Patan. The Mokhias say these are statues of the Nawar rajas who built the durbars and temples.

Beneath the projecting eaves of many houses are hung jars of Ganges water such as pilgrims carry, also what I suppose are *muntras*, of clay or metal something like a small crown hung by a chain, often also flowerpots. While we are stopping to look at some of these objects a crowd gathered round my *jampan*. A great crowd, and I hardly knew why, till I observed they seemed remarking the pencil and memo book I had in my hands. These I then prudently put into my pocket, but I hope no misfortune will befall the city in our time or it will surely be attributed to the *feringhee* woman having done some *jadhoo* with her writing. Flying kites is as favourite an amusement here as elsewhere, and the hill paper, wonderfully strong and light, is an excellent material for making them.

We saw many people beating out rice from the bush. Rice is tied into small sheaves before it is cut. The sheaves are laid on a smooth clean earthen platform and beaten out, not trodden by cattle as in the plains, nor yet threshed as with us, I have seen nothing like the joint of a flail. The never failing bamboo staff is used and great must be the additional labour of using so unyielding a tool. The straw is stacked up. The grain is then put into a huge stone or wooden mortar where two people, women generally, thump it with bamboo pestles to loosen the husk. I suppose it is afterwards winnowed.

The town, take it all in all, has more clean and open streets and spaces than I expected. Our progress brought us to a temple which the Raja is building on the spot where his grandfather Run Bahadur

Swami was murdered by his own brother. While you took the boys to look at the building, I felt cold sitting in the *jampan* and drew on my cloak. A *fakir* came up to me who, though he had long matted hair, a plentiful sprinkling of cow dung ashes over his body and the strip of orange cloth round his shoulders characteristic of *fakirs*, was not so revolting as most of his class. He came up to me and said "Are you cold, Mai?" (Mother) "Yes, I am." "Then, I'm very cold, Mai, and have nothing to put round me. Give me something to buy a *chudha*". I gave him an eight *anna* piece. "This won't buy a *chudha*." I gave him another. "Now, let me have one more, and I'll buy a warm *doputta*." I turned my pocket inside out, to shew him I had no more money about me. "Come tomorrow to the *kote* and you shall get some more money." He came next day with our regular beggars.

Passed by Mahtabar's house and underneath the drawbridge, which he had made across the road to connect his two gardens. Over which just a year before his murder he had so politely led me by the hand. It is all tumbling to pieces now. Poor Mahtabar, he was a great wretch but he was not the cowardly, mean spirited contemptible being most of them are.

We had been projecting a return to Koulia for some days, but 'tis no easy matter to get coolies in these festival times. On Tuesday last, however, we got off about 7 a.m. The fields had changed colour since last we came up this road and the rivers had greatly fallen. There was more of bustle and business everywhere. There are in this valley many streams, the principal, the Baghmati and Vishnumati join below the town. Wide beds but shallow water. These streams do much mischief bringing down during the rains quantities of sand which when deposited on arable land destroy it. At the beds of the rivers where overflow is most apprehended, the people drive in small wooden stakes and weave oziers between them. This looks a frail defence but it is so elastic that the stream passes over it and it forms a barrier to the sand.

The morn was delightfully fresh and cool like a few lovely September morns at home. Saw at a pool in a bend of the river women washing clothes; never remember having seen any but men. They did not whisk the clothes against a stone in the unmerciful way *dhobies* do, but put it in a heap on a large flat stone and beat it with something like a cricket bat.

Sunday October 12th

Our darling Moggy is now just the age that Moonia was when God took her. A perfect model of health, intelligence and happiness are you my sweet baby. And your *dhai* is in her way as good as yourself. Alick is, I think, somewhat more what we wish to see him than he was two or three months ago. Less languid and baby-like, still weak and overgrown but not so easily moved to tears nor seeming quite so bullied. Lawrie greatly improved. There is now some prospect of his, in time, thinking English. He is biddable and docile but it is the docility of a dancing dog. There is neither mind nor heart in it and I do not think he has the slightest fondness for any human being, black or white.

Koulia, October 17th

When we entered Nepal, I was every hour asking myself how the valley had ever been discovered, ever populated, so then, as one is seldom satisfied with not knowing without forthwith spinning a theory to "account for the milk in the coconut", I took for granted that the passes from the other side were more accessible. Now that I see the barrier that stands up on the hilly side I confess myself as much at a loss as ever to conjecture how this lovely valley was ever discovered.

I wonder whether there ever was timber of any size to be found in Nepal. At present so far as we have seen of the place, [it] presents a wonderful contrast to the corresponding level of the West hills. There, there are varieties of pine and fir, walnut and oak growing to a great size and a little interior, so near as Mahasao I believe, and all along the bed of the Sutlej above Belaspoor as fine timber as any in the world. *Sal*, oak, deodar, walnut, horsechestnut. I suppose nothing of the kind exists in any of the surrounding hills here, as every timber long enough for the beam of a house is brought from the Terai. It is perfectly astonishing how the timber for the Residency was ever brought up. Native buildings, durbars, temples etc., although they have a great deal of wood in their construction, contain I fancy no rooms of any wide span.

This Koulia hill is the only place where I never saw any chance passenger. There are some villages in the nooks all below us. Just now there are a great many passengers thereon but the inhabitants have no occasion to cross this hill. The high road from Nyakot to Kathmandoo runs about a mile below us.

The last day we came up here, as we halted at the Brahminee Patee, we had a good view of the Bhootias who came pouring in from the snowy land of Bhootan to pass the winter in the genial climate of Nepal. I suppose that unless among the Kraals of the Hottentots it would be impossible to find lower specimens of humanity. I never saw countenances so devoid of intelligence. There was quite an intellectual expression in the little shaggy goats and long horned sheep that they drove along. We had just surmounted a steep ascent before we halted, and before us was another pinch in the road leading through a narrow gorge. Through this gap appeared troop after troop of Bhootias, sturdy and muscular in their make, their long hair matted in elf locks over their bare heads, no vestige of beard or moustache and the dress of all very much alike, so that it was quite impossible to distinguish between men and women. There were no children of the party. Their costume in general was a long loose bedgown of blanketing girt around the loins with a leathern girdle, in the breast a huge pocket which seemed a miscellaneous depot for all their worldly goods. Many of them wore loose breeches gathered below the knee where it met a legging of a very useful kind. The shoes or rather sandals seemed woven of hemp and from the ankle upwards the leg was covered with what seemed a boot of woollen felt. I could not look at the care these hardly human creatures took of their extremities without a bitter thought of the infatuation that left our troops to march bare foot among the snows of Kabul. The Bhootias have decidedly Tartar features, but not so flat as the Nawars. They have a much fairer tint than the Nepalese and many of them a curious red complexion, or rather on each cheek a red patch so bright and so defined that it is difficult to believe it not painted. The Bhootias bring large flocks of Bhootan sheep and goats generally loaded with small wallets of salt and other commodities guarded by large dogs of the mastif kind. There were no dogs with the people we saw on the day I speak of, but the winter we came here I saw at Kasi Chit some dogs very like the engraving of a Bhootan dog in the Zoological gardens [of] the Society [for] Useful Knowledge. The Bhootias likewise keep up the traffic with China in furs, silks and toys. Moorcroft describes the sheep in his *Thibet*, and at Simla I have seen flocks regularly laden, driven by men with features like these Nawars and their hair plaited in a long tail.

There is no immediate war contemplated, but peace can hardly be preserved beyond next year, if so long. Some change for you is probable next season.

Sunday October 26th
This morning had a decided cold weather feeling. We have been shutting up doors and letting down *purdahs* and otherwise trying to fence out the wind. This huge ill designed house is the whirlpool of draughts of air during the cold weather. Indeed, it shewed no small ingenuity to lay out so much money and build up so much material with so little comfort resulting. But except Dr. Steel's I never saw a comfortable cold weather house in India.

ELEVEN

To the Punjaub

In December 1845 the Lawrences left Nepal. Honoria had a miscarriage and then went to England with Alick and Harry. Henry saw them on the way for the first stage of the journey. Henry was to return to Nepal, but on December 11th the Sikh army invaded British India and he was immediately called to the scene of action.

The First Sikh War was an unprovoked act of aggression on the part of the weak successors of Ranjit Singh, so far as any aggression is entirely unprovoked. Ranjit Singh's settled aim was to keep the peace with the British but to have a free hand with his other neighbours. In the process of conquering the Punjab, and some very extensive adjoining territories, he had built up a formidable army, more formidable than even Henry Lawrence realised. This army was the Sikh people in arms, a militant incarnation of their religion. Ranjit Singh died in 1839. He could control his army. His successors could not. They were in bitter and bloody enmity with each other, and the story of these years is a tale of treachery, murder, and assassination. But all of the Sikh Sirdars were united in fear of their army. Eventually they tried to solve their problem by launching this army on British India, calculating – so it was said – that the result would in any case be favourable to themselves. If the army was victorious, their domains would be increased. If it was defeated they would be safer at home. Some such conclusion had been foreseen for some time and there was speculation among the British at Delhi about what should be done with the Punjab after the inevitable clash. The campaign was short and sharp. It ended in a decisive British victory. The Punjab was not annexed but British soldiers remained in the country.

Henry Lawrence was appointed British Resident at Lahore, the capital of the Punjab, with the task of keeping the peace. The titular Maharajah, Dhuleep Singh, was a small boy. His mother and her lover, exercising power in his name, intrigued mercilessly until renewed anarchy seemed likely. Terrified of this, the Sikh Sirdars beseeched the British to help them govern the country until Dhuleep Singh came of age. A Council of Sirdars remained nominally the governing power, but Henry Lawrence was by common consent the uncrowned king of the Punjab.

Meanwhile Honoria had taken the boys home and was absent from India for nearly three years. She divided her time between London, Henry's family at Clifton, her beloved brother William at Bridgnorth, her parents in Ireland and her friend Mary Cameron in Scotland. Then in March 1848 she was joined by Henry who had been sent home on sick leave, travelling with Lord Hardinge, the retiring Governor-General, who had become a close friend.

When Honoria left India, Henry had been making a creditable career for himself but now he had become famous. He had not only brought peace to the Punjab, but had begun to change it from a desert with strings of cultivation along the rivers into a peaceful, prosperous land. He was moreover renowned for making his subordinates rise above themselves, for choosing exceptional men to work under him and for a remarkable ability to delegate authority without losing control. On his return to England Henry was knighted and lionised.

This was the only time that Henry Lawrence had been in Britain since his youth. He needed a long furlough for his health, but he and Honoria never rested for long. Henry had wanted to leave the Punjab in the hands of his brother John during his furlough, but Lord Hardinge had already been criticised for undue partiality towards the Lawrences, and the claims of Sir Frederick Currie were judged superior. He was an able man with some knowledge of the Punjab, but as events showed, not enough understanding of Sikh reactions. He had been desk-bound in Calcutta too long and was insufficiently agile to grapple with problems posed by a country that had yet to be tamed. At the end of April trouble broke at Mooltan, and two British officers were murdered there. Moolraj, the Governor of Mooltan, revolted and the trouble began to spread.

When this news reached England, Sir Henry Lawrence felt that, whatever the doctors said about his health, his place was back in the Punjab. So after less than seven months in England, he returned with Honoria, their son Henry – or Harry as he was usually called – and Sir Henry's sister Charlotte, then aged thirty-four. They left by steamer for Egypt, where Honoria observed that "it was new and pleasant for me to feel among Orientals just on an equality." The Suez Canal was not yet cut. So the journey through Egypt was by land and they then joined another steamer to continue on their way to Bombay. Here Henry pushed off at once by boat for Karachi, leaving Honoria and Charlotte with Harry, to follow as and when they could.

Henry arrived in the Punjab to take part in the final stages of what had now become the Second Sikh War. It ended with the complete and final defeat of the Sikh army. After this the new Governor-General, Lord Dalhousie, was glad to annex the Punjab to British India. He took a strong personal interest in this new province and placed it under a Board of Administration consisting of Henry Lawrence as President, John Lawrence in charge of finance and a third member, who was first C. G. Mansel and then the Lawrences' old friend, Robert Montgomery. The work of the Board of Administration was one of the wonders of its age,

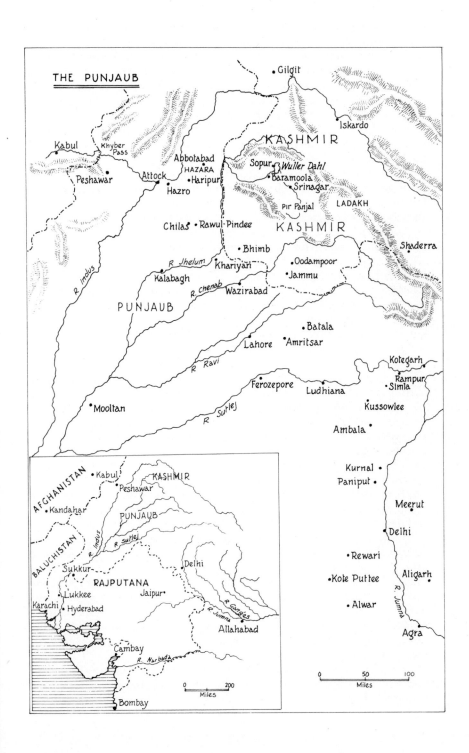

THE PUNJAUB

Gilgit

KASHMIR

Iskardo

Kabul
Khyber Pass

Peshawar
Attock
Abbotabad
HAZARA
Haripur
Hazro
Sopur
Wuller Dahl
Baramoola
Srinagar
Pir Panjal
LADAKH

Chilas
Rawul-Pindee
KASHMIR
Shaderra

Bhimb

R. Jhelum
Kalabagh
Khariari
R. Chenab
Wazirabad
Oodampoor
Jammu

PUNJAUB

R. Indus

Batala
Lahore
Amritsar

R. Ravi
Kotegarh
Rampur
Simla

Ferozepore
Ludhiana
Kussowlee

R. Surlej
Mooltan

Ambala

Kurnal
Paniput

Meerut

Delhi

Rewari
Kote Puttee
Aligarh

Alwar

R. Jumna

Agra

0   50   100
Miles

AFGHANISTAN
Kabul
KASHMIR
Peshawar
Kandahar
PUNJAUB
R. Indus
R. Surlej
BALUCHISTAN
Delhi
Sukkur
RAJPUTANA
Lukkee
Jaipur
Karachi
Hyderabad
R. Ganges
R. Jumna
Allahabad
Cambay
R. Narbada
Bombay

0   200
Miles

but it is peripheral to Honoria's journals. Here it is enough to say that the constitution of the Board had a fatal weakness. It was not made clear what was to happen if its members disagreed. Henry and John loved each other, but they had different views on some important subjects and they were both too masterful not to express their disagreement with vehemence. For a time the complementary gifts of the two brothers worked for the good of the people they ruled, but eventually a point came when they could work together no longer. Then, Dalhousie, who had upheld John Lawrence's views throughout, moved Henry to Rajputana, leaving the Punjab under the sole charge of John.

Meanwhile poor Alick aged ten had been left behind in the care of his uncle and aunt, Dr. and Mrs. Bernard at Clifton, to be joined by Harry a few years later. When Honoria first met Dr. Bernard in 1837 he was already married to Henry's sister. At that time Honoria summed him up as "a person to be admired and esteemed but not likely to be loved by any but intimates. There is in him something very hurting to one's self-esteem. He seems to take for granted that you have a high opinion of yourself and forthwith begins to pull you down. I think he could with great difficulty enter the feelings of another. He is one who goes on his own path and sees that clearly enough, but is apt to forget that other men have each his own track." Honoria seems to have forgotten this first opinion of hers, assuming without question that Uncle Bernard would be a perfect mentor and congenial companion for their small sons. But Alick was miserable.

The Bernards brought up their own children with others entrusted to them. The nursery and schoolroom were lively but the Bernards were hard and cold with a distorted piety that left deep scars. It was easy to choose the wrong guardians but at a distance of several thousand miles it was not easy to diagnose the mistake or put it right. A generation later this common tragedy of Anglo-Indian life is the subject of Kipling's semi-autobiographical tale *Baa Baa Black Sheep*. In that case the parents came back five years later and discovered with horror what they had done by entrusting their children to the wrong people. Between her tears the mother cries out, "Oh, my son . . . ! It was *my* fault . . . and yet how could we help it?" Henry and Honoria never saw their sons again in this life and never discovered what they had done to them.

Sanawar school, which figures largely in the following chapter, was the first of the hill schools founded by Henry Lawrence for the children of other ranks among the British troops in India. Hitherto they had been dragged up in degrading and death-dealing conditions in the plains. Henry financed this work partly by generous gifts from his own salary and partly by public subscription. Sanawar stands on a hill 5,000 feet high opposite the hill of Kussowlee. It has now become a public school (in the English sense) for Indian children, where the traditions bequeathed by Henry and Honoria are very much alive.

The following letters, journals and descriptions are written to Alick – and later to Harry. Occasionally, however, Honoria forgets this and addresses Henry.

Bombay, Thursday December 14th, 1848

My darling boy, many days have passed without my writing, for I have been busy and my heart has been very sad. Papa is gone. Papa's heart is very sad about the Punjaub. He had laboured with his brothers to establish peace in that country, to deliver the people from the miseries they had for generations endured from war. While we remained, the work prospered. Now all is destroyed. Besides the actual battles and slaughter we read of in the public papers, there is misery in whole provinces and the time of their tranquillity is now removed very far.

If Papa finds all quiet, he will write to us to proceed up the Indus. Otherwise we must wait here for a steamer to take us to Ceylon, thence to Calcutta and so up the Ganges.

January 16th

Harry is a great delight to me in what would otherwise be very sad loneliness, and he is a good boy. Everyday we talk about brother. I allow him as a favour to kiss your picture and he will soon know all your Indian life. "Now, tell me what brother did when he was a little boy." He remembers every body at home and talks to Anne but he is very happy with black servants. I have got a nice *ayah* called Begum, a good head manservant called Mohammed Hooseyn.

I can shut my eyes and think that I see you darling, in the room upstairs, in the library, in school, in the downs, at church, at meals. Everywhere my thoughts and prayers follow you.

Karachi, February 3rd, 1849

On January 20th we embarked on board the steam frigate *Sesostris* at Bombay. The ship was filled with troops, treasure and ammunition. No ladies but ourselves and Mrs. Cracklow wife of the Colonel commanding.

January 24th, Harry's birthday

We dropped anchor off Karachi about three miles from the shore, the strongest possible contrast to the shore we had left. Here, as far as the eye can reach is one vast bed of sand, except the North-West; there a ridge of barren mountains runs to the sea. Desolate and barren all looks, as the desert. Yet is there in this boundless tract, with its pure atmosphere a sense of freedom and elasticity that I greatly prefer to more civilised scenes.

There is but one great drawback here as in all similar places I have been in, Egypt, Aden etc., and that is bad water. Here it is brackish and dark coloured. We landed at a *bundee* or embankment, begun by Sir Charles Napier, and left unfinished but even so a great convenience.

Three carriages were waiting and in these we went to Captain Fennemore's house. We had brought with us bedding, bathing tubs etc., and we were put into empty rooms, where we made ourselves very comfortable compared to what we had felt on board. We cannot yet have the luxury of a good cup of tea, the water being so bad, but on the whole we are not starved.

What a busy time Papa has had since we landed in Bombay on December 8th. But thanks be to God, so far from suffering from all this, he is better in health, and I feel very hopeful that a blessing will rest on all he is doing for the unhappy country that is so largely placed in his power.

On board the steamer *Napier*, February 21st, 1849
Yesterday we sent off all our baggage to the steamer and this morning I was up at three o'clock. We went for six miles over barren sand, very heavy for the horses; here and there a peep of the blue sea seen between the sandy ridges. It looked like the mirage in the desert. At last just as the sun rose we came in view of the open sea, where lay the steamer *Napier*, hissing and smoking for us. She is an iron vessel with only two and a half feet draught of water, ninety horse power, one hundred and twenty feet long and thirty-two feet broad with two funnels.

Thursday February 22nd
We are now in the river Indus, having completed the navigation of the tidal creek and entered the river by the Kihawaree mouth. This flat-bottomed boat could not stand out in the open sea, or cross the bar at the river's mouth. She therefore winds in and out through a network of salt water channels formed by banks and islands, gradually deposited by the river at its mouth. This delta is supposed to have arisen chiefly since the time when Alexander the Great's fleets came down the Indus. When the tide is full, most of the islets I have mentioned are under water. The low tide leaves deep winding channels, some of these very narrow, through which there was hardly room for the vessel to pass. The soil is generally clothed with verdure, large tracts of mangrove, a low spreading tree of dark fresh green that grows only within the influence of salt water. A good deal of light feathery tamarisk jungle. Where the ground is more elevated it is covered with fine grass and on the highest spots stand clusters of reed huts inhabited by herdsmen. This is a vast pasture district. We saw troops of buffaloes, some grazing, some reposing up to the neck in water, great herds of camels looking very much at their ease. It was delightful to see these creatures enjoying themselves. I never before saw them except laboriously employed and often suffering sadly. Little shaggy ponies

frisking about in companies, oxen, sheep, and goats. Here and there groups of wild looking men who attend to these cattle.

At 3 p.m. today we got fairly into the Indus and soon came up to a flat, which we have taken in tow. A large unwieldy looking vessel she is. We stop about sunset each evening, and set off at daylight in the morning. The climate hitherto is delightful. On deck at 2 p.m., the thermometer 75° with a fresh breeze. I feel very happy to be at last moving towards Papa.

Saturday February 24th

We are now on board the flat which is lashed alongside of the steamer. Here we have a cabin each and a spacious saloon. Yesterday we lay to all day at a place called Unnee, where we took on board stores that had been brought over land from Karachi. The greater number of troops and stores that are sent up the Indus cannot be sent the way we came by the tidal creeks, because these vessels could not carry sufficient fresh water for so many people, and in the creeks none is to be had for a considerable distance inland.

The banks of the stream as far as we can see are an unbroken level, generally covered with low brushwood, chiefly tamarisk. No habitations in sight except here and there clusters of reed huts, shelter for the people who herd the large droves of cattle and who one way or another find employment from the river steamer. In the midst of this waste it was curious to see great pyramids built of shot and shell, guns dismounted lying by the side of their carriages all taken to pieces, besides bales of clothing and other stores.

The Scindees we have seen are a fine looking race, well sunned and hardy, with hair and beard like a lion's mane. They wear a very funny cap, shaped like an English hat, only with the brim placed round the crown and of bright colours. They were hard at work all the day and as darkness came on it was pretty to see them separating into groups according to their castes, kindling their fires and cooking their food, partly rice and partly unleavened bread of wheat or millet with various little condiments of *ghee*, turmaric [sic], onions and spice with which the poorest class in this country contrive to make a savoury meal. We sat on deck and sipped our tea, looking at the groups on shore. Their dark forms very scantily clothed looked exceedingly picturesque, as they crouched around their fires, sometimes the red glow of the embers leaving the figures hardly visible, and sometimes a fresh piece of wood thrown on lighting up a blaze that illumined all.

When they had done eating, one of the party brought out a rude sort of guitar on which he played, while the rest joined in a song, very monotonous and dull to our ears, but they must have liked it, for these hard worked men were still sitting there at their concert when I came downstairs at nine o'clock. This morning they are all bathing with great delight, a dozen black heads seemed rolling about in the water near our boat. Some men were standing ankle deep with the scantiest clothing possible on, washing their principal garments and which, when wrung out, they put round them to dry. They looked a well fed, cheerful, active set and I wish it were possible to supply the wants of the poor Irish as comfortably as these people are supplied. This is a climate, where clothing, lodging, and fuel are of comparatively small importance and the want of these is the principal misery I have been used to see at home.

I enjoy almost everything in India, because here I have a feeling of health and comfortableness that I never had in my own cold and uncertain climate. I always liked India and now I like it better than ever.

Monday February 26th

We are now near Hyderabad. I wonder if the camel in the [Zoological] gardens looks like the camels of which we see troops here. Long strings of them, the rope in the nose of one tied to the tail of the next, the huge creatures moving along perfectly noiselessly, for their soft spongy feet come down very gently on the sand.

Lahore, April 5th, 1849

We arrived here on March 31st and found dear Papa looking better than I expected after all the fatigue and anxiety he has had. At present Papa has the work of forming a completely new government, civil and military for the Punjaub. Uncle John is here looking very well; he and Papa work together all day long.

Lahore, April 23rd, 1849

The Indus is but a dull river to navigate. The banks are either a jungle of tamarisk or an extent of barren sand, very few fields or houses in sight. Our fuel was wood and we took on board as much at a time as kept us going for ten or twelve hours. As we always anchored for the night, it was very nice when we reached a wood station about sunset. Otherwise, we lost an hour or two stopping to wood. As soon as we came alongside and threw out an hawser the Baluchis came flocking down, some to help the work but most only to look at us. They are a wild looking race, long shaggy hair and beards, and their clothes consisting chiefly of pieces of cotton cloth, not cut or sewed but huddled about the head, shoulders and loins, sticking on one could not tell how.

I have not told you about fishing for *pulla* in the Indus. The *pulla* is shaped something like a salmon, but smaller. The flesh is white and delicate, but is so full of oil that I could never eat above one or two mouthfuls. A man takes a large globular earthen jar, with a small mouth. He sets this jar afloat, and then lays himself across it, bringing his chest over the hole. Thus balanced he floats down the stream, holding a net, of which the mouth is kept open by a stick like sugar tongs. When he feels that any fish are taken, he lifts up the net, shutting the mouth, and it is pretty to see the glittering creatures taken up out of the water. He raises himself a little so as to admit of putting the fish into the jar, then adjusts himself again for another catch. Hundreds of men are thus employed the whole day. They pay a tax to government for the right of fishing. Morning and evening I used to watch them coming across the wide level of white sand that borders the stream. Slender black forms almost naked, each man balancing on his head the large fishing pot with long handles of the net sticking out of it like horns had the oddest effect you can imagine. This is the mode of fishing from Hyderabad to Lukkee.

Thence to Sukkur it is done in boats, and this is also very pretty to watch. Small black, flat-bottomed canoes raised high at each end and a little tent or hut of reeds in the middle. This appeared to be the house of the whole family. At night we saw the boats made fast to the shore, with the families asleep in them. In the morning they loosed anchor, the women took a clumsy oar as helm and stood steering, while the men at the stern managed a large net and the children amused themselves in the cabin. Thus they glided about our large steamer that made the way against the stream and looked like an elephant among so many mice. The *pulla* fish is not found above Sukkur, the natives say that it comes so far to salute a saint's tomb there and then goes back to the sea without turning round lest it should dishonour the saint by turning its tail.

From Mooltan Major Edwardes marched with us here. Our camp consisted of between three hundred and four hundred people, our escort, baggage and followers. We used to get up at one or two o'clock in the morning, take a cup of tea and set off. Palanquins, elephants and horses carried us. Overnight we had sent on our tents and, when soon after sunrise we reached our ground, we found all ready for us. Breakfast, bathing, sleeping, dinner, tea and bed took up our day. The last part of our journey we made in a carriage that Papa had sent out for us with four horses. We left our camp at 5 p.m. and got in here at 8 a.m. next morning.

Lahore, Wednesday May 2nd, 1849

I wish you could see the garden★ Papa has got for the European

★The "Lawrence Gardens" eventually became a beautiful park. Since Independence they are officially called the Jinnah Gardens, but their old name survives.

soldiers here. Very likely you may hear soldiers spoken of as drunken, disorderly people. So very many of them are. Papa does all he can to give them employment and amusement. There was a pretty bit of ground near this with some fine trees and old tombs. Papa had it enclosed for a garden and is gradually enlarging and improving it. There is a building for coffee room and library. There are racket courts, fives courts, ball courts, swings, whirligigs, gymnastic poles etc. By degrees we are getting workshops of all kinds, carpenter, shoemaker, smith etc. where the men may practise any trade they know. We hope soon to have baths. A military band plays in the garden two or three times a week. It is pleasant to see men, women, and children who otherwise would have no place but the barracks, the parade ground, and the bazaar with every temptation to idleness and drunkenness happily and innocently employed. Papa has applied to Government to have a garden of the same kind in every place in the Punjaub, where there are European soldiers.

A few days ago we had a gay sight there. About thirty of the principal men who had served with Major Edwardes in his campaign last year were to receive *killuts* or dresses of honour. When we went into the great room these gentlemen were sitting on chairs in two rows facing one another, their relations and servants sitting on the floor or standing behind the chairs. The chiefs were mostly a clumsy, hard featured set, burley figures bunched up in short waisted dresses, with interminable rolls of shawl and muslin, long curling hair and beards, armed with swords, daggers and shields. They all stood up as we entered and the room had a strong scent of people who never bathed. On the long table at one side were arranged neat parcels put up in white muslin. Beside them stood the man in charge; and another tall slender man dressed in white with a reed pen and a piece of paper in his hand was keeping the account of what was given. As each bundle was laid at Papa's feet he rose up, went to the gentleman who was to be dressed, embraced him, spoke of his services, and then put on him the dress of honour, just as Pharaoh did to Joseph, I suppose. Pearl necklaces, gold bracelets, shawls, embroidered cloaks and such like with swords, and watches were bestowed. Harry was greatly amused at helping to adorn these Pathan officers.

Mahasoo, near Simla, May 30th, 1849
We are on one of the thousand hilly ridges, that intersect one another, and we look down upon gigantic waves as it were turned solid. I hope you do not forget the little hill, where we used to sit when you began to learn "Lars Porsena of Clusium" and there we could look down on one side to the green fertile level of Nepal, studded with villages and

with temples, on the other hand down the abrupt slope of the hill to the valley of the Raptee.

We enjoy the perfect quiet of this place after the perpetual turmoil of Lahore. We are staying now in a nice bungalow, but tomorrow we intend to move deeper into the mountains and pine forests. The only thing we wanted is water, which never forms a feature of the scenery and at this season is only found in the streams that trickle in the bottom of the deep gorges or *khuds* that divide the range of hills.

I wrote to you by last mail closing the letter at Kussowlee, but I did not tell you about the school.★ The boys and girls in the school are healthy and happy. They are perfectly clean and well cared for. Three times a week they have clean underclothes and once a week clean bed-linen. The boys wear as dress: checked trousers of strong cotton cloth, a jacket of checked woollen cloth, in summer a blouse and a cap of grey cloth with the number of the boy in scarlet. The girls wear frocks of dark checked chintz in summer, woollen in winter, white tippets and bonnets. For cold weather short cloaks and hoods. Both boys and girls are divided into companies, and the elder ones in charge are called Corporal, Sergeant, and Sergeant Major. These are responsible for the behaviour of their divisions, for reporting anything wrong to the superintendant, for clean hands, faces, and hair. If they hear an improper word spoken to say that it must be reported, and various other matters of discipline. Thus perfect order is kept up.

At night when they turn into the dormitory each Sergeant Major stands beside his division, each boy standing at the foot of his bed. The word is given "Jackets off"; off go all the jackets: "fold up jackets"; in a moment all are folded and laid smoothly at the foot of the bed; "shoes off"; then a rattle as all the great strong shoes come off and are placed under the beds: "kneel down"; all kneel down each by the side of his bed, and there is perfect silence for three or four minutes. Then they finish undressing and get into bed. Nearly the same goes on with the girls upstairs. We hope on June 28th to have a feast at the school, that the children may have pleasant thoughts of dear Papa's birthday.

Magoo, June 1st, 1849

Here we are in one of the rude travellers' bungalows that form our Indian hotels. I have just been preparing for dinner one of those camp stews you used to enjoy with us, meat, potatoes, seasoning all put into a stewpan together, the lid fastened down with paste. Bye and bye this will be taken off the fire and set on the table. Potatoes are abundant here, and very good indeed, though they get little care; furrows scratched in the soil wherever there is a little clear space among the pines and fir trees, but the ground is not cleared or manured.

★Sanawar.

The whole country is clothed with trees chiefly of the fir species, several varieties, larch, Scotch fir, spruce fir, one that grows like a cedar, and other kinds that I don't know. The trees stand so close together having never been thinned that though they shoot up into tall stems, there are no fine spreading trees. This is the most unfavourable season for seeing the place. The ground is so parched that there are scarcely any wild flowers, but only the remains of the moss with which the pine branches are fringed and of the numerous ferns, some almost trees, and others the very minutest with which these hills are clothed after the rains. Still I spy a few wild strawberries, and pretty pink dog-roses, and there are yet some of the wreaths remaining of a creeping white rose that a few weeks ago spread from tree to tree. Here and there a few tassels remain of the scarlet tree-rhododendron, with which in March whole hill sides seem in a blaze. It is curious as the road winds from one face of the hill to another, to observe the sudden change in the vegetation. One aspect all pine; another all oak, the evergreen or Spanish oak; another all rhododendron.

There seem few creatures to enjoy these beautiful woodland glades. The dear sweet cuckoo indeed sings here, as much as in Lee Woods, and just now I hear a note much like the linnet. But the chief living things are flies, which strange to say in this uninhabited region, swarm as if in a butcher's or a confectioner's shop. The higher parts of the hills which we resort to for coolness are not inhabited by the natives. Save here and there near the roadside, a hut of rough planks, forming a shop for one of the *banias* or grain dealers, who follow in the track of civilisation, however scanty. The mountaineers cluster in villages built of stone and flat earthen roofs down in the ravines, which we should find intolerably hot, but where they can more readily obtain water. The sides of these ravines are terraced with fields, sometimes only a few feet wide, the sides built up with stones and the soil often artificially laid. These slips of land are very fertile, producing wheat, rice and several other grains, ginger and other garden crops.

The people appear a thriving and contented race. We have not met one beggar. They are small made, not very dark and with Tartar faces with scarcely any beards. There are some very funny looking little fellows who come from the higher regions. North of this they remind me somewhat of our old friends the Bhootias at Nepal, but these are a much more diminutive race. The women seem to work as hard as the men. I saw the other evening a little woman with a face like a monkey's. Her hair tied at the back, hanging down her back in a long plait, the ends decorated with red tassels, a dirty rag rolled round her head. Her dress was loose trousers of coarse blanketing and a wide shirt of the same girded round the waist with a hair rope, shoes of plaited twine. Round her ancles and wrists she wore huge rings, or rather fetters of copper, which must have weighed several pounds. Of which I suppose she was very proud as well as of her silver ear-rings and nose-ring. Well this little body carried on her back three large planks, the common load for a man. The servants I asked told me women carried such loads into Simla, six or eight miles.

Matiana, June 3rd, 1849

Before eight o'clock reached our tent. I never had been in a tent with Papa before, since the sad, sad day, January 7th, 1846, when he left us at Segoulee going to the wars while we were on our way to England. In this tent we found breakfast. Tea, bread and butter, eggs, grilled fowl, rice, and a "country captain", a kind of dry curry. There we bathed, having with us the big sponge bath Papa got at Clifton. At 5 p.m. set off again as in the morning and got here about nine o'clock, to a nice clean bungalow. Had tea and bed. Lord Gifford and Captain Fane are in the room adjoining ours, and I hear Harry in the verandah with them chattering away.

Nagkunda, June 10th, 1849

My darling boy. We are very much pleased to find you use the microscope. I send you some things for it. The moss is what Harry calls "the beard and moustache of the trees". The wood-roof I send to show you that we have here some of the very same wild flowers that grow at home. The wool is perhaps the most interesting thing. It grows on long eared, long tailed goats. Mrs. Procknow told me that at Rampur she had seen the making of *pushmeena* shawls. One takes just a year. A poor woman keeps a shawl goat, and when the shearing time comes the wool is shorn. All the hair is picked out by hand from the soft wool. The woman then spins the wool on a clumsy little wheel. Next she sets it for weaving. Her loom is only some sticks set up in the open air to the length required for the shawl. On these the warp is laid and then she stands weaving in the wool till her work is done. At Rampur the shawls can be bought at from twelve to twenty-two rupees. Uncle Bernard will tell you about the division of labour and its benefits. The people who live among these hills, and have very little intercourse with the world around them continue in their rude way to live comfortably and are far better off I believe than most of our manufacturers at home. Certainly a hundred times better off than our poor Irish peasantry.

We are very happy in a bungalow consisting of two rooms. This window has got three panes of glass left out of eight. The floor is of rough planks, and so is the ceiling. Looking up I can see through the planks and then up through a very rough slate roof to the sky beyond. The house stands on a little level halfway down a ridge of hill.

On Monday at 6 a.m. we left Matiana for Nagkunda. The road was beautiful, winding above deep gorges and among hills. Carefully cultivated, patches and stripes of deep brown grain ready for cutting, or of yellow stubble, were mingled with masses of pine forest. Some of the houses with projecting balconies were just like the model Uncle brought of a Swiss cottage. We had a tent pitched halfway and rested during the heat. Just before sunset we rounded the spur on which stands the *dak* bungalow – public rest-house. Close by were pitched some small tents. In one we saw Lord Gifford and Captain Fane at dinner. They had come by a more difficult road than ours, and were resting comfortably in some kind of undress that prevented their rising to come out to us, so we nodded in passing.

Tuesday we rested here, and on Wednesday went to Kotegarh a place near where the river Sutlej leaves the hills, a good deal lower and warmer than this, and where there is much more level ground. The only Christian inhabitants are some missionaries. When at eight o'clock we reached the mission house, we were glad to stop. The full moon had risen some time from behind a wall of mountain that fenced our view, but the deep shadows cast on our path made torches necessary. Four men accompanied us carrying large splinters of blazing pine and shewing the narrow zig zag path, while the silvery moonlight showed the surrounding hills. Thursday and Friday we halted but saw little, for the mist was gathering thickly around. Saturday morning was clearer after a storm the night before, and we went down to breakfast at the missionaries. They are Germans, quiet earnest people who live there generally in perfect seclusion, giving themselves to the work of trying to benefit the people and persevering, though seeing little result of their work. We went to the girls' school, a small room where sat eighteen girls, four to twelve years old. Meanwhile, Harry was in the verandah learning phrases in German from the little Procknows and highly amused with a funny little creature, a bear of a week old, the ugliest, but drollest young thing I ever looked at, big head, short legs, black rough skin and a wide sprawling walk. He let the children play with him and was able to lap milk.

Simla, June 17th, 1849

I wrote last from Nagkunda which place we left on the 13th for Therg. Halfway the bearers put down my *dhoolie* to rest and drink water. A woman came up to me. She was young, very pretty. Her hair was plaited in a long tail that hung below her waist. On her head a white handkerchief folded cornerwise, the ends tied behind. She wore a dark woollen jacket open at the bosom with a red striped petticoat, heavy silver bracelets, anklets, and ear-rings. So I supposed she was of the wealthy sort. She sat down familiarly, but not impertinently, and began to examine me and Harry, much amused with my bonnet and the fringe of my cloak. She carried over her shoulders an axe for felling trees and in one hand a sickle. I asked her what she had been doing? "Cutting corn and firewood," she replied. And after a while she said she had once had a needle and asked if I could give her one. I gave her some needles, pins and buttons with which she was delighted. "Wait," she said, "and I'll fetch you some milk." She ran off and brought a great bunch of poppy heads, the capsules of which while green had been pierced for the milk of which opium is made and which afterwards ripen. The seeds, small and dry, taste rather like nuts and the natives are fond of them. *Ayah* had the poppy heads, and I made haste to get away lest more applicants should come for my haberdashery.

Kussowlee, June 29th, 1849

Here is a day of pouring rain. All our windows are shut and the wind moans among the trees. I have no boy with me now. We resolved not to take Harry to the plains during the heat, and we thought he would feel the separation less leaving him with Aunt George, than if we brought him here and sent him away to Simla. So on Tuesday I came away leaving Harry. But I am with Papa and that makes up for everything.

Now I have to tell you how Papa's birthday feast went off. I arrived here on Wednesday, but Papa did not come till next morning. Found everybody very busy preparing plum-pudding and other good things. Before breakfast time I espied Papa coming along the winding road by the hill side and felt very happy. After breakfast about a dozen people came from Kussowlee and we all went to church at eleven o'clock. Service is held in the school room. The children looked very nice, boys in white trousers and blue jackets, girls with brown chintz frocks, white bonnets and tippets. When I looked round at the children rescued from the worse than heathenism of the barracks and removed to the happy home they were in, I felt what an honour it was to be allowed to help such a work. Mr. Parker★ preached on "Train up a child in the way he should go". About two hours were thus occupied, and then all the young things rushed out to enjoy themselves till dinner was ready.

Each child has a metal bowl for water, a plate, knife, fork and spoon. They sit in order, and the servants who carve at the side table, set before each a mess, roast mutton, curry and rice with loads of plum-pudding. This finished, they went to play. The boys had cricket in the play ground and the girls in their day room had press in the corner, blind man's buff and so forth.

★The headmaster.

By and bye came the distribution of sweets. A man went round with basket after basket, which the gentlemen served in handfuls to the children, the girls holding out their pinafores, the boys their caps; mangoes, walnuts, sugar-cane, almonds, raisins and sundry Hindustanee sweet-meats. We left the children to enjoy themselves.

When it was dark we went out to see the fireworks. For an hour or two there was a ceaseless blaze and bang, crackers, rockets, etc. and a grand bonfire. The natives enjoyed all this mightily. Some of them flung about the fire and tossed up the squibs in a way quite surprising, considering their light cotton garments. But nobody was hurt. and about nine o'clock we all broke up after a very happy day. Papa made a little speech to the boys, promised at Christmas some prizes should be distributed not to the cleverest, but to the best, and told them that he had never passed so happy a birthday and would always remember them on that anniversary. June 28th is henceforth to be the anniversary of the "Lawrence Asylum".

Kussowlee, Saturday July 7th, 1849

We have remained with the Parkers and have had a great deal of pleasure in observing the school. Last Wednesday we went out gipsey-ing with about forty of the children down into a deep, deep glen and we stopped by a spring of clear water near a village. Already the rain has brought out a good deal of vegetation. It was pretty to see the children coming in lines and groups down the steep face of the opposite hill, the girls' white bonnets and tippets gleaming among the trees. At last all assembled and refreshed themselves with drinking and washing at the fountain. We had brought several hundred of mangoes which were put in a heap before Mr. Parker. The children passed in single file each getting a share of the fruit which they sat down to enjoy. The girls on one side and the boys on the other. Presently they all began to sing. They ended with the anthem "Lord of all power and might". While they were singing the sun set, the full moon had quietly climbed up above the hill opposite, and it was time to move homewards. It was almost as bright as day on our return, but the ascent was a weary one to some of the smaller ones. Papa walked, putting two of the children by turns on his pony, and all were safely back before ten o'clock, very tired but very happy.

You know the cow is held sacred by the Hindoos. A poor man near Kotegarh accidently killed a calf and was looked upon with horror by all his neighbours. Nobody would eat or drink, or smoke with him and he became in fact, what in England we only read of, excommuni-cated. The man's life was very miserable, when at last a priest told him that he might be restored to society if he was first buried and rose again. Accordingly, a place was dug in which the culprit lay down and he was earthed over all but his head. Over his head a thatch was placed, just leaving room for him to breathe and to receive the food his friends brought him. On the thatch, earth was laid and mustard seed was sown. The man remained buried until the seed began to grow. When it was pronounced that he was purified, he was taken out of the grave and restored to society. As you read the history of Europe in the Middle Ages, you will find many instances of superstition as blind as this and like another that has just happened. You know that Moolraj has been tried and pronounced guilty and sentenced to death for the murder of Vans Agnew and Anderson. He writes to Papa that he is innocent, but since those who tried him think differently, he appeals to the ordeal of fire, requests to be allowed to go into the fire, and that if he comes out unhurt his innocence may be acknowledged. Of course our Government will not allow this but I hope Moolraj may not be hanged,* for I don't think his guilt has been proved.

Lahore, September 23rd

Dear Papa left me on the 26th to go to Kashmir. So here I am in our two big rooms without one of my own people. The illness that Papa had made him very weak, and he did not much recover while here, so that I was very glad when he consented to go to a cold climate, and to a place where he could not have such hard work as here. Some days before he started he sent off elephants, with tents, servants, all things for food, cooking and bedding. When he set out it was in a *dhoolee*, a litter in which he can sleep, but when he gets among the mountains he must travel on a pony, or in a chair carried by men. The weather is growing very cool and pleasant now, and I feel much better.

October 6th

When the late war ended some of the chiefs surrendered. Among them were Chuttur Singh, and Sher Singh, the father and son, the former who held Uncle and Aunt George prisoners, the latter who with his troops had left Major Edwardes when he was before Mooltan and went over to the enemy. These, with several others, were very leniently dealt with by our Government, being allowed to go and reside on their estates on terms that they would not go beyond a certain limit, not collect arms, not correspond with other insurgents and some other conditions. It was a very impressive scene here one day last April, when they were all assembled in our large room, seated round, while Papa and Uncle John explained the terms to them. Each man gave his solemn assent, on which, they were escorted to their homes. We could not suppose that they had any principle of truth that

*He was not.

would make them keep their word, and Papa was often made anxious by secret intelligence that the *moofsids*, rebels, were transgressing their rules. Just after Papa went away, Uncle got further accounts of their doings, and resolved on seizing them. This required a good deal of caution, for if the *moofsids* had had any notion that they were discovered, they would have escaped, and it was necessary to sally forth the same night from Lahore, Wuzeerabad and Amritsar to places twenty or thirty miles distant and pounce upon the different *moofsids*.

All was arranged very secretly. Mr. Saunders and another gentleman from Amritsar, Mr. Inglis from Wuzeerabad, and from Lahore Uncle John, Mr. Montgomery, Major Edwardes and Lieut. Hodson. On September 30th troops were ordered to be ready, but they knew nothing of their destination. A squadron of cavalry, a wing of infantry and two guns. It was a brilliant moonlight night. Uncle and Aunt John, Mr. Montgomery and Major Edwardes and I sat till late talking over the expedition, but not a soul of the other people living in the house knew about it except Aunt Charlotte. The troops marched at nine o'clock with Mr. Hodson.* At one o'clock the gentlemen set out in a carriage and very anxious were Aunt John and I till ten o'clock next morning, when we got a note saying all was well. It was just daylight when they reached Batala, the *moofsid* village. Troops were thrown around the place, and the fort within was surrounded. Everybody was taken by surprise, and there was no resistance. With Major Edwardes were some of his Pathan troops who had been with him when Sher Singh went over to the enemy, and they would gladly have wreaked their vengeance. The traitors not resisting were as safe as if they had been friends. Old Chuttur Singh was in his bed and Major Edwardes with a party kept guard over him. Sher Singh and his brothers had gone out to ride. Uncle John and Mr. Montgomery went after these, while Mr. Hodson remained with the troops outside. The men returning from their ride were taken quite by surprise and gave themselves up at once. Their timely capture has probably averted much bloodshed and misery.

The last account I had of dear Papa is dated September 29th when he was between Jammu and Kashmir, travelling in a kind of tray, padded all round and carried on men's shoulders. He was in beautiful scenery about six thousand feet above the plains, mountains covered with forests of oak and pine, and the ground enamelled with violets, buttercups, clover and other home flowers. Distant views of snowy peaks between the river Chenab foaming through a rocky channel below. They had crossed the stream where it was 150 feet wide, by a *sanga* or rope bridge, where they were pulled across in a basket, in a

*Of Hodson's Horse.

very rude way resembling the bridge at Clifton. But at Dodampoor the clumsy structure required a long time to cross. Papa sat in a loop of rope with his feet resting on another and holding by a third.

Lahore, December 6th, 1849

On the 28th of last month dear Papa returned from his travels after ten weeks absence. Just as he returned came two great camps, the Governor-General's and Commander-in-Chief's, and this set every body in as great a commotion as it would do if the Queen came to stay in Clifton. I have often mentioned the gardens that Papa made for the soldiers here. There is every thing to amuse and occupy the men and their families. Besides, there is a fine vegetable garden, whence the soldiers get turnips, carrots, beetroot, cauliflowers, artichokes, peas, and other vegetables, a comfort such as you can hardly imagine in a climate like this. There is a pretty entrance with a lodge where a sergeant lives, and an iron gate and railings. Those railings I look at with great pleasure, for they are made of the barrels of the old Sikh guns. Formerly every man in the Punjaub went about armed. Last year their arms were taken from them for they are now under the protection of a regular Government. And the long muskets that used to commit so much mischief are now peacefully standing up as garden railings.

In this part of the world our gardens require continual watering, every little plot of ground has a canal of its own from one of the deep wells, where all day long the bullocks pace round and round working a large clumsy, creaking wheel by which the water is raised. In the middle of the soldiers' garden a sort of raised terrace [was] built, and over this was stretched a gay awning for the little Maharajah.* Lord and Lady Dalhousie and a few others sitting on this, the sight was very pretty. A clear, bright, calm day, the gardens crowded with people, soldiers with their wives and children, native chiefs, both Mohammedan and Hindoo, with their armed followers gay with jewels, shawls, and every coloured costume. The gay staff officers of the Governor-General and Commander-in-Chief with crowds of ladies and gentlemen. The pleasant part was to see the soldiers' enjoyment. Papa had got quantities of fruit from Kabul and Kashmir, grapes, apples, pears, quinces, pomegranates, oranges. There were three hundred dozen of tartlets, as much bread and cold meat as they could eat, with tea, coffee and ginger beer. As evening drew on the gardens were illuminated and there was a grand display of fireworks.

The little Maharajah is just your age. He is a pretty and gentlemanlike little fellow, and looked very well in his robe of yellow silk

*The putative grandson of Ranjit Singh.

and turban of gold tissue all glistening with jewels. But better than all this finery, was it to see his happy look and familiar manner towards Dr. Login★ who has the charge of him, a kind and good man, very fond of the boy. Some time, perhaps, little Dhuleep Singh may know how much better off he is brought up safely under kind instruction, than if he had still been called a king with a daily chance of being murdered as so many before him were. But I am afraid that it is more likely that as he grows up people about him will make him discontented with his humbler position. Meantime he is quite delighted at the coming move to Fatehghar where Dr. Login goes with him and where Tom Barlow, your cousin Willy's cousin, is to be his companion.

Let us always have happy accounts of your conduct and, my boy, try to shew us how well you can write. I thank Uncle and Aunt for sending your letters just as they are written and I do not want you to put off writing till you can get pens and ink and leisure to write slowly. But I do not like to see how little care you take in writing to us. You slant your letters away with such long heads and tails that they are hardly legible.

January 5th, 1850

We have had a great many visitors, both in the house and to dinner. Indeed we have dined alone but once, since Papa returned from Kashmir. One visitor we are very glad of is William Arnold who remembers you at Fox How and whom I hope you remember, for I should like you while you live to remember that you passed your ninth birth, 1847, at Fox How amidst the scenes so dear to that wonderful and good man, Dr. Arnold.

I wrote to you about the chiefs who were seized on October 1st, because they had broken the terms of the promise on which they had been allowed to live at their own houses. A few days ago they left this place under an armed escort to go to the Fort of Allahabad. Moolraj too was sent at the same time and so all those who a year ago were fighting against the Government are now sent out of the Punjaub. And now we earnestly hope and pray that a time of peace is come, that the Government will be able to attend to making roads and canals and improving the conditions of a poor people who for years, aye for generations, have been ground down and oppressed by armies marching through their country. Papa would indeed be happy if he could see the country, [which] he has a large share in ruling, great and prosperous. A good soldier always loves peace. And if Christians govern the people

★The same Dr. Login, afterwards Sir John Login, who was physician to the king of Oude (see Chapter Eight).

justly and mercifully there may be a hope that they may think our religion the true one.

Poor little Maharajah Dhuleep Singh is also gone. He went off as merry as a cricket, delighted with the bustle of marching, and riding gallantly with his hawk on his wrist. He is, I believe, rescued from much misery, to be placed under kind good treatment, but still there is something melancholy in the complete breaking up and sweeping away of a powerful Government.

By the time you are reading this Harry will have a little brother or sister to play with.

Lahore, March 31st, 1850

You are still feeling bitter cold in England, I suppose. Here the heat is just beginning. We have got up the *punkahs* which is not as pleasant an event in the year as taking them down in October. However we hope not to be here in the hottest part of the year, though where we shall go is uncertain. We hope to Kashmir. I should like to see that strange and beautiful country and write to you about it.

Twelve

The First White Woman in Kashmir

Honoria continues her journal to her son Alick in England who is now nearly twelve. Her youngest child, Honoria Letitia (Honey or Norah) was born on April 26th, 1850. In June she set off for Kashmir with her baby daughter and Dr. Hathaway to join Henry and Harry who have gone on ahead. Kashmir was an outlying part of the Sikh dominions which became a separate native state as part of the settlement at the end of the First Sikh War. Henry Lawrence had been travelling in Kashmir on a working holiday. His health benefited from the climate and it was useful for him to see those mountainous regions for himself.

Lahore, June 13th, 1850

Papa set out on the 3rd taking brother Harry with him. I am to go from Wazirabad to Bhimb and Papa is to meet me at Pir Panjal pass, 10,000 feet high. No white faced woman has ever visited Kashmir,* nor had any entered Nepal till I went there.

Kashmir, July 3rd, 1858

On the morning of June 17th at daylight we reached the foot of the hills, Bhimbur, where Maharajah Ghulab Singh had ordered all to be ready for me. The heat was stifling, and I felt weary and worn after twelve hours in the *palkee*. Only for the hope of soon meeting Papa and Harry in a cool climate I could have laid down and cried. But we soon got a kettle boiled, a goat milked and a delightful cup of tea, on the strength of which I was able to set off once more. We had now got hill men to carry us, strong, active, and sure-footed as goats. The litter

*It was almost a dead heat but Honoria has priority by a narrow margin. A very pretty, brave and eccentric British young lady, travelling with a young man whom she seems to have kept at a distance from her bed, entered Kashmir by a circuitous route through Tibet and met the Lawrences on her journey. This strange incident is not mentioned in Honoria's journals, but it is described on pp. 394–7 of *Honoria Lawrence* by Maude Diver.

used in Kashmir is about four feet long by three feet wide and extremely comfortable no doubt for people who know how to sit like tailors, and rest by leaning forward. But I looked with dismay at being put like a dish of cold meat on a tray, and determined to remain in my own *dhoolie* as long as possible. 'Tis but a rough looking thing made of bamboos lashed together with a coarse curtain thrown over. But it is long enough to lie down in. And *Dhai* was exceedingly delighted at being promoted to the tray that had been sent for me painted and guilded like a Lord Mayor's coach.

Our course, for there was no road, lying just along the bed of a river and then up and down, over huge boulders, and up and down such steeps as no one without seeing could imagine. It was up this very road that Papa brought a Sikh army with artillery in the year 1846 when the former Governor of Kashmir Sheikh Imanm-oo-deen refused to give up the kingdom to Ghulab Singh.★ The large force that Papa brought prevented any bloodshed. When the Sheikh found he was to be thus dealt with, he surrendered and disclosed the plot of Lal Singh, the Vazir at Lahore.

The road to Kashmir has been little of a throughfare since the downfall of the Mogul Empire, but in the palmy days of Akbar and some of his descendants the emperors resorted thither for the hot season. Try and get *Bernier's Travels*. He tells of his journey with Shah Jehan from Delhi to Kashmir, of all the pomp of that time nothing remains, save the halting places built at about every ten miles for the emperor. These exist still, some in absolute ruins, some partly habitable, all built on the same plan: a large open quadrangle, corridors, serving for stables and such like running along two sides, the side facing the gateway containing the royal apartments. The material is stone with a small proportion of brick, scarcely less durable. The cement where it still holds, seeming as indestructible as either. Yet decay has been here. In some places where the site chosen has been near a stream, the sudden torrent seems to have carried away some of the foundation. Elsewhere a seed has fallen in a crevice and the roots of a tree have gradually loosened the stones that battering rams could hardly have brought down. About two hours ascent brought us to the Ada Tuk, the summit of the first range of hills, lying between the plains and the level land of the valley.

Ghulab Singh has this year built halting places for European travellers. Oh what a falling off! In one corner of the old Serai enclosure are four earthen walls with earthen floor, rough plank

★After the First Sikh War it was agreed between the British and Sikh governments that Ghulab Singh should be the Maharajah of Kashmir but the Vazir, Lal Singh, who was the lover of Ranjit Singh's widow, tried secretly to keep Ghulab Singh out by supporting the former governor.

ceiling and doors; such is the place that now felt a welcome shelter. All along the bungalows were much of the same fashion and to improve their comfort the clay floor had just previous to our arrival been well soaked with water and covered with a coarse white cloth so that every step one sank as on snow.

As to provisions, we have never seen bread since we left the Punjaub, beef in every form is prohibited under a Hindoo king, the mutton and Punjaub poultry are very poor and the fish indifferent. But as we approached the valley we began to get fruit and ice, and now daily feast on these and somehow continue to live very comfortably with the help of such English stores as we brought with us.

The fame of an English *hakim* (Doctor) soon spread. Dr. Hathaway had medicines with him and was surrounded by patients. Here he removed a cataract from one woman's eye, and had many other cases. At every stage indeed he has been besieged by sufferers and here has quite a dispensary.

The rest of this halting place was broken by a visit from a great man Jowahir Singh, the Rajah of Poonch, son of Dhyal Singh and nephew of Ghulab Singh. See as to these brothers, Papa's book, *The Adventures of an Officer in the Punjaub*. The Rajah had, I am sorry to say, been waiting to meet me at Ada Tuk the previous morning. Dr. Hathaway then told him I was tired and probably asleep in the *dhoolie*. Unfortunately not knowing this I put out my head and asked for some water and then the Rajah said he had seen I was awake. With many apologies for my fatigue and so forth the interview was then staved off. But now he sent a messenger saying that he had been waiting for twenty days, having come all the way from Poonch in hopes of even a moment's interview. I sent my best compliments *"bohut, bohut, salaam"* that I should be happy to see him. The envoy brought a present of unripe mangoes, apples, and apricots with some bags of rupees. Any eatables may be taken and our servants were too happy to get them ripe or unripe. About the rupees there was the usual fight, I reminding him that we could not keep such a thing. I was really loath to take the money, which probably the Rajah could ill spare, merely to have it transferred to our government's treasury. This time I escaped taking the money. Gholam Ally Shah had been sent to meet us at Ghimitur and take charge of my camp all the way up. He is a portly middle-aged Mussulman of gentlemanly manners and few words, who took excellent care of me. Riding or walking alongside of my *dhoolie*, getting provisions etc. Shah Jee, as he is familiarly called, was master of the ceremonies and, among other merits, understood my unidiomatic Hindustanee, and polished up my broken sentences into proper court guise, when I was conversing with any of the great folk we met on our progress. Shah Jee had it now much at heart that the

Rajah should be received with due honour, that Dr. Hathaway should go to the proper distance to meet him, "at least half a mile the Rajah was entitled to." "Might not a hundred yards do in the heat of the sun?" "If the Doctor will alight from his horse that might do." Then "the Rajah must sit by the lady's right hand, his son opposite." It was comical enough to have these étiquettes arranged upon a mud floor, the seats being some cane stools and pack thread *charpoys*, over which I spread a shawl. Presently I saw winding towards the green bank rising on the opposite side of the stream by which we were located a host of matchlock men, spearmen and orderlies, some on foot some on rough little ponies, all scampering about as if to increase the importance of the interview.

On an elephant in a silver *howdah* sat the Rajah and his son. The doctor rode forth to meet them, both parties dismounted with due formality and embraced and then proceeded to the hut where I was sitting. I rose, met the Rajah at the door, shook hands with him and his son – I was spared the embrace – desired them to be seated, and we had some of the usual conversation. "Are you well?" "Perfectly." "Are you happy?" "Through your kindness I am." "This is a beautiful country your highess has got." "Not my country, but yours. I am but your servant." After a brief time I said "I am but a traveller and must soon move. So your highness may go." "Not till you have received something from me." "Have I not received your fruit and your kindness?" "But this is for your daughter." "Quite impossible." "Nay in the way of friendship." "Is it not friendship to bring my children here?" and so we went on much as if we had been acting a charade, ending however, in the Rajah actually leaving on the threshold two great bags of rupees, though we escaped the shawls and the pearl necklace. The money was a charge till we got here and could make it over to the treasurer. A sample of every meeting with a chief, amusing for once or twice, but becoming very tiresome.

Papa is better, and becoming more so, but he cannot in a few weeks shake off the fatigues and cares he has so long undergone.

Kashmir, July 13th, 1850

On such a day as this I long for you beyond the power of words to express, that you might share with us the beauty, almost beyond that of earth, of the scene we are in. It is noon, but under the broad shade of the *chenar* trees we do not feel the sun. We are in one of the old imperial gardens formed in terraces between the mountains that surround part of the lake and the lake itself, a slope of about a quarter of a mile. Down this a stream flows in an artificial channel bordered on each side with gigantic *chenars*. At each successive terrace, the water tumbles down an artificial cascade. The whole length of the stream is studded with fountains. Above each flight of steps leading from terrace to terrace, something of a pillared portico, with rooms on either hand.

I am now seated in my *dhoolie*, or litter, which is set down close to the fountains. To my right I look up the stream to a line of swelling hills, clothed with grass, but with masses of rock protruding. To my left I look through the pillars and still follow the stream with its bordering *chenars* till it is lost in the lake. Next come two tiny islets connected by a bridge, the arch of which terminates the vista. Beyond, the view expands. The lake lies like a mirror, bordered by green upland and orchard, beyond which rise conical isolated hills. And beyond all, quivering and twinkling in the noonday mist, rises the snowy battlement that we crossed in order to reach this happy valley. The hills crowned with snow, and the blue sky with its fleecy clouds hardly distinguished from one another. Among the trees near us is a group of Kashmiris with their picturesque flowing drapery, some standing, some sitting in all sorts of easy, graceful attitudes, commenting on our white skins and uncouth dress. Some children, just such as Murillo would have delighted to paint, are playing with a flock of goats, and now and then one making a rush towards the fountains, partly for the fun of a sprinkling, partly to get a nearer view of us. Under the trees stand horses and mules picketted. Our servants in the many coloured garments sit, stand, and lounge. Close to my *dhoolie* Papa lies stretched on a *charpoy*, reading. Harry runs about in ecstasy pitching some tiny tents sent him by the king, just big enough for him to creep into when they are pitched. And beside me lies sister in her own little swing cot, which makes a snug nest for her whether sleeping or waking.

We have been for a week past in another garden house also bordering on the lake. There we had a spacious verandah, supported on pillars of polished black marble, all evidently the work of Italian artists, who in the days of the emperors beautified Agra with the Taj and other monuments.

This morning after an early breakfast we got into our boat, such a fairy-like skiff, long, narrow, sharp at either end. In the centre a cabin open all round with lattice work to close at pleasure. Thirty or forty boatmen with green shovel-shaped oars pull us along, an oarsman at either end steering. No necessity for turning the boat as either end is bow and stern.

I was called to go and look at the fun in the large pond just below bordered with green sward, and there was Papa, the doctor and Harry tumbling about like porpoises. He had on a swimming belt with which he floated merrily about in water about four feet deep, making off however when Dr. Hathaway turned the gush from a great fountain right against him. Harry sends you a snake skin which I hope will be an acceptable contribution to your museum.

August 10th, 1850

We have got what is my great delight, an out-of-door life. Close to the garden house which is our headquarters is an avenue, a mile and a half long, perfectly straight, about fifty yards wide. It is bordered on either side by poplars standing like lines of soldiers, not one wanting in the ranks and their height equal from seventy to eighty feet. Poplars they are but such Brobdignag ones that nothing you have ever seen called by the name can give you much notion of them. Under these trees the ground is carpeted with green sward kept close by the nibbling of the sheep. At one end the vista terminates in a barren, rocky hill, on the top of which stands a lonely grey temple of great antiquity and, from its peculiar elongated dome, evidently of Hindoo origin. But the Mahommedans as they conquered, gave all places and events as far as possible a Mahommedan version and accordingly this hill is named the Tukht-ee-Sooleeman or throne of Solomon. And there is a legend of Solomon, whom they chiefly consider to be a wonderful magician, having built the temple by magic.

The other end of the vista is lost in green fields and picturesque huts, thatched with the long reeds of the lake. At this end of the avenue are offsets, clumps of the *chenar* tree and under the shade of these I have taken up my abode for all except sleep. *Sutrinjees*, thick cotton carpets spread on the ground, and an awning supported by tall poles overhead. A camp table, a wicker chair, and a couch, a gaily painted *charpoy* belonging to the Maharajah, with shawl, scarlet bedding and coverlid.

Honey has fairly played herself to sleep and I am tired too of laughing. Two or three hours ago a man and boy came up the poplars, leading a bear, a monkey, and a goat. I don't much fancy these exhibitions, but this man looked so good natured with his black beard, and white teeth, and parti-coloured raiment that I yielded to Harry's desire to see the fun. Bruin was a remarkably large and intelligent fellow, and his master and he seemed very affectionate. The man said the bear was eight years old, had been caught young, and had never been beaten. The monkey was like other monkeys, which I greatly dislike looking at when tamed. The goat had a glossy black skin and a necklace and tassels of cowrie shells and scarlet worsted. They went through the usual tricks and soon had a large audience. The sentries whom the king rather persecutes me with, intending to guard every step I take, rested on their long matchlocks, and grinned with delight. Our own Afghan horsemen, the most picturesque of mortals, with their regular Jewish features, flowing beards, massive turbans, and profuse drapery looked more "melancholy and gentlemanlike" but equally well pleased. The sound of the drum had attracted a crowd of Kashmiris. They always remind me of the Spanish peasants in Murillo's paintings. Just the same lazy, well fed, dirty, good humoured, grateful look. And the children are perfectly beautiful, with large black eyes and drooping lids and skin not much darker than Spaniards, and the extraordinary easy polished demeanor that we are accustomed to connect with high rank. The women have coarse features. They do all the hard work, and soon look aged but with all that they step out in all their rags and dirt with an air that I can fancy like Mrs. Siddons. There was soon a crowd gathered to look at the bear etc., not the least part of the spectacle being little Sissy's delight, as she crowed and clapped her [hands] and was set to take a ride on Bruin's back, her little waxen hands grasping his rough hide, while his master led him along.

Kashmir, August 21st, 1850

Dear Papa has gone on a tour on the Chinese frontier. Ladakh, Iskardo, Gilgit. I get his letters almost daily. He is greatly enjoying the strange land he is in and gathering strength daily. He is moreover doing all he can to heal enmities and to relieve oppression among the tribes.

Today is Papa's and Mama's wedding day. Yes, thirteen years have we been married and each of those years have drawn us closer together. Great was [sister's] delight on the present occasion. As great as that of her *dhai*, a fine tempered, handsome, young woman, who will soon be sorely encumbered with all her jewels. She has high pay and no expenses, and all her spare money is turned into jewellery. Tinkling and shining she looked very pretty in her drapery of white muslin edged with scarlet.

Just here I was interrupted by a visitor, not a very wealthy one, but one to whom I stood up and shewed all respect. He is called the Shah-Sahib and is descended from the ancient Moghul Emperors. He is a well-bred intelligent man. He brought according to his small means a small offering, a china cup, a paper fan, and a small packet of incense. I asked him about Solomon and his throne here, telling him that Solomon was mentioned in our Holy Book. He said he was a great king and a magician. That as he was flying through the air, he passed over this valley, which was then a lake and the hill now called Tukht-ee-Sooleeman standing up as an island on which he alighted, and kissing the place sent for a jin – demon – and ordered him to clear the surrounding hills. Whereupon the Bara-moola Pass was opened, and the lake was drained off by the river Jhelum. The jin's name was Kash and his wife's Meer and the valley was called after them. I asked the Shah-Sahib if, as he was a great scholar, he had ever read our Holy

Book, which is translated into Persian. He replied yes, and it was a pure doctrine. He was ready to talk on the subject. Indeed I never met with an educated Hindoo or Mussulman, who had any objection to listen or even to assent to what we say. But then they had "That doctrine is good for you. Our own and our own fathers' faith is for us."

For some weeks the heavy rains swelled the streams into torrents carrying away the bridges and cutting off our intercourse with the plains for ten or fifteen days at a time. The Jhelum river, which flows through this valley, flooded all the surrounding country and for some days people went in boats from one place to another. When it had somewhat subsided, the first time I went out in a boat we glided among trees up to their waists in water over fields of Indian corn with the heads just visible and close to houses built on piles, now standing like islands. I believe no lives were lost and but little damage was done. The people are prepared for such inundations which are rarely accompanied by wind and, as there is a long level for the Jhelum to flow over before it comes near Srinagar, the capital city, it does not rush violently. Even a flood is managed quietly in this quietest of places. The very mosquitoes instead of buzzing sharply and making a fuss about what they are doing, alight quietly, and look about them before they begin to bite. The only exception to this quiet is the noise of quarrelling. Both men and women make noise enough then, but do not seem ever to come to blows. A great part of the population live entirely upon the water. Long, large, unwieldly boats thatched over, not an uncomfortable dwelling in a climate like this. An earthen fireplace for cooking, a very rude spinning wheel, a hutch for fowls, a fishing net and a few earthen cooking pots seem the sole furniture. I don't know what becomes of the men belonging to these boats, for one seldom sees in them any but women and children.

The women here row stoutly and the children are quite amphibious. It is strange to see the swarms of little things, dark and shining like tadpoles in the shallow water near the banks. Rice is the principal diet, but they have no scarcity of fish, fowl and milk. The king does levy very heavy duties in kind, but still, provisions are cheaper than anything I ever met with. Fruit is a mere drug.

Since we came here we have had cherries, mulberries, apricots, melons, apples, pears and quinces. But the glory of the land is the grapes like "the clusters of Eschol". It is a treat even to look at them. What will it be by and by to eat them? The vines grow to the height of sixty or seventy feet, climbing up and along rows of poplars. The poorest cabin is beautified by its vines, and as we glide down the stream in a boat, the clusters of grapes actually hang over into the water where we could pluck them. But there is no temptation to steal what is so abundant. You might as much think of stealing hips and haws in England.

Kashmir, August 23rd, 1850

Last evening came the English mail with your letter from Dublin of June 30th. I can think that I see you and the girls landing at Kingston, though I can hardly believe in the stick-ups and shooting coat that have made such men of you and Willie.

Aunt Hayes* sent Harry a carriage and four. You can hardly imagine the sensation it creates here where no sort of wheeled conveyance was ever seen.

This afternoon, as we sat under our poplar shade, I received a visit from an old *mullah*, or Mahommedan priest, an old man that is a treat to look at. This old man is seventy years of age and has a beautiful snowy beard. He is dressed in perfectly clean white clothes, with a neat white turban and a staff in his hand. Papa had sent and procured for him with some difficulty a pair of spectacles, which arrived from Lahore yesterday, and he came to receive them. He spoke only Kashmiri and Persian of which I know but a few words, so our interpreter was Meerza, who could not help claiming my admiration for his *choga* of English stamped flannel, which he valued as much as I should a Kashmir shawl. Of course a large following accompanied the visitors, and the *mullah* said he had heard of the arrival of the English carriage, and begged to see it. He had once been in the plains in his youth, but had never seen anything on wheels. The Meerza had never been out of Kashmir. So there was Harry in great glory explaining the mystery of a coach and horses and, of the lady and gentleman sitting in it. I rather think the *mullah* is convinced that in England the carriage seat has a sharp iron spike, for the passenger to sit on, just as he saw in this carriage. For as there are no roads in Kashmir, nothing but footpaths, he could not understand how a carriage could be drawn along by horses, without the people in it falling out. Harry who has picked up Kashmiri very quickly was all energy explaining the matter to the *mullah* and Meerza. Were it not for writing and talking to Harry, I might forget the English language in this place. I feel the benefit of being obliged to talk Hindostanee and of listening to its being read to me.

The said Meerza is gentleman-in-waiting at the court, and he brings the court circular regularly to read to me. This is the style of it:

"On the 10th day of the month the king worshipped as usual in his own temple, and then gave audience. Sirdar – Thakoor Dass offered for a monopoly of soap. He said 'O king. I am a well wisher to the

*Henry's sister Lettice had married the Rev. H. H. Hayes.

state, and for the royal benefit I offer to pay fifteen thousand rupees a year for the privilege of being the only one allowed to sell soap.' The king was pleased and put his seal to the bargain. A beggar came up and said 'O king, I have been trying for three days to come and present my petition but the guards sent me away.' The king said 'It is not good to oppress the poor,' and made the soldier give the beggar some money.

"It was then reported to the king that the great and illustrious Lady Lawrence on the preceding evening went out as usual in the royal barge with her children. She was very happy, but said the evening was cold, and so she turned back before she reached the last bridge. This morning intelligence came that through the good fortune of having the noble, the excellent etc., etc., Sir Henry Lawrence here, a son has been safely born to the *Meean* (king's eldest son). There was great joy. The *Meean* according to custom went to conceal himself, being ashamed, but the king said 'O my son this is a great happiness, do not hide your face.' Then the *Meean* came out. Gifts and feasts were sent to all the priests, the Mahometan as well as Hindoo. All prisoners who were in for heavy crimes were released, and the Brahmins were ordered to cast the horoscope of the new born child, before fixing his name. The king sent a new suit of clothes, very fine to the mother, and others less beautiful to all the ladies of the establishment."

In a boat on the Wuller Dal or Great Lake of Kashmir, Thursday
September 19th, 1850, 11 a.m.
At daybreak Papa left me at Sopur for a circuit by land in the neighbouring hills. I stood for the last time in the balcony overhanging the river. The Jhelum here is about as wide as the Thames at Richmond. We looked down it at the rude bridge supported on piles, at the shabby and ruinous but still picturesque town of Sopur, where the whole population were turned out to look at us. Down away, away the windings of the clear stream; its banks sloping green into the water, flocks and herds grazing the rich pasture; villages nestling amid clumps of trees, fields ripe for the harvest, of every shade of yellow, brown and cinnamon, orchards of apple, quince, and pear loaded with fruit thickly as the berries on a holly branch, the grape vines festooning among them. Overhead a sky, such as England could not see, forming a dome that seemed on every side to rest on the surrounding hills, whose sides were sometimes barren and rocky, in other places undulating, clothed with green, their summits bristling with forest and the highest peaks glistening with snow.

With Harry and Norah embarked on our pinnace, long, low and narrow with the cabin rising in the centre, the roof flat and railed round, where I have spent many a pleasant hour gliding about on these beautiful waters. It was not eight o'clock yet, when I asked some questions of our Commodore Mulfuttah and he opened his store of learning. He is a good looking middle-aged man, dressed in a loose gown and turban, very dirty, intelligent and talkative. He stood on the upper step of the ladder leading to the sort of poop whereon I sat and leaning over the low rails thus began:

"Long, long ago, on the top of that low hill which you see over there lived a Peer (saint). Where the lake now is was then all land cultivated like a royal garden. For his prayers and good deeds it was given to the Peer – his name was Baba Shooken-oo-deen – to know future events, and he told the people of the valley of a flood that would come to punish them for their sins, that all who wished to escape must flee to the mountains, taking only what they could carry on their backs, and never look back to what they had left. Most laughed at him. A few listened. They fled and escaped. Among the inhabitants was a *koomar* (potter), a good man and just, regular in prayer and giving alms to the poor. He and his family fled. All they carried with them was a little victuals, and the wheels and other implements required for his trade. Some of his family when leaving looked back. They were carried away by the flood. Some went halfway and then just looked back for a moment, but the potter himself went right on till he reached the mountains. When he took the load off his shoulders it seemed very heavy. When he opened it lo! all was turned to gold. His children came up and as each put down his load there was gold in it, some more and some less. Then they remembered where each man had looked back. He who had looked back halfway had half his load gold half earth, and thus each man found a reward according to his obedience."

Several of our servants had gathered round and applauded the tale. Then said Mulfuttah, I can tell another, if the lady will give me permission, far more wonderful. "Speak on" said I and he began:

"After the flood the whole lake was governed by a snake named Burnâg. He had great power and wisdom and dwelt in the middle of the lake.

"Why should the lady smile? Why should her servant tell a lie? This is no tale of mine. Every one in Kashmir knows it. I heard it from my father and I teach it to my son.

"At this time a stranger came, no one knew from whence. He went to a fisherman whose boat was moored by the shore and said to him, you are a poor man, take me in your boat and shew me where Burnâg dwells, and I will give you ten thousand rupees. The fisherman consented, and took the stranger to the spot in the midst of the lake where the snake had his dwelling where the water bubbles up to this day.

"There the stranger took out a book. He read, he made signs, he repeated charms, and then plunged into the water. In about an hour he returned bearing with him the snake, about as long as my finger, and as thick as a reed. He put Burnâg into a *lota* (a metal water pot) and shut the lid close, lighting a lamp underneath. Now said he I shall be king of the lake, and make Burnâg my servant. But I must go and catch his children. You sit here O fisherman, and watch the *lota* and you shall have another ten thousand rupees. So he said and plunged again into the water. The fisherman sat watching the *lota* when Burnâg spake and said to him: 'O my brother, open the vessel and let me go. The stranger has promised you ten thousand rupees. This is little to what I can give. Let me go my brother.' Then the fisherman listened to the snake. He blew out the lamp and opened the vessel. 'Now,' he said, 'before I let you go tell me what I am to receive.' 'Let me into the water,' said Burnâg 'and the first thing you see floating on the water take up and it will be wealth beyond counting.' So, he let the snake go; and lo! as he gazed on the water a quantity of charcoal came floating by. Then he wept and said 'Burnâg has deceived me, he promised me much wealth, and here is charcoal.' And he wept again. His wife was sitting by, and she was a wise and careful woman and said: 'Take up the charcoal my husband, I want some for my fire-pot,' (*rungaree*). But he grew angry and said 'Burnâg has deceived me, I won't touch this charcoal.' 'I will,' said she, and she gathered some before it floated past.

"Then as they looked, they saw rise from the water the head and the limbs of the stranger. So they knew the snake had slain him. Then the woman went to put some charcoal into her *rungaree* and behold it was all turned to gold. She approached her husband and said, 'It was you who refused to listen to me when I told you to gather the charcoal, then we should have had much more wealth.'"

Mulfuttah then paused, and I asked "What happened next?"

"After that, please your ladyship, Burnâg had a son and daughter. He wished them both to marry, and he sent them forth saying: 'Search for a good place for me to dwell in. Go to the lake above us and the lake below and bring me word again.' The daughter brought word and said: 'The Manns Nag Bul★ (a small lake at some distance) is a good place. Go there my father.' And he said, 'You have spoken truly, and you shall marry Manns Nag, the snake of the lake. The son went to the other lake and saw that it was large, with clear sweet water, and he said in his heart I will be king here. Then he came back to his father and said, 'That lake is full of weeds and stones, the water is bad, it is not fit for you to go to, my father.' Burnâg answered: 'You have told a lie and now you shall dwell in that lake. It shall become even as you said, and

★Now called Manastral.

you shall dwell there and become Manns Nag's servant evermore.' And so it is to this day. The place is called 'Khooshapoor', the place of gladness. At first it was so called because of its beauty and is now so called in ridicule."

"A very pleasant tale," said I, "but are there nowadays any *fakeers* like those of old times?" "None, none in our time," said Mulfuttah. "All men cheat and tell lies and no such men can be *fakeers*."

By the time Mulfuttah had ended his tale we were in the middle of the lake and going so slowly that I said, "I think Mulfuttah you have forgotten to salaam to the *fakeer*, and the boat is stopped." "No", said he, "but now we are near Burnâg's dwelling." And in a few minutes we stopped where the water looked dark with a rippling, bubbling, spring rising. "There is Burnâg's house," said Mulfuttah, and thereupon every man in the boat threw out a handful of rice and sugar to him. Sister's *dhai* in great haste opened a bundle, and took out a little sugar to throw. I stopped her and said, "Your master gave you a *boodkee*, a Venetian gold coin, when baby cut her first tooth. Throw that to Burnâg if you care about his favour. He will take sugar and rice from those poor men, but depend upon it he knows that you have gold." She laughed and said, "I won't give away what my master gave me."

Thirteen

Hills and Plains

Henry Lawrence liked to go on tours of his enormous kingdom during the cold weather. Honoria goes to meet him on his return from one of these tours and describes how she and the children accompanied him on another tour. They travelled with a large retinue but it was smaller than most people in their position would have taken with them. On tour, Henry had a rest from fierce disagreements with his brother John, which were the more painful because the brothers loved each other. This journal is addressed to Alick.

Lahore, November 6th, 1850

Dear Papa has not been so well for some days. He has double work now as Uncle John is absent and there is much of the public work of a very annoying kind. Government do not very often take his view of what is just and kind to the people. He has however been able to avert many harsh measures, and the peace of the country continues.

Lahore, November 20th, 1850

The sickness of this year is quite unexampled in my experience of India. Such has often appeared at one or two stations from local causes, but now it extends from Peshawar to Delhi. Our house has been an absolute hospital and I rejoice to say all our patients are better, thanks to Dr. Hathaway.

Papa is bestirring himself even more than usual about the jails, where the sickness has been great, and it requires no small watching to make the keepers attend to the wants of these poor wretches. So Papa has been pouncing in at unexpected hours morning and night.

What are called the "gay doings" of the cold weather are now beginning, but I feel so sick at heart from all the suffering around, that such doings are even more than usually distasteful to me.

Lahore, Sunday February 23rd, 1851

My own son, the thoughts that fill my soul regarding you are pre-vailingly solemn and anxious now that you are on the eve of so great a move as that to a public school. We will ask Aunt to get a copy of Arnold's sermons to give you from us.

Shalimar Gardens, Lahore, March 5th, 1851

We have moved our camp out to these gardens, in hopes that the change of air will remove the obstinate low fever which for more than a month has hung about Papa. Our new house is springing up quickly.★ The cookroom is just outside. The house stands on a *chabootra* or raised platform about twelve foot high. The centre room is the original native building, lofty and domed, into which we have put a skylight. The rooms and verandah all round, we are building. They are twenty-four feet high. Every bedroom has its bathroom, for here we should be very uncomfortable if we did not go into a bath every day. We have a place built that does for either a fire place or a thermantidote; the latter being a huge box upon an axle, in the centre of which turns a wheel with fans, something like the sails of a wind-mill. The outer side of the box is filled up with a frame supporting a thick mat of *kus-kus*, kept constantly wet. The wheel going rapidly round carries in a tide of cool air through the mat, and sends a current into the house. Windows near the roof keep up the draught. And thus the temperatures may be kept as low as 80° in the hottest weather. For very large thermantidotes bullocks are used to turn the wheel; smaller ones a man can turn.

Lahore, May 15th, 1851

I have been very ill, and thought that I should die.

Lahore, July 12th 1851

I did not think last month that I should ever be able to write to you again, but God has again reprieved me from the very brink of the grave. At present I believe all alarming symptoms are over, but I have intense pain from rheumatic fever, which has left me only the use of my left arm.

Lahore, July 29th, 1851

Since I wrote you a few lines by the last mail I have greatly improved in health and strength, and am now sitting up to write. This letter will probably find you at Rugby. We have heard many particulars of the

★Their house was called Alhenho after their three children, ALick, HENry and HOnoria. See p. 227.

place from William Arnold⋆ who lived in the very house you are going to.

We are now preparing to set off for the hills, Kussowlee and Simla. At Kussowlee we hope to find Harry blooming and happy and to see our two hundred children at the Asylum thriving. I am glad you have seen the wonderful Crystal Palace.

Kussowlee, August 18th, 1851

Our journey is safely over and we are rewarded for its great discomforts by finding ourselves in a delightful climate. Could we choose our own part of India to live in there would be nothing left to desire in climate. Little sister looks very much the colour of a spermaceti candle, but I hope she will be very different in a week or two hence, for she is out of doors the live-long day. I am still very feeble, and feeling that I have had a crushing illness, but I am free from any severe pain.

While at Loodhiana we saw the American Mission, the girls' Orphan School, containing twenty children, seven of whom are among those Papa rescued from Kabul.

Kussowlee, August 27th, 1851

I am staying at the Asylum and enjoy the sojourn very much, having a set of rooms to myself where I can be quiet, looking at the school when I feel able. We have now ninety-six boys and sixty-five girls, all in excellent health. Some slight cases of ophthalmia are the only ones in hospital. The organisation is much like that of Rugby, I fancy, only with different names. The boys wear uniform like the artillery. The girls have checked gingham frocks with white bonnets and tippets.

We have just completed a building for the chapel and school room, one that we planned when we were up here rather more than two years ago. Mr. Parker had to design all, to teach the workmen, and indeed to shew them with his own hands how every thing was to be done. The chapel is of pointed Gothic Architecture, all built of a durable grey stone and the fittings of cedar pine. We are soon to have a regular opening of it, which we hope will be largely attended and funds collected to go on with another building, a separate one for the girls. For this we want 15,000 rupees (£1,500), and we do not despair of collecting the money. If this building were completed, we could receive 400 children. Besides the school family, Mr. and Mrs. Parker have six children of their own and among these Harry has passed four months very happily.

⋆The son of Dr. Arnold, a member of the Indian Civil Service and the future biographer of Dalhousie.

Kussowlee, September 8th, 1851

It seems like your entrance on life that you should pass a birthday quite away from home. Now I must tell you how that day passed here. Harry was very full of its importance and of his own, too, in being master of ceremonies. There was a holiday in the school and each child got an *anna* (about three halfpence) which here purchased a fine amount of sweets. There was to be an illumination in the garden, oil lamps and Chinese lanterns of coloured paper.

In the evening the elder boys and girls were assembled in the garden. The plum cake was cut and distributed and your health was drunk in negus. I must not forget that all our servants too ate your health in sweet meats.

Kussowlee, September 18th, 1851

You say you were to enter Rugby on August 21st, and I inwardly rejoiced that such should be the day, for it is the anniversary of our wedding.

Yesterday was a pleasant day for us here. The first opening for Divine service of the New Chapel and the laying of the first stone of the girls' separate house. Sir William and Lady Gomm, our Commander-in-Chief and his wife, came to the opening. We hope to get the funds for the new building considerably enlarged by yesterday's doings. We have already got about three thousand rupees (three hundred pounds) and hope for more.

Lahore, December 31st, 1851

Papa was to arrive in the evening, so I went in the carriage to the Ravi, taking Honey and her nurse, while Harry galloped on his mule, Tim. The late rains had swept away the bridge of boats and now the river was covered with ferry boats, the banks gay with parties wanting to cross. Herds of bullocks, buffaloes, sheep were waiting by the brink and every few minutes a clumsy flat-bottomed boat pushed off with a freight of bipeds and quadrupeds. I was amused watching a fine looking young man with naked legs and shoulders who was waiting and, to pass the time, squatted himself down on the sand, opened a leather jar of *ghee*, took out a lump and stuck it on his knee. Then he unrolled a large dirty turban and shook down a head of hair like Absolom's, long curls almost smothering him. These he parted with his fingers and rubbed them with the *ghee*, till all the hair was saturated. The remainder of the grease he rubbed over face and neck, twisted up his hair and the filthy turban again over it, stood up and stretched himself before me, as much as to say "Don't I look well?" But I was chiefly looking across the stream across the long shadows of the four slender towers that adorn the tomb of the Emperor Jehangir at

Shaderra. The beautiful tomb raised over him by his beautiful wife Noor Mahal, who as a widow came to Lahore and here lived in retirement, spending her wealth on this tomb for her husband and a humble one beside it for herself.

Lahore, Christmas Day, 1851

We have just had a visit from Haidi Hoosein, a native gentleman for whom we have a great regard. Papa has known him for sixteen years and has gradually helped him on from being a writer in the survey to his present position as judge of the city of Lahore. He understands English perfectly, and Papa had been talking to him about the administration of justice, befriending the poor and not dreading the rich.

Camp Janee-Ke-sung, February 3rd, 1852

Here I continue the journal of which the first part was dispatched yesterday. I marked the package "paid throughout", and there was four rupees charged for steam postage. So I hope that it will reach you without any heavy pull upon your pocket.

Yesterday's was a long march, fourteen miles over rough raving ground, very trying to the feet of camels and elephants. The country is wild almost uninhabited, stony and undulating with a low scanty jungle of thorns and wild sloes. It is said to abound in wild hogs, very large and ferocious, that come in troops and root up such cultivation as there is. The villagers keep packs of a large hill dog with which they hunt the pig. Great numbers also of hares, and a good many grouse and partridge.

Our latest event is that we have a foundling added to our establishment, a little girl of four years old, whom two of our guards found yesterday with two men from Kabul, who could give only a very lame account of how they came by her and were contented to give her up. Probably, they had stolen her to bring her up as a slave. Papa is sending notices to all neighbouring towns, in case the child is enquired for, and if no one claims her we will send her to the missionary orphan school at Loodhiana. Child stealing, especially of girls, is a common crime throughout India.

One evening while at Rawul-Pindee, we were out for the air and were attracted by a crowd, seated in an open space. It was a *panchayat*, or assembly of elders to administer justice. The case was one of theft; a man accused of having stolen some jewels belonging to a woman. He stood up in the middle and vehemently denied the charge. Witnesses came forward to prove his guilt, and at last he acknowledged and actually produced all except a gold nose-ring. Night drew on so the court adjourned, the culprit giving security that he would appear the next day. In the midst of the circle was placed a pair of shoes with which I fancy punishment was to be administered by smiting on the mouth. But the *panchayat* possess stronger power than bodily chastisement. They can excommunicate a man, so that none of his kindred or friends will smoke with him or eat with him, and moreover they can threaten him with being handed over to the English courts of law, the delays and complications of which are looked upon with great terror. We were struck with the good temper and justice of the proceedings we witnessed. And they cost nothing, save that the plaintiff paid a rupee for the tobacco smoked during the conclave.

In many things the simple ways of the people are far more effective than our elaborate systems. As Colonel Napier* said the other day, when we noticed a very rude breakwater in the bed of a torrent, merely some bushes kept down with heavy stones, "Now, if I had been called on there, I should first have taken circles, then prepared a map and sections, next made an estimate and applied for an assistant. And my work might have been done next year."

Haripur in Hazara, February 8th
The road to this place has a great deal of beauty in the distant prospects. In every direction the crust of the earth is cracked, as an earth ball might be in baking, into fissures many miles in length and from fifty to two hundred feet deep. Sometimes nearly wide enough for the loaded camel, at others extending many yards, but always with the same dreary clay surfaces, "of the earth earthy". I believe a circuitous road avoids these ravines, but we got fairly into a network of them in our last marches. On the 3rd we marched from Janee-Ke-sung to Oosman Kalta, traversing the last of those low ranges of hills that intersect the Punjaub, pretty nearly East and West. This last pass bears the ominous name of Margulta, which being interpreted is cut-throat. The hills here are more rocky, less crumbly than in the other ranges and at this lowest part a passage has been cut through the rock, an extraordinary work, for the times it must have been done in viz. under the Moghul Emperors. Emerging from the pass a beautiful plain lay before us, almost surrounded by mountains, not the giants of Kashmir which though very grand rather overpower one. They are so large there is no taking them in in groups, but the Hazara hills are nowhere above ten thousand feet high, and they are grouped together so as to give every variety of tint from the deep brown to the far off delicate blue just tipped with snow.

Here we were greeted by Major James Abbott, an old friend and a remarkable man. About ten years ago he made a journey from Herat

---

*The future Field Marshal, Lord Napier of Magdala, the great constructor of roads and canals in the Punjab.

to Khiva to negotiate the liberation of some Persian slaves. A work of simple benevolence. Then by the Caspian to Russia and from St. Petersburgh to England. All which he has written in a very interesting book. He is now in charge of a district bordering on the Indus, and inhabited by a race of Mahommedans remarkable for their manliness and simplicity. It is a fair land watered by brooks that run out of valleys and hills and consequently exempt from the dearth so often caused by failure of rains.

It is grievous to see so goodly a country denuded of timber, but the Sikhs were thorough barbarians in destroying the trees of every country they invaded. Thousands and tens of thousands are now planted here, as everywhere else in the Punjaub, but these are for our successors to benefit by. Here in Hazara there are a profusion of orchards, limes, peaches, apricots etc. And the vine twines from tree to tree. There is no absolute poverty in the whole place. The people press to look at us, especially at me and the children, for till now only two ladies have ever visited Hazara.

Among these people Major Abbott lives as a patriarch. It is delight-ful to see a British officer loved and respected as he is and the province he administers, larger than all Wales, so peaceable and prosperous. I do not mean that he is perfect, for he has some failings that make it difficult to deal with him officially, and he gives Papa more trouble than many a man of not a tenth part the merit. The more so because Papa has so high a regard for him. Abbott is morbidly sensitive, and he has lived so long without coming in contact with other educated minds that he cannot apprehend any views but his own. He is aged about forty, small make, with eager black eyes and well marked features. I suppose it is many years since shears or razor approached him, and his hair and beard are silver white. A broad-brimmed white hat, coat and trousers made after the taste of a Hazara tailor, a spiked staff about seven foot long, and the whole man alive with energy, a remarkably sweet and gentle voice. He lost the two first fingers of his right hand at the time he was made prisoner on the shores of the Caspian.

I mentioned our little foundling, and now her mother has appeared. The men, from whom we took the child, had not stolen her but had, as they said, received from the mother three rupees to carry her to Peshawar. When talking on the subject they admitted she would be worth two horses, if they took her to Kandahar. The mother's story is characteristic enough. Imagine a weather worn, spare blind woman, not really I suppose more than forty, but so emaciated, shrivelled and sun burnt, that she might be sixty, her only clothing a tattered petti-coat, a coarse old sheet about her head and shoulders. She was seated on the ground, a fine lad, her son, standing by her, and the little girl nestling up to her recovered mother. She spoke in a low chanting tone, rocking her body to and fro, interspersing all with invocations to Allah and the Prophet, and prayers for blessings on us, stroking Harry and Honey with her poor withered hands. I sat beside her on a low chair and the servants gathered round to listen and to interpret, for her Hindustani was so mixed with Persian and Pushtoo, that I could hardly understand it.

"I am a *Hadjee*," that is a pilgrim to Mecca. "The fourth year is coming round when we set out on our *Hadj*, pilgrimage, to the holy city of the Prophet. We went forth eight. We return two and a half, myself my son and this child. We took our old parents to die at Mecca. On the road my husband died and my two brethren. We had saved some money and said in our hearts we will go to the holy place and obtain pardon for our sins. Happy are those who die in the city of the Prophet. They shall without doubt go to heaven. But they must go with their whole hearts.

"When they meet with hardship on the road, they must not say in their hearts 'Why did I leave my home to suffer this distress? He who says so has no merit. Am I not going on the service of Allah? Will he not care for me?'" "Very true" said my old *ayah*, "but a good man carries Mecca in his heart. Where the heart is clean, there is the holy place."

"Go on, my Mother" (*Maee* or Mother is the term used in addressing an old woman), said Ibrahim who, looking as handsome as ever, leaned over the *Hadjee* and interpreted where I could not understand, while Honey played with his sword and shield.

She went on, "We embarked on the Indus at Kababagh and got down to Bombay. There three rich Mahommedans chartered a ship for pilgrims. They fed us till we reached Mecca. One of them gave us bread and meat in the morning, one of them fed us at noon, the other at night. At Mecca every rich man gives alms to poor pilgrims. Since we left Mecca every good Mussulman has given us a morsel of bread for the sake of the Hadj. I became blind at Aden on my return. It was as if a curtain fell before my eyes, since then I have not seen even my hand. One by one my friends died. But by the help of Allah I reached Ferozepore. There a *syud* lent me a camel to take me to Lahore. I walked on and was weary carrying this child. So I agreed with two men from Kabul to carry her to Peshawar. They did not like going so slowly as I and left me behind. I went on after my child weeping as I went. A man met me and said 'Mother, why do you weep?' I answered 'Why should I not weep, when wicked men have stolen my child?' He answered, 'Is it not then your child of which notice is given in all our towns? Behold you will find her in the great man's camp.' So here I have come and found my lost child."

Hazro, February 14th, 1852

Papa quitted me the day before yesterday. I watched him with all the crowd of horse and foot that accompanied him down from our camp over the rough shingly ground and through the deep sand to the Indus, then into the boat across the river and through the sand on the other side, till he was lost among the hills.

We remained at Hazara for five days, all full of interest. Lord Stanley* came to us and is now gone on with Papa. He is a young man of great energy and intelligence. No beauty as to his outer man except a fine forehead and eyes. He is a Rugbyan and every one who does credit to that place seems in a manner a son to me. Lord Stanley absolutely devours information and in the few months he has been in India has learned more of it than many men do in a life time. Two or three very pleasant, intelligent officers joined us and I wished often you could hear the conversation. Lord Stanley telling of Nova Scotia, Jamaica, the United States and all Europe; Major Abbott about Central Asia, the people and their ways; Papa full of India, Burma, and China; conversation never flagged. Abbot is an enthusiastic antiquary and I was delighted with seeing his collection of antiquities and coins. He has dug up innumerable specimens of sculpture, from the purely Greek time on to when Buddhist traces are mingled with the Greek, yet still retaining the graceful form, and ending in the hideous many armed deformities of Hinduism. Not one of the images was perfect. The Mussulmen are devout image breakers, and every figure that is exhumed unless kept under a guard has its head knocked off or at any rate its nose. Countless numbers have been powdered up for lime. Indeed one is quite lost on thinking of the myriads that must thus have been destroyed, the tumuli and sites of old Greek and Bactrian cities serving as a mine during these thousands of years. And in like manner with coins, gold, silver, and copper which have been dug up and circulated and melted down having no value beyond their weight in metal until the last fifteen or twenty years when Europeans began to collect them.

Papa was busy upon the murder of Mr. Cain and Mr. Trapp and trying to apprehend the murderers. Some of the tribe among whom the murder was committed have been kept as hostages. Papa summoned Jehan Dad Khan the head of the clan and his minister Boostan Khan, both of whom have been suspected of instigating the murder but against whom there is no proof. The chief is a poor frightened looking creature. Boostan is a fine bold ruffianly looking fellow, who came in, knowing himself charged for his life, with the air of a prince,

*Lord Stanley (1826–93), 15th Earl of Derby, he became the first Secretary of State for India and later Foreign Secretary.

sat down on the ground and answered all Papa's questions in an easy off hand way that looked very much like innocence. I confess I was glad when the examination was over and the men let go, for they had a following of five or six hundred men, all stalwart fellows who had accompanied their chief and would have enjoyed exceedingly a good scrimmage with the chance of plunder. They sat and stood outside round the tent, and every now and then there was a stir among them that made my heart beat as I sat at the table with Papa, and I looked very suspiciously at Boostan, thinking that a dagger or pistol might be hid in his girdle. Papa, myself, the children and Captain Gordon were the only Europeans in the tent and, though we had a good escort, there was no extra guard placed. However, the whole went off as peacefully as any ordinary visit. How the affair will end is uncertain. Papa ended by saying to the elders of the tribe "If you give up the murderers they will be hanged, but your hostages will be released with honour and gifts. If you refuse to give up the murderers, the hostages shall be taken to Lahore, perhaps to Hindustan and I will come with an army to burn your villages and give your country to another." The old fellows folded their hands and said with some fun, "We should consider your presence an honour, but our country is rather a difficult one for your army." Papa dismissed them, and we heard a salute fired from over the water, when they arrived there safely. We earnestly hope that they will give up the murderers.

The next stage was to Torbela just above the Indus, a very beautiful little amphitheatre commanding a fine view of the hill Mahabund, supposed to be the Aornos of Alexander.

While on this frontier we travel with quite a little army. Most of my share of it I hope to dismiss tomorrow at Hussan Abdal. You would be amused to hear me, when we move, marshalling my troops. "Let ten horsemen and ten footmen keep close to the young lady's *palkee*. The young gentlemen are to be under the charge of the *kazee* and four horsemen. Let two horsemen accompany the elephant with the *ayahs*. The remaining troops divide in three, one party with the advance guard, another with the rear, the third to keep by my *dhoolie*." And so we go making a sad dust, but with no more molestation than you meet between no. 16 and Gile's shop. The case might be otherwise were we without our guard.

The valley of the Indus along which we have been travelling winds very much between rugged and lofty hills, about a mile apart. I am reading Chapman's Homer, carrying it in my *dhoolie* and often think whether Alexander read Homer on the very ground where I am now reading him. I never understood Homer till reading Chapman. Pope's translation wearies me, seems always like a piece of acting, but Chapman brings before one the very men and women. To return to the valley of the Indus. In former times, that is fifteen or twenty years ago, it was a perfect garden many miles in length. The stream winding among fields, the hills studded with villages and fringed with forests. Indeed these hills chiefly supplied the Punjaub with timber floated down the stream, and the valley swarmed with inhabitants. In the year, I believe, 1836 a tremendous shock was felt, whether it was the cause or effect is not known, but at that time a hill fell down between Chilas and Gilgit and blocked up the river, so that only a small stream trickled through and men passed on a high and dry road, where had formerly been the bed of a torrent. This lasted for four years. Then the people above Hazara heard one morning a dreadful noise and, while they wondered what it was, behold the whole valley where they dwelt was overswept by a torrent. The river had at last worked its way through the barrier and the accumulated waters of four years rushed down, filling the valley almost to the tops of the hills. Those few who escaped by getting to the top of the very summits, describe it as like a wall of mud advancing with a dreadful noise and smell, carrying along forests, villages, men and cattle. The flood subsided but left the valley what is now a perfect desert, a mass of stones and sand through which the river makes its way and the bordering hills without a tree. Gradually soil is forming in some recesses and cattle find scanty grazing. A few huts are rising and in the course of years the ruin may be forgotten. But now it is a wilderness of the most forbidding kind, the shingle and boulders making it dreadful work for the cattle especially elephants and camels. There was great difficulty in finding a tolerably clear space to pitch our tents.

The old *Hadjee* has left me today. I gave her over in charge to the *Moulvee* who is going towards Peshawar, and as a good Mussulman, will take care of her.

Camp Kala Serai, Monday February 16th, 1852
At Hassan Abdal I dismissed my footguard and a score of horse, the latter wild looking fellows, many of them clothed in chain armour with spear and shield. The armour is only for time of peace, being a terrible thing for the wearer when there is a chance of a gunshot wound carrying any portion of the armour into the body. These fellows looked well in steel caps, with heron plume and turban twisted round the brim, long matchlock slung behind, buffalo hide shield on the back, long spear in the right hand, long crooked sabre by the side. And the dress a mass of so many swathings and danglings that no European can imagine a man so encumbered, using his limbs.

Dummuk, February 27th, 1852
When travelling with Papa I took small heed of distances, provisions,

state of roads, and such like. But now I must be quarter master for the camp, and you would be amused at the arrangements I have to make and the complaints that come before me. The washerman comes in with a complaint that the water carrier has touched his food and so defiled it, which the carrier stoutly denies. I know it would be useless for me to find out the truth, so I say, "Summon a *panchayat*. Each choose two men and they choose a fifth. Then in the presence of your brethren let it be settled." In ten minutes the plaintiff and defendant come in quite satisfied. The award of the jury was that the water carrier was guilty and should pay three *annas*, the price of the defiled food. The washerman said, "He did not want the money. Only he could not put up with the insult." And so all were friends again.

Another day comes one of the guard to say that his wife's sister, a widow whom he supported, was coming to meet him on the road but was waylaid and carried off beyond Hazara. "Get the *pundit* to write a statement of your case and I'll send it to Major Abbott." This is done and it turns out that the lady had been carried off by her own consent. Another time I heard loud weeping and wailing and cries for *insaf* and *dohai*, justice and mercy. It is some villagers come to complain that one of the elephants got loose in the night and destroyed part of their crop. "Let the villagers be paid for their loss, and the elephant's keeper be fined." So in this little community is the law administered.

At Pukka Serai, the last stage, there had been some rain, but I thought it might clear, and set off. In an hour the cloud poured forth, and this in a country intersected by ravines, which shortly became the beds of torrents. The road such as it was, as slippery as if it had been soaped. I gave an hour's start to Honey's *palkee*, and hoped she would reach the tents before the worst of the rain came on. Harry and William cantered on. They must be drenched.

About halfway, in the midst of a ravine, I saw three of the camels sitting down under their loads, which the rain had made hopelessly heavy. A little further on three elephants were stuck fast in the slippery bog, and a crowd of men assembled with pick axes, bringing gravel and stiff clay from a distance, which the poor elephants had the sense to shuffle under their feet with their trunks. By this time darkness was coming on, and there was a bad prospect for the night.

It was about 8 p.m. when I arrived, and was thankful to find a tent pitched, though in the midst of a slush of wet. Honey was quite dry and warm. The boys had changed their clothes and were soon comforted by a cup of tea with a little brandy in it. The beds being well covered with tarpaulins were not very wet, and we all have flannel nightdresses. So to bed we went, my bed in a corner screened off. And as many servants as the tent would hold crouched in at the other side. Happily the stove had arrived and a blazing fire was very consolatory.

As I padded my way over a wet floor to a damp bed, I thought of all English notions of "a well aired bed" as one of the first requisites, and lay down with some misgivings.

The children were soon fast asleep, but I lay listening to the thunder and wind and very much dreading that the tent which had been hastily pitched in a loose wet soil might come down on us. How thankful I was when on awakening in the morning I heard all the cheerful little voices! Honey as merry as a cricket, and the boys answering "quite well" to my enquiries. And I could hardly believe when I stretched myself and found no rheumatism.

Khariyan, March 4th

There has been much rain. I have been sadly hindered on my road. However the rain has been a blessing to a thirsty land. As a native said to me yesterday, "Last week the crops were so high," touching his ancle, "now they are here," touching his knee.

Alhenho, Saturday March 20th, 1852

Pleasant as was the march, I was right glad to return to my own pleasant dwelling.

Lahore, Saturday April, 1852

Our grand event has been that dear Papa returned on the 15th after fourteen weeks wanderings, during which he had traversed thousands of miles and not met one accident or serious illness to himself or his camp.

Lahore, July 25th, 1852

Dear Papa keeps wonderfully well, and works almost as wonderfully hard as he did in the cold weather. He and his fellow labourers are now very busy drawing up a report of what has been done in the Punjaub since it became a British Province, with a sketch of the country and people. I suppose the documents will come before parliament next year, when the renewal of the Charter★ is discussed.

Unless there is any other work you prefer we should like to give you as a birthday present *Creasy's Sixteen Decisive Battles of the World* . . .

Lahore, October 17th, 1852

Do you ever hear people talk about emigrating? I mean people with any serious idea about going? We have lately been reading a great deal about New Zealand, and the Canterbury Settlement, and our hearts turn with great yearning towards that fine climate and young country,

★The Charter of the East India Company.

where we might live with our children. We have a vague idea of Papa's taking a year's leave and on going there to look at it. Would you like to go as a colonist? The climate braces people for work, and all have room enough. You may perhaps be beginning to understand the difficulty of finding room to work in England.

Lahore, October 31st, 1852

Riding on horseback is of great importance, and we would fain have you saddle and shoe your own horse. You cannot think how foolish and uncomfortable Lord Stanley looked for want of being a good horseman, when he was riding with Papa round the border. He lamed Papa's favourite horse for want of knowing how to manage him, and was sadly annoyed; indeed, I suspect frightened, when Nicholson or Lumsden or any of the young men with Papa proposed a scamper.

By this mail papa has written to Sir James Hogg, Nicholson's uncle, to ask a writership for you. Our thoughts about New Zealand are still too vague for us to be indifferent to your having India secured. We shall see how the new Charter★ affects the India service.

★The Charter of the East India Company.

FOURTEEN

Rajputana

At the end of 1852 Dalhousie moved Henry Lawrence from the Punjab to Rajputana (or Rajasthan) where he was to be Agent to the Governor-General. Here his duties were not to rule but to advise native rulers, who were independent in their internal affairs but recognised Britain as the Paramount Power. This gave the British representative vague but formidable powers. Henry exercised these tactfully but firmly. He and Honoria were cut to the quick when they were forced to leave the Punjab but in writing to Alick she expresses herself with restraint. As she put it in a letter to her friend, Emma Edwardes "I have given all my feelings chloroform and ignore all subjects but *rupees, annas* and *pice*".

Some of these letters are to Alick and others are to Harry who had left India to be with his uncle and aunt Bernard at Clifton.

January 1st, 1853

The last few days have changed the prospect of our lives a great deal. The Governor-General has written appointing Papa to Ajmere which is the capital of the Rajputana States. He is very sorry to leave the Punjaub, where his long experience fits him for greatest usefulness, and where he feels a personal interest in every chief and family, where too he has originated a number of great works which he hoped to carry out. Besides all this we give up the prospect of again seeing the Asylum. The change is therefore very far from our wishes.

We have got fairly into our hot weather way of life. At four o'clock the house is stirring. The children are called and before five they are washed, dressed, tea-ed, and out of doors. On the elephant go Honey, Mona, Billy and Marianne with *dhai* and a *chaprassi*. Harry and John go out to ride if they like. Otherwise they play in our own grounds, harnessing a goat to a little carriage working in the garden, visiting the stable or anything they like. After six they are confined to the western side where this tall house casts a shadow for many yards, where they play, but they must be in the house by seven. Meantime Papa and I have got up and generally sit in the beautiful western verandah to read and write, and I potter about the house seeing after the many things so large a family require and very happy and thankful thus to be able to occupy myself. At eight o'clock Bell comes to teach the children, and lessons go on, interrupted by prayers and breakfast till two o'clock. By one o'clock Harry's lessons are ended, and he too lies down for a siesta. One by one the children and attendants drop off, so that about two or three o'clock there is a lull all over the house. After three the little voices are heard again. Four o'clock dinner. Then play till nearly six – go out again as in the morning – home soon after seven, tea and bed. And the seniors do not sit up much later.

> Camp Hursuroo, twenty-four miles from Delhi,
> February 14th, 1853

This is the first time I have had the heart to begin a journal to you, although we have been travelling since January 21st. Harry's impending departure quite overcame me. Now it is over. Though I feel sorely bereft of him, yet can I better gather up my thoughts.

At 8 p.m. on February 10th he and Papa got the carriage. I stood at the door to watch what almost felt like a funeral going away, while the young moon set behind the trees. Papa took him as far as Aligarh, whence he turned off to Agra. And now I am altogether in a new world, where Papa never was, where I never was before.

Aunt Charlotte, Honey and I are in a tent pitched on the sand. All around are hillocks and plains and waves of sand. Just in one spot is a green patch of about half an acre of wheat, where a well affords water. We have a large camp, the Alwar Rajah, one of Papa's new lieges, having sent servants and troops to meet us. Sentries are pacing round, the horses are neighing for their evening food as they stand in their pickets. Herds of camels are snorting and munching their thorny supper, [with the men] hubble-bubbling as they squat down in a circle. And over all, the moon is shining. We travel, mamma in a *dhoolie*, aunt, sister and *ayah* in the carriage which is pushed by a score of men.

> To Harry, Camp between Delhi and Rewari, February 15th, 1853

You never saw such sand as we are come to, except what you saw for a mile or two on each side of the Ravi and Chenab. Here the whole country is such and our carriage with its narrow wheels sinks deep, where the native broad wheeled *gharrees* get on. My *dhoolie* is the best conveyance and gets on at the rate of three miles an hour. The carriage pushed by twenty men makes scarcely two miles. All about us is sand,

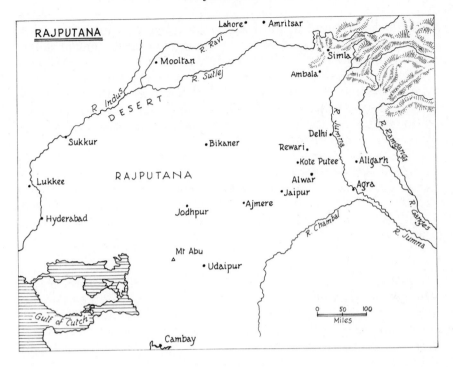

with a few stunted trees. Yet there are a great many wild peacocks, wood doves and green parrots.

To Harry, Rewaree, February 17th

We arrived here yesterday morning after a long night's march. I have had visits from some native gentlemen, who all ask about you. Thakoor Omed Singh, brother to the Alwar Rajah, whose territory we shall enter tomorrow, offers all his possessions and says his prosperity is blossoming since our approach. I asked one of these gentlemen if it looked like rain. "God never would send rain while your highness is travelling, but when you are safely housed your servants hope for rain." They have brought us some delicious oranges, quite different from those in the Punjaub.

Continued at Googul Kote, February 18th, 1853

We left Rewari at 5 p.m. last evening and got here, only twelve miles, after a pleasant march of only three hours by moonlight. I came in my *dhoolie*, having seen the carriage go off in grand style with Aunt, Beebee etc. The Rajah had sent eight horses, with comical harness of ropes and patches. An old coachman with a white beard and sky blue turban mounted the box. A half naked man with a long, bare, black, back mounted one of the leaders, and off they went followed by horsemen dressed in scarlet and green. We have entered a hilly country, reminding me of some of the hills we were among last year, only here we skirt among them instead of going through the passes. There are many fine trees still green, but the general face of the country is burnt up, sandy, and brown and a hot wind sweeps over it. At 2 p.m. in the tent the thermometer is just 90°. Last February we were glad of a stove lighted in the tent.

The sentry walks up and down looking very hot and, as soon as he is relieved, sits down and in two minutes strips off his English cap and coat and trousers and looks comfortable in his light white muslin clothes. A tray of toys has just been sent to Beebee, figures in clay, ivory, silver and gold. The latter I returned assuring the *thakoor* I could not keep them, and she is very happy with the others.

Monday February 21st

In the country we have come to, they no longer use the Persian wheel that you remember. The water is nearer the surface, the wells, I fancy, not more than thirty feet deep and the water is drawn up in the skin bags by a rope passed over a wheel and pulled by two bullocks walking down a slope.

An easy march of nine miles brought us to Kote Puttee, a very pretty place. The night was a lovely moonlight one and all was pleasant until we went to bed, and then we were sadly off for we were put into beds swarming with bugs. After midnight I got up and caught thirty-two, but this did not discourage the survivors.

The grove is full of living things, all tame and sociable, for we are now in a Hindoo country where animal life is respected. So there are swarms of peafowl, now bringing out their young ones to take the air and screaming most inharmoniously, ring-doves without number, cooing and walking close under our feet, squirrels running up and down like lightning, green parrots chattering, mynahs singing after their fashion and a pretty little tame bird hopping about, which I never saw before, like a robin redbreast with a black cravat.

March 3rd

Saw some real *banyan* trees, the first for many a year. Even the comparatively small ones are beautiful, and I always think it interesting to watch the roots as they spring from the boughs or wave in the air, dry and unhappy looking, like unsatisfied desires craving for they know not what till they touch the soil that is their natural home, where they take root and spring into verdure.

Ajmere, March 4th

On Saturday the 5th we got here. Our house is a bungalow, not a comfortable one but it does not much signify, as we expect to be here very little. Our time will probably be spent on Mount Abu during the hot season, and the rest of the year marching about.

I have never told you about a Durbar Papa held at Jaipur. You must know that Rajputana or Rajastan or Rajbaree as it is variously called, all names signifying "the abode of kings", consists of a number of independent principalities, all under a sort of allegiance to our Government, and Papa is now the agent to manage the affairs of these small kingdoms. In the middle of Rajputana, if you look on the map, you will see a little red patch called Ajmere entirely belonging to the British. This is under a separate officer, Col. Nixon. Now these Rajputs claim to be children of the sun and moon and, knowing very little of the rest of the world, have a vast opinion of their own importance. Being ignorant and idle they lay as great stress on all matters of étiquette as the courtiers of Lilliput did. There is a little Rajah at Jaipur who thinks himself a great man, and he came to return Papa's visit.

We were staying at Major Richard's house, in front of which there is a paved courtyard. On this was spread a thick cotton covering, and over it a white sheet. In the centre was an awning, raised on four gilt poles, where was set a heap of embroidered cushions. Troops were drawn off in line, and there was a great deal of hurrying to and fro of men dressed in enormously full white petticoats, with short quilted jackets, their chops tied up in cotton pocket handkerchiefs, anything but like the warlike Rajputs I expected to see.

Papa and Major Richards went on an elephant to meet the king who was in a great litter, and brought him to the awning where the little fellow sat down on the cushions, Papa, a little lower on his left, and Major Richards on the ground, all crossed legged and without shoes. This was very unlike the style of real great durbars [in the places] where Papa was used to be, such as Nepal and Lahore where all sat on chairs, and English gentlemen wore their shoes. A crowd of petticoated natives stood around. Behind the Rajah two men bearing *chowries* of peacock's feathers. A band of dancing girls came with the royal party all decked out in tinsel and tissue. They performed their monotonous movements to music about as sweet as what you hear with Punch and Judy. Presently, a man brought a basket full of garlands of flowers, long necklaces of roses, jasmine etc. The Rajah put one round Papa's neck, one round Major Richards' and then the Prime Minister, garlanded all the greatest people. I did not like to see Papa looking like a mountebank, without his shoes, decorated with flowers and smelling of otta of roses.

233

To Harry, Mount Abu, April 14th, 1853

Now I want to tell you about this new place we are in. Look on the map between the Gulf of Cutch and Cambay, and rather east of them and you will find Abu. Perhaps it thinks itself a very high hill, for it never saw anything higher. But if it were to see Simla and Kussowlee it would cry, "What a little thing I am, hardly higher than the table." It is 4,500 feet above the sea and stands nearly isolated. There is a very pretty lake studded with little wooded islets and each edged with tiny, rocky, wooded bays. The houses are all small and thatched. There are many fine trees. Altogether Papa and I think this the prettiest place we ever saw in the hills. Some of the old servants are with us. Papa has the old horses, Urbee, Ladakhi and Foujdar Khan.

To Harry, Mount Abu, May 12th, 1853

Papa has a great deal to do, though not so much as he had at Lahore. He generally sits in the verandah reading or writing for an hour or two before breakfast. Then he is in the *dufter* after breakfast till three o'clock when we drive. Towards sunset we go out and very often remain out till nine o'clock having tea and reading on the *chabootra*, a raised platform on a rock overlooking the lake and with a lovely view of the mountains, trees and open glades. This house is not like Lahore, the rooms are few and small and we seldom have strangers.

Do you remember Mr. and Mrs. Newton, the missionaries? I heard lately from Mrs. Newton who is at home in America. She tells me that the book *Uncle Tom's Cabin* is a very faithful picture of slavery. I was in hopes it was exaggerated.

Henry adds:

Honey runs in and out of my office, as you and Alick used to do, and picks up torn paper to carry away. My office is a nice little room fourteen feet square with three windows and two doors. All round are bookcases, and maps, and I sit in a corner at a table between two windows.

To Harry, Mount Abu, Rajpootana, June 5th, 1853

Honey has a nice little friend now, Sophy Shakespear. They meet every morning and evening for their ride and walk, and last evening they looked very nice. There is a pretty valley with rocks, trees and grass where the band plays twice a week and all the people resort to listen. Lady Shakespear had Sophy before her on her horse, and Papa on his beautiful grey Arab had Beebee, who was dressed in white with a large leghorn hat. Sophy also in white with a pink bonnet. Her Papa, Sir Richmond, is an old friend of Papa's and it is now very pleasant to have him here. He was knighted for being very brave and good when he went to Khiva, and got the king of that country to release some Russian families, whom he had captured and made slaves of. Sir Richmond had the pleasure of taking them back to their own country. You remember Major Abbott at Hazara? That kind gentleman who shewed you so much armour and sent the *kazee* with us when you and I came back from the Indus without Papa? Well he went first on that same errand about the Russian slaves, though he did not succeed. Do you remember how his fingers were cut off, and he used to write with only the thumb and little finger? He was wounded at that time.

Mount Abu, Rajputana, June 6th, 1853

We read very anxiously dear Alick, all the newspapers say of the probable changes about Haileybury College,* and the more enlarged examination of young men for the Civil Service. Papa thinks the plan a good one, and I hope that you will bear it in mind as a fresh stimulus to exertion. If Haileybury be closed, the outside examination will most probably be much harder. It would be a sore trial to us, were you to fail. Now is the time to work and to strengthen both mind and body. Remember too that Harry will do as you do. If he sees you active and energetic he will stir himself and vice versa. You would not do him harm, or set him a bad example. But remember there is no medium. You must do him good or harm.

Of course there will be much more honour in winning it,† but remember my boy that the struggle will be great, not greater than you can make, but what you may easily fail in. If you lose this excellent provision in life, I really see nothing suitable open for you, besides the bitter mortification to you and to us. Gird up your loins then my boys and *strive*, that is the one word that includes all.

Formerly a civil employment was a ripe apple plucked and laid on your plate. Now the fruit will be left on a high bough where numbers will be invited to strive for it.

To Harry, Mount Abu, July 5th, 1853

Our cottage is much like a haystack with doors and windows in it. Most of the people go back to Deesa when the rains begin. The houses are built only for fine weather, but we hope to stay here till the cold weather begins.

October 3rd, 1853

After two months that I have not had a pen in my hand, I am once

---

*Haileybury was the training college for entry to the Indian Civil Service.
†i.e. a place in the I.C.S.

more able to write thus much that I commend you to God's holy keeping. And that you are day and night in the prayers of your mother.

Henry adds:

October 4th, 1853

The above few lines will show you that dear Mamma is better. She has been very, very ill indeed. I often thought during the last two months that she was dying. Mamma is now able to sit up for half an hour twice a day, and lies out in the air morning and evening. I hope she will be able to go into camp with me by the end of November, for she always liked camp life.

I was sorry to hear that you did nothing but play last vacation. I do not want you to work in the holidays as at other times, but a little work must make the play more pleasant. Even to hear that you played energetically would be pleasant, but to hear that you were listless and apathetic vexes us.

Mount Abu, Rajpootana, November 6th, 1853

I was sorry not to have a line ready for you or Harry to send by the mail yesterday. But after writing a little for the preceding mail, my faintness returned. Today I feel better and hope by degrees to fill a letter for next mail. I write lying down. So fear I may not be very legible.

We were much pleased to find that you had got on a step in form this half. I do not understand how your place in the class varies so much from week to week. Sometimes your standing shows that you can get near the top, at others that you get very far from it. This would not be if your diligence was steady. I am very glad that you seem to get on in mathematics. I do hope you have pleasure in reading, not merely story books but such as history, biography and travels. In India a young man without such taste is at best a cumberer of the ground and rarely escapes low habits.

I hope you will never touch tobacco, never take up the wretched puppyistic notion that it is manly to smoke.

November 19th, 1853

Let me add to the above that your father has had to meet every hardship of climate, from Burma to Kabul and has never used tobacco in any way.

On the 16th we had the happiness of receiving the English mail up to October 8th. We like all the particulars you give of the athletic games, and all other school matters, but I want to know what part you personally take in it all. You write more as if you look down upon it from the top of a tree than if you were a sharer. Which do you like best, running, riding, bathing, cricket, football or lying on your back?

We long to hear of you and Harry being together. I do not fear your bullying a little fellow but more than this I want to hear of your being to him by degrees all an elder brother may be.

We want to know something of your inner mind, your likes and dislikes. Do not fear your parents will be severe judges. We wish to have a high standard for ourselves and you.

I continue free from relapse, though far from strong. Dear Papa goes next week out to camp and 'tis a great disappointment to me to stay behind. You have sometimes mentioned having the choice left to you of things you are to learn by heart. I wish you would learn the forty-third chapter of Ecclesiasticus in the Apocrypha. It is a noble hymn.

This is the last letter written by Honoria Lawrence. She died on January 15th, 1854. As early as October 1853 she had written "I have no feeling that can be called a presentiment about my confinement. But my reasonable conviction is that I am likely to die then." She had had rheumatic fever and she was pregnant again.

Epilogue

After Honoria Lawrence died in 1854, the widowed Henry was broken hearted and went through a phase of self reproach such as nearly always follows bereavement. His love for her, so he felt, had been a half love. But to those who saw him, it seemed that, more and more, he lived in the next world, near to her. His sister Charlotte took over the running of the house and looked after Honey while Henry continued to lead an active life, soothing the grievances and gaining the affection of the rulers of Rajasthan, who feared Dalhousie's policy of modernisation and annexation. At the same time he watched over their conduct with resolute vigilance. His sister, Charlotte, acted as his hostess and was "very fairly assisted by darling wee Honey, so far as it was possible for a little thing like her to do so".*

In 1856 the once great kingdom of Oude was annexed to British India. The issues were tangled but outright annexation was not a just solution. And the first year of the new rule was grossly mismanaged. So the annexation of Oude became one of the causes of the Indian Mutiny. Too late to avert disaster, Henry Lawrence was appointed Chief Commissioner at Lucknow, the capital of Oude in 1857. He realised that an outbreak was imminent and in the few weeks remaining made many enemies into friends and prepared to defend a scarcely defensible position with tiny forces. He was killed on the fourth day of the siege of Lucknow.

Alick (1838–1864) did enter the Indian Civil Service. In 1858, after his father's death, he was made a baronet in recognition of Henry Lawrence's services to India, with a "special remainder" providing that, if his male descendants died out, the title would go to his younger brother, as if their father had been the first baronet. Alick married in

---

*Reminiscences of Sir Henry Lawrence by Y, published at Dehra Dun in 1893. "Y" was Robert Young of Culdaff, who lived with Henry Lawrence at Mount Abu.

1862 a beautiful and gifted but wayward Irish girl, Alice Kennedy. Two years later Henry's brother, John, became Viceroy of India. Alick went to join his uncle John at Simla for the hot weather.

That summer there was a great gathering at Simla which included George and Dick Lawrence and Sir Herbert and Lady Edwardes. Lady Edwardes, whose account I follow, tells us that Alick was "much beloved for his many personal attractions and highly honourable qualities" and that with his young wife there was "a sweet babe of six months old". However, one night there was a quarrel and Alick left the next morning for an expedition "into the interior" with his uncle Dick whose duties took him there. About ten days' march from Simla, Alick was riding ahead out of sight round a turn of the road. There was a sound like a falling tree and then perfect stillness. Dick hurried his horse on but, when he turned the corner, there was neither sight nor sound of Alick. At this point the "road" was a wooden gallery supported by stakes driven into the wall of a precipice.★ A few planks seemed gone at one point and Alick's little dog was there, looking down and whining. It transpired afterwards that someone had stolen the nails which supported the planks. Dick looked down. The bottom was thousands of feet below and he could see nothing. Eventually Alick and his horse were found far below. His uncle travelled day and night for four days to bring his body back, so that his young wife might have a last look at his face. He appeared to have lost consciousness while falling and the smile on his face "spoke of joy".

Alick and Alice's "sweet babe" grew up epileptic and died young leaving three small daughters, so that the title went under the special remainder to Alick's younger brother Harry (Sir Henry Waldemar Lawrence, 1845–1908, my grandfather). His childhood with the Bernards was miserable and seemed to break something within him. His later life was not unhappy but he did not do full justice to his ability. He has left to his descendants the memory of a wise philosophy that was gently stoical and a little ironic. He was called to the bar and then, in partnership with one of his cousins, invested in a rice mill and wharf in Rotherhithe on the Thames. With characteristic disregard for Victorian convention he used the wharf as a place to entertain his friends, a custom that was kept up by my father. During the sixty years of its existence Lawrence's Wharf never had a strike.

Honey or Norah (Honoria Letitia Lawrence, 1850–1923) was everybody's sweetheart as a little girl. When her mother died she was not yet four and was brought up for the next three years with her father and her aunt Charlotte in India. She was then sent to England

---

★The most likely spot for this famous Anglo-Indian tragedy is somewhere between Sarahan and Chini on the Hindustan–Tibet road.

where she spent much time with her uncle John, while he was in England after the Mutiny and before returning to India as Viceroy. Once when she was naughty, he held her over the banisters and said he would drop her. "No, you won't," said Norah, "because that would be murder and then you would be hanged." So the stern ruler of India had to give in to his small niece. In 1873 she married Henry Hart,★ another Irishman of an Anglo-Indian family. The marriage was childless but very happy.

I remember my great aunt Norah well, as a much loved old lady, vigorous and bright-eyed, with a strong look of her mother, the first Honoria and the author of these journals. I can still see her smile and hear her chuckle.

★See his biography *Henry Hart of Sedbergh: a Victorian Schoolmaster*, by G. G. Coulton, the great medievalist.

Glossary

of Indian and Anglo-Indian Words

Hobson-Jobson, a Dictionary of Anglo-Indian Usage, is the prime source for all glossaries of this kind. The footnotes to the novel, *Adventures of an Officer in the Punjaub*, written by Henry Lawrence with the assistance of Honoria, give some pithy definitions which I have incorporated; all quotations are from the footnotes to this book. We have not tried to standardise Honoria's spelling of Indian words but this should not present much difficulty, if the reader bears in mind the features of Indian pronunciation referred to on the last page of the introduction. We have omitted the names of many trees and plants and some animals, because the reader will often know already what they are and, if not, the correct name of an exotic plant will not help him much. A few words are omitted because they only occur once in a context where they are sufficiently explained.

In a few cases it is impossible to be sure of what Indian word is represented by Honoria's spelling; where doctors differ, I have chosen the meaning which seems to suit the context best.

Akali A member of a body of militant Sikh zealots. "Literally immortals (or without death). What may be called Knight-errants among the Sikhs."
Ankoos An elephant goad.
Anna A coin, one eighth of a rupee.
Atta A coarse wheaten flour.
Attar, uttur Otto of roses.
Attar dan A container of attar.
Ayah A native lady's maid or nurse maid.

Baba A child.
Baboo A clerk; often a clerk who writes English.

Baksheesh, bakshish A tip.

Balatee, blighty Britain.

Banghy A bamboo placed across the shoulder with a load suspended at either end.

Bania *See* bunniah.

Banian A flannel waistcoat.

Banyan tree A European name for the Ficus Indica, whose branches send down shoots that take root in the earth.

Barat That part of the Hindu marriage festivity when the groom takes home the bride.

Bashaw Pasha.

Bastee, busty An inhabited quarter, a village, a slum.

Baston A large bag or portfolio, generally of leather, commonly used by a canango (q.v.) for his papers.

Batta An extra allowance made to the army when in the field.

Bawarchee A cook.

Bearer A palanquin carrier. A valet.

Begum Lady.

Bell of arms The place where the arms and accoutrements of native regiments were kept.

Betel *See* pan.

Bhatkurro To greet a great man with proper respect.

Bheestie A water carrier.

Bholia, bhotia A long narrow boat.

Biparree A trader.

Boccas–waller, boxwallah, boccaswallah One with a box. Therefore a pedlar.

Budgerow A lumbering, keelless, Ganges barge.

Budhie Tangible thanks, a gift.

Buggy A two wheeled gig with a hood.

Bukoo A Nepalese long-sleeved coat like a Tibetan chupa.

Bund, bundee Any artificial embankment, a dam or causeway.

Bundook A musket.

Bunniah, bania, bannia, bannian A Hindu trader, moneylender, often a corn chandler.

Buris A charitable gift or tip.

Burra Big, great. Burrah Sahib = great Lord.

Bus Enough. Stop! Used precisely as the Italian *basta*.

Buston *See* baston.

Canango, canangoe A subordinate native revenue officer responsible for keeping the accounts and recording the circumstances of the villages within his pergunnah (q.v.)

Canat, kanat, conaut, connaught The side wall of a tent.

Caste A European name for the hereditary divisions of Hindu society.

Chabenee Parched grain.

Chabootra A raised platform.

Chadder, chudder, chudha A sheet, a square piece of cloth or other textile.

Chapatee *See* chupatty.

Chaprassee, chuprassi A messenger, who wears a chaprass or badge of office.

Charpaee, charpoy "A bedstead formed of a light wooden frame, on four short legs, and laced over with twine or a broad tape called *nawar*."

Chatha An umbrella; generally one carried as a symbol of rank.

Cheek The wall of a tent.

Cheela, cheelah A servant or disciple.

Chenar A plane tree.

Chiccau–wallah One who fixes prices or pays promptly.

Chichi A person of mixed blood.

Chillum The bowl of a hookah (q.v.).

Chil(l)umchee A brass basin.

Chit A note, letter.

Chobdar An attendant who bears a staff.

Choga A long, sleeved garment like a dressing gown.

Choola(h) A portable cooking stove. "Travellers erect a temporary one, generally of mud or stones."

Chopper Thatch.

Choukee A low square seat or pedestal.

Chowree, chowrie The bushy tail of a yak, used as a fly whisk.

Chudder *See* chadder.

Chukee A hand mill.

Chumar A tanner, which is a low caste; "chumars are ready to turn their hand to anything that promises gain."

Chuna Fresh lime.

Chunam A smooth plaster made of lime.

Chupatty, chapatee A flat cake of unleavened bread.

Chupkun The long dress worn by men in northern India.

Chuprassee *See* chaprassee.

Clashy, Kulashee A surveyor's chain man, employed to measure fields for the survey; a tent pitcher.

Cooly A hired labourer or burden carrier.

Coprah The dried kernel of the coconut.

Cos A measure of distance "varying from a mile and a half to five miles but usually equivalent to two English miles."

Country Native born or made.

Cowry A small white shell used as currency.

Cranchee A kind of ricketty and sordid carriage drawn by wretched ponies and harnessed with rope.

Cranny A clerk who writes English.

Cuddoo A creeper.

Cummerbund A belt, a cloth girded round the loins.

Cutcha Soft, unripe, raw; the opposite of pucka (q.v.). A cutcha building is one of sun dried bricks.

Dak, dâk, dawk Letter post or any arrangement for travelling or transmitting articles by relays.

Dal A pulse, lentil.

Dand An oar.

Dandy, dandee 1. A boatman on the Ganges.
2. A conveyance consisting of a hammock slung on a bamboo staff and carried by two or more men.

Degchee Saucepan.

Dhaee, dhai, dhay A childrens' nurse or midwife.

Dhoby, dobee, dobie, dhobee A washerman.

Dhooli(e), dooly A covered litter, cheaper and lighter than a palanquin. The usual ambulance of the Indian army.

Dhoon A flat valley parallel to the base of the Himalays. The dhoon = Dehra Dhoon.

Dinghy, dingy A small boat, skiff or canoe.

Dollee, dolly A complimentary offering of fruit, flowers etc.

Doodh panee Milk and water.

Doputta, dooputty Literally "two breadths", a wide scarf, veil or stole.

Dost Friend.

Dufter Office.

Dunga A row, argument. A dunga wala is a mutineer.

Dunkah Kettle drum.

Durbar A court, the levée, of a king or any great person, and those who attend the levée, namely the government, or the government building.

Durzee A tailor.

Dustoor Custom. Hence any customary payment or commission.

Eedgah A place of prayer and assembly outside a town for Muslim festivals.

Fakir, fakeer Literally poor, generally a religious mendicant, sometimes, a title of respect; is with Peer (a Saint) and other such titles "often arrogated by men whose holiness or poverty lies only in the name".

Feringhee A European, literally a Frank.

Ganj A market place.
Garee, gharry, gharee A cart or carriage.
-gee *See* -jee
Ghat, ghaut A pass or passage, a landing place or path of descent to a river.
Ghee Clarified butter.
Ghurrah, gurra(h) A clay water pot.
Gram Chick pea.
Griffin A newcomer to India.
Guddee The throne or seat of royalty, literally a cushion.
Gurak A cow keeper.
Gurreeb, garib Poor, chétif, put in one's place.

Hackery, hackerry A bullock cart.
Halwai *See* hulwai.
Hasir Ready, present, alert; always used for a subordinate.
Hatee, hatty, hathi An elephant.
Hookah A pipe for smoking through water.
Houndie A bill of exchange written in a native language.
Howdah A framed seat carried by an elephant.
Hubble-bubble A rudimentary form of hookah.
Hulwai A maker of halva, or sweetmeats.

Imambara A building for the celebration of Mohurrum (q.v.).
Istikbal A ceremonial greeting.
Izzut Honour, pride.

Jadhoo Magic, witchcraft.
Jamawar A piece of cloth fit to make a dress or other clothing.
Jampan *See* jompon.
-jee, -ji An honorific termination. Dhaijee is Madame Nurse. The root *ji* means life.
Jemadar 1. The second rank of native officers in a company of sepoys.
2. A Major Domo.
Jheel A sheet of stagnant water.
Jhool The housings of a horse, elephant or other domestic animal.
Jillmills Venetian blinds.
Jompon, jampan A kind of sedan chair.
Jomponny A man who helps to carry a jompon.
Jungh War. Junghee Lord is Commander-in-Chief.
Jungle Uncultivated land, forest, any wild growth.

Kanat *See* canat.

Kazee, kajee A subordinate law officer. A title used for Ministers of State in Nepal.

Kellut A dress of honour.

Khalifa, kalifa Literally the Calif or successor of the Prophet Mahommed. Also a king, a cook, a tailor or a pedagogue.

Khalsa The religious community of the Sikhs.

Khana 1. A house, receptacle.
2. Food.

Khansamah, khannsamah A house steward or chief table servant.

Khitmutgar, kitmutgar A Moslem servant who waits at table.

Khoda God.

Khoosh Pleasure, enjoyment.

Khud, kud A precipitous hillside or deep valley.

Kincob Gold brocade.

Koomar A potter.

Kote House.

Kuddo(o) *See* cuddoo.

Kuhur, kahar A bearer, domestic servant or palanquin carrier.

Kulashee *See* clashy.

Kumerbund *See* cummerbund.

Kunaught, kunnaught *See* canat.

Kuskus Fragrant grass on which water was thrown; used in various cooling devices.

Kusrah A part of surveying carried out by natives.

Kutchery An office of administration, a court house.

Kutora A small brass bowl or cup, literally a full blown flower.

Lagao, lagow A Ganges word for mooring a boat.

Lakh One hundred thousand, especially 100,000 rupees.

Log People. Sahib log means the gentry. Sikh log means the Sikhs.

Looee Flannel, also a local word for a light blanket.

Lota A brass or earthenware water pot.

Maite, mati An assistant under a head servant.

Malee A gardener.

Manjee The master or steersman of a boat.

Masjid, musjid A mosque.

Masoola, masoolla A heavy surfboat made of planks sewn together used for landing on the Coromandel coast.

Maund A measure of weight (the Greek *mina*) generally about 80 lbs.

Mehtur A sweeper or scavenger.

Mesh A pulse.

Metahee, meetai Sweetmeats.

Michaun A tree refuge from wild elephants; a stage or scaffolding erected to watch a tiger, to guard a field or what not.

Mida A form of flour.
Mina, mynah A name applied to several birds of the starling family.
Minar A tower, a minaret.
Mistree A foreman or master workman.
Mofussil The country districts, and smaller towns.
Mohant The head of a body of Hindu religious mendicants.
Mohout, Mahout The rider in charge of an elephant.
Mohur The chief gold coin of British India.
Mohurrum The Shiah commemoration of the death of Hussein and Hassan.
Moofsid A malcontent, rebel.
Mookhia, mokhya A Nepalese official, a village headman.
Moonshee A secretary or interpreter.
Moorghy, moorghi(e) A chicken, likely to be very small and skinny.
Mootsuddy A native accountant, writer, secretary.
Mora A stool.
Moulvee A judge, a learned man.
Mulla, mullah A schoolmaster, a learned man, especially one learned in Islamic law; also the bond still connecting a freed slave with his former owner; hence, inter alia, the slave himself.
Muntra, mantra Properly a Vedic text or formula but also a charm.
Musalla, mussalla Spices.
Mushk, mussuck, mashak The goatskin water bag carried by a bheestie (q.v.).
Mussalchee A link boy.

Nawab Literally a delegate. Hence a Viceroy of the Great Mogul and, later, a title of high rank.
Neoza Pine kernels, also a spice used in making sweets.
Nullah A water course, often a dry one.
Nuzzer An offering from an inferior.

Onseeree A message containing greetings, salaams.
Oosur An evil spirit.
Otta *See* attar.

Paharri, Paharee The hill people of the Himalayas.
Pajamas, pyjamas Loose drawers fastened by a string round the waist. Hence pyjamas as night wear.
Palkee Palanquin.
Pan, paun The betel leaf used in combination with nut, lime etc. for chewing.
Panchayat An assembly of villages elders, arbitrators. Literally, a fivesome.

Panee Water.

Patee A Hindu religious building with shelter for travellers and cattle.

Pavah A synonym for patee (q.v.).

Peer A Moslem saint or tomb of a saint.

Pergunnah, pergannah A subdivision of a zillah (district).

Petarrah, peteras A box used in travelling by palkee, two such being slung to a banghy (q.v.).

Piang A small oval box, a small pot made out of hollow sections of bamboo.

Pice A small copper coin, one twelfth of an anna.

Pindi A camp.

Poojah Hindu worship.

Pucka, puckah Ripe and therefore anything that is all that it should be in its own kind. Thus a pucka house is one built of kiln-baked bricks and mortar.

Pultun A regiment or rather brigade of native infantry.

Punkah A fan and more particularly the large swinging fan of cloth stretched on rectangular frame and suspended from the ceiling which is used to agitate the air in hot weather.

Purdah A curtain or screen, especially a curtain screening women from the sight of men.

Purwasty, purwustee Special favour and indulgence. "The favouritism that knaves ask and fools bestow."

Purwusteekur, parwastikar To entice by purwustee (q.v.).

Pushmina, peshmina A warm soft shawl made from the wool of the hill goat.

Puttoo A length of cloth.

Pyah kuring, piar kur, pior kur To make love.

Qui hi Is anyone there? Europeans of the Calcutta Presidency; so called because they summoned their servants by shouting "Qui hi".

Rana A rajah.

Raotee A small quadrangular tent or small room on top of a house.

Razee Contented, at ease. Razee bazee means thoroughly at ease.

Resai A thick wadded quilt.

Rukshea, rukshee A spirit distilled from rice.

Rupee The standard coin of the Indian monetary system, roughly equivalent to two shillings.

Ruttle A car in which idols are carried on feast days.

Saees *See* syce.

Sahib The polite Indian address to persons of consequence, especially Europeans. The usage is closer to Monsieur in French than to Sir in English.

Salaam, salam A salutation. Literally peace, c.f. shalom in Hebrew.

Sanga A rope bridge.

Saree The cloth which constitutes the main part of a woman's dress.

Sati, suttee The rite of widow burning, a wife who sacrifices herself on her husband's pyre.

Seer A measure of weight, generally about two pounds.

Sepoy, sepahi An Indian soldier dressed and disciplined in the European style.

Serai A building for the accommodation of travellers.

Shalimar gardens The name applied to the royal pleasure-grounds in most oriental capitals.

Shiah That branch of the Moslems which specially venerate Ali, and his martyred sons Hussein and Hassan.

Shikaree, shikary A sportsman, hunter.

Shooldarry, shooldarrie A small tent with two poles and very low side walls.

Shooter sowar, shuter sowar The rider of a dromedary or swift camel.

Sirdar 1. A chief; a Hindu title equivalent to the Mussulman Khan.
  2. A valet. The head of any group e. g. palanquin bearers.

Sooparee Betel nut.

Soorhai A large earthenware pitcher.

Sowar A trooper, any rider.

Sowari, suwaree A train of attendants, cortège.

Subadar The chief native officer of a company of sepoys.

Sudder Board Board of Revenue.

Surwan A camel driver.

Sutringee A striped carpet of thick cotton.

Suwarree *See* Sowari.

Sweeper *See* mehtur.

Syce or saees A groom.

Syud A descendant of the prophet Mohammed.

Talee A metal plate

Tanghan The strong little pony of Tibet.

Tank An artificial pond or lake made by excavation or damming.

Tattoo, tat A native bred pony.

Tatty A mat of fragrant grass, on which water is thrown, used to fill up door or window openings during the season of hot winds.

Thakoor A term of respect, a Rajput noble.

Thana, tana A police station.

Thanadur A police officer in charge of a thana.

Thermantidote A sort of winnowing machine fitted to a window and encased in tatties (q.v.) so as to drive cooled air into a house. See p. 216.

Thugs A widespread secret society of robbers and murderers devoted to the goddess Kali.

Ticker, ticcah, tickah Any person or thing engaged by the job.

Tiffin Luncheon.

Tomasha A public spectacle, a "happening".

Tope 1. A grove or orchard, especially a mango grove.
2. An ancient Buddhist monument.

Tota A parrot, a term of endearment.

Tukleef Trouble, distress.

Tulwar A sabre.

Tussah Tussore silk.

Urra A pulse.

Uttur *See* attar.

Vakeel An authorised representative, a lawyer.

Zemindar A landlord in the sense of one who holds land on which he pays revenue direct to the government.

Zenana The women's quarters.

Ziafut, ziafat A banquet or ceremonial present.

Zillah An administrative district.

Index